MOMENTOUS MOBILITIES

Worlds in Motion

Edited by Noel B. Salazar, University of Leuven,
in collaboration with ANTHROMOB, the EASA
Anthropology, and Mobility Network.

ANTHRO
M⊕B

This transdisciplinary series features empirically grounded studies that
disentangle how people, objects, and ideas move across the planet. With
a special focus on advancing theory as well as methodology, the series
considers movement as both an object and a method of study.

Momentous Mobilities

Anthropological Musings on the Meanings of Travel

Noel B. Salazar

berghahn
NEW YORK • OXFORD
www.berghahnbooks.com

First published in 2018 by
Berghahn Books
www.berghahnbooks.com

© 2018, 2020 Noel B. Salazar
First paperback edition published in 2020

Library of Congress Cataloging-in-Publication Data

Names: Salazar, Noel B., 1973- author.
Title: Momentous mobilities : anthropological musings on the meanings of
travel / Noel B. Salazar.
Description: New York : Berghahn Books, 2018. | Series: Worlds in motion |
Includes bibliographical references and index.
Identifiers: LCCN 2018001776 (print) | LCCN 2018017553 (ebook) | ISBN
9781785339363 (ebook) | ISBN 9781785339356 (hardback : alk. paper)
Subjects: LCSH: Tourism--Anthropological aspects. | Quality of life.
Classification: LCC G156.5.A58 (ebook) | LCC G156.5.A58 S35 2018 (print) |
DDC 306.4/819--dc23
LC record available at https://lccn.loc.gov/2018001776

British Library Cataloguing in Publication Data
A catalogue record for this book is available from the British Library

ISBN 978-1-78533-935-6 hardback
ISBN 978-1-78920-803-0 paperback
ISBN 978-1-78533-936-3 ebook

It is not our feet that move us along—it is our minds.
—Ancient Chinese proverb

For Keila Luna and Eva Yani

Contents

Illustrations

Foreword

Vered Amit

One of the most productive aspects of the emergence of "mobility stud-ies" as an interdisciplinary field of scholarly investigation has been the way in which it has afforded interrogations of the convergences and interac-tions between different types of mobility. As Noel Salazar's volume cogently demonstrates, there is much to be gained from bringing different forms of mobility—intra-national and international labor migration flows, tourism, educational mobility, highly skilled expatriate moves, and spiritual quests—into a common analytical frame. It provides opportunities to consider ques-tions of imaginaries, choice, compulsion, scale, pacing, and alternations, as well as overlaps of and divergences between different forms of mobility. But probing these questions is not only a matter of pursuing analytical abstractions. What is particularly compelling and original about the nar-rative journey on which Salazar takes readers of this monograph are the ways in which it combines memoir, ethnography, and theory. This potent combination grounds Salazar's analysis in his own life course, in the lived experiences of his many different interlocutors as well as in the histories, institutions, discourses, landscapes, contexts, and boundaries with which they must contend.

Noel Salazar's monograph thus vividly reminds us that the interface between different mobilities isn't simply a dry matter of schematic classi-fication. The interactions between different types of mobility happen over the course of people's lives as they embark on journeys or contend with the comings and goings of other travelers. One journey may transition into a very different type of voyage. A person you've known or met in one place may elicit a visit or a move to a different locale. Relationships, statuses, and/or resources developed in one milieu can shape possibilities for mobil-ity and immobility miles away or years later. Who gets to leave, who gets to stay, what kinds of journey they can contemplate or undertake, and which circumstances shape these "(im)mobilities" are matters not only of larger or smaller institutional and systemic pressures/constraints but also of numerous personal calculations and improvisations. In short, these kinds of questions are thoroughly embedded in ongoing dialectics between structures and intimacies, between aspirations and enactments of mobility.

Until recently, the organization of the scholarly investigation of mobilities often preempted the interrogation of many aspects of these interfaces. It preempted them by limiting the spectrum of mobilities that were being subjected to scrutiny. Social science investigations of the movements of highly skilled professionals or students are now beginning to burgeon, but not too long ago they were exceedingly rare. It preempted them by segregating the study of those forms of mobility that were being investigated into separate silos. While the current organization of mobility studies has significantly moved away from these two orientations, we still risk preempting the scope and modulation of our investigations if we assume that we already understand the hierarchies, geographies, and ideologies of privilege, resources, and choices shaping contemporary movements. How voluntary are the journeys of the "middling" travelers whose education, jobs, or family networks may increasingly suppose some degree of spatial mobility? Do discourses that trumpet the advantages of "international experience" position mobility as a means to an end—skills, connections, advancement—or is it becoming a hollowed-out, but no less avidly sought, end in and of itself? These are just some of the questions probed in Noel Salazar's versatile investigation of the "travails," opportunities, and becomings of contemporary forms of mobility and immobility, a testament to the contributions that anthropological enquiry can make to the development of a multidimensional and interdisciplinary field of mobility studies.

Vered Amit is professor of anthropology at Concordia University. She is the author or editor of fourteen books, including *Thinking through Sociality: An Anthropological Interrogation of Key Concepts* (Berghahn Books) and *Mobility and Cosmopolitanism: Complicating the Interaction between Aspiration and Practice* (Routledge, coedited with Pauline Gardiner Barber).

Preface

Travel is useful, it exercises the imagination. All the rest is disappointment and fatigue. Our journey is entirely imaginary. That is its strength.

—Louis-Ferdinand Céline, *Journey to the End of the Night*

There are well-founded reasons why I am interested in human mobility. My own family and personal history are deeply marked by multiple mobilities and border crossings. My Flemish mother met my father while on holidays along the Costa del Sol, in the south of Spain. This encounter, in turn, led my Spanish father to migrate to Bruges, Belgium. I was born in between, in France, and spent most of my formative years shuttling between Belgium and Spain. After a career working in Spanish hotels, and having started in Belgium as a restaurant waiter, my father ended up as a horticulture laborer in the family business of my mother (who herself alternated doing secretarial tasks with helping in the greenhouses).

Although not common in the 1970s–1990s working-class and lower-middle-class environment in which I grew up, my parents liked spending at least part of their holidays exploring Europe's cultural wonders. As a kid eager to learn, I happily joined them. As soon as student jobs gave me sufficient economic resources, I started traveling abroad with friends. Thanks to scholarships and zero-interest student loans, I had the good fortune to study in the United Kingdom and the United States. The family contacts in England dated back to the time my Flemish grandmother sought refuge there during World War II. Across the United States, be it on the West Coast (San Francisco), East Coast (Washington), or in the Midwest (Chicago), I met distant relatives—third generation descendants from poor Belgian peasants who had migrated to the "promised land" at the beginning of the twentieth century.

It was just before the dawn of the new millennium, after having finished my studies in psychology, that I ventured for the first time in my life outside of Europe (not counting the trip with my parents to the Spanish enclaves of Ceuta and Melilla in northern Africa). I was in my twenties and had just graduated as a foreign degree student in the UK. The earnings from an interim position in Brussels gave me the financial means necessary to travel overseas. I also had enough time—a couple of weeks before starting a full-time job in Italy. The trigger for my first transatlantic trip was an invitation from an Italian friend to attend his wedding in Baja California, Mexico. Since I considered it too extravagant to travel such a distance merely to attend a party, I checked out whom else I could visit "in the area," and carefully prepared an entire road trip. I flew from Brussels to San Diego (via an uneventful stopover in Cincinnati) because flights to the United States were cheaper than those to Mexico. I vividly remember the scenic drive along Highway 1, where an unconventional traffic sign near the border caught my attention. It depicts a family on the run and, in large capital letters, the word "caution." This road sign along the US-Mexican border alludes to the "danger" of people trying to enter the United States illegally. Entering Mexico at the infamous Tijuana border crossing went remarkably smooth (traversing in the opposite direction, I would experience later, was significantly more cumbersome).

The wedding gathered an interesting mix of people, both from a geographical and sociocultural perspective. When the parents of the Mexican bride heard that I would be based in Rome, they told me about a family friend who was working as a Catholic missionary in Uganda. The priest occasionally traveled to the Vatican, and they asked me to convey to him their best regards. I thought it quite a stretch to assume that I would ever meet the man. After the party, I continued traveling through Mexico. I first visited some Mexican friends with whom I had collaborated as a volunteer in France the year before. One of them lived along the border with Texas. I was naively surprised to see a house replete with cultural indices to the United States. The father of the household was absent as he was doing some seasonal work in San Antonio (a pattern the family had been used to for many years).

The other Mexicans I visited grew up in the old colonial cities around the capital and were moving back and forth, depending on job opportunities. I also met with a Belgian school friend who was working for a global consultancy firm in Mexico City. Our paths would keep on crossing in the years to come as he would be reassigned to different countries surrounding the Atlantic Ocean. Before returning to Europe, I paid a visit to a retired American couple in California whom my parents had met during a cruise holiday on the Nile in Egypt. The man had served as a pilot in the Korean War back in the 1950s. Despite his age (82), he was still very sharp and raced around in his shiny Ford Mustang convertible. I returned to Europe with a bag full of mobility-related memories.

As planned, I started working in Rome for an international NGO dealing with refugees and other forcibly displaced people. As part of my job, I visited detention centers and refugee camps and settlements around the globe.

One year after my memorable trip to North America, I was sent to Nairobi, Kenya, to help with a training for refugee aid workers from across Africa. Afterward, the trainers were invited to visit a refugee settlement in the north of Uganda. We flew to Entebbe and spent one night in the country's capital before continuing the trip north. In Kampala, the unimaginable happened: by total coincidence, I ran into the Mexican missionary who was a friend of the bride's parents I had met at the wedding the year before. The Belgian schoolmate I had visited in Mexico City would keep surprising me too. When my spouse and I moved to Philadelphia in 2002 so that I could start my graduate training in anthropology at the University of Pennsylvania, he was the one to pick us up at the airport and to guide us around the city (he was temporarily posted in Wilmington at that time).

Although I returned to university to make sense of the intense refugee-related experiences of (im)mobility I had witnessed, I ended up doing research on tourism. My doctoral project brought me to the Indian Ocean region. I conducted ethnographic fieldwork in Indonesia and Tanzania. After obtaining my Ph.D. degree in the United States in 2008, I started working as a postdoctoral fellow in geography at the University of Leuven in Belgium, continuing to work on tourism. However, I soon had the opportunity to join an anthropology research unit specializing in migration. This move forced me to think about how I could combine research on migration and tourism. Using mobility as an analytical lens seemed to offer great possibilities in this regard. I currently live in Brussels, a city in which migrants count for more than half of the population. Not surprisingly, my interest in boundary-crossing mobilities is heavily influenced by my personal background and life experience.

This monograph has been many years in the making (and, as such, it is a nice example of "slow science"). The original idea arose around 2010, but I also draw on materials from earlier periods of research and observation. Most data were collected during projects that were generously sponsored by the European Commission and the Research Foundation Flanders (FWO). However, I continued gathering information long after the funded projects were officially finished. It may be hard to categorize this work because it blends elements from various genres. It contains ethnographic data as well as analyses of secondary sources and personal, autoethnographic reflections. The writing up took a long time and happened piecemeal. In fact, many parts were written while I was traveling. I wrote in trains (my favorite place-in-movement to write), in airport lounges, in hotel rooms, at deserted beaches, and at my sit-stand office desk back home.

Bringing this project to an end would not have been possible without the help of many people, including family and long-term friends, colleagues from all corners of the globe, and people I met in passing during one of my many trips. I decided not to give a long list of names here, because I would forget to mention some people. Additional input came from the many university and nonacademic audiences to whom I presented parts of this book and from peers in virtual space (through the intermediary of various social media platforms). I particularly want to thank the present and past colleagues and students at the Cultural Mobilities Research (CuMoRe) cluster in Leuven and those from the EASA Anthropology and Mobility (AnthroMob) Network for their constructive feedback and endless inspiration. Thanks also to the people at Berghahn for their professional handling of this manuscript.

Noel B. Salazar
Brussels, fall 2017

Mapping Mobility

> We hear much talk of roots .... Of the roots of our societies and historic communities. Of our deep-rooted traditions in particular geographical areas since the dawn of time...
>
> But Man is not a tree—he has no roots; he has feet, he walks. Since the time of *Homo erectus* he has moved about in search of pastures, more benign climates, or places where he can seek shelter from inclement weather and the brutality of his fellow men.
>
> —Juan Goytisolo, *Metaphors of Migration*

In 2006, UN Secretary General Kofi Annan released the report *International Migration and Development*, in which a "new era of mobility" was identified, characterized by a "back-and-forth pattern" (General Assembly 2006: 7). No matter where you are on this planet—somewhere in the largest metropole or on the most remote island—you encounter people who are "on the move." The journeys undertaken vary widely in terms of distance, time, and motivation, and point to the diversity of what social scientists have come to call human "mobility."[1] The way the term is being used in scholarly circles, mobility entails, in its coinage, much more than mere physical motion (Marzloff 2005). Rather, it can be understood as movement infused with both self-ascribed and attributed meanings (Frello 2008). Put differently, "mobility can do little on its own until it is materialized through people, objects, words, and other embodied forms" (Chu 2010: 15). Importantly, mobility means different things to different people in differing social circumstances (Adey 2010).

Practices favoring "flexibility, mobility, and repositioning in relation to markets, governments, and cultural regimes" (Ong 1999: 6) seem to have become commonplace. Mobilities including temporary relocation—"any form of territorial movement which does not represent a permanent, or lasting, change of usual residence" (Bell and Ward 2000: 98)—are promoted widely as being a desirable and even normative path toward "success" in life: educational achievement through studying abroad, career achievement through transnational work experience, and quality-of-life achievement through lifestyle mobilities, pilgrimage, and international tourism. In many parts of the world, such practices have become central to the structuring of people's lives (Bauman 2007). While definitions and descriptions overlap and contradict each other, a common characteristic is that these types of mobilities are undertaken "for a specific motivation and/or purpose with the intention that, afterwards, there will be a return to country of origin or onward movement" (European Migration Network 2012: 128).

Mobility research in general calls attention to the myriad ways in which people become parts of multiple translocal networks and linkages. Notwithstanding the many kinds of involuntary or forced movements (typically linked to situations of poverty, disaster, conflict, or persecution), most "back-and-forth" travels are positively valued. Many people link "voluntary" geographical mobility automatically to some type of symbolic "climbing," be it economically (in terms of resources), socially (in terms of status), or culturally (in terms of cosmopolitan disposition). In other words, mobility is used as an indicator of the variable access to and accumulation of these various types of symbolic capital (Bourdieu 1986). Of course, there are many underlying assumptions regarding the supposed nexus between spatial and symbolic mobility, while the mechanisms producing mobility as well as immobility are poorly understood (Faist 2013).

As I show throughout this book, it is important to identify various forms of boundary-crossing mobilities. In anthropology, a "boundary" generally refers to the sociospatially constructed differences between cultures or categories (Barth 1969), whereas a "border" generally stands for a line demarcated in space (T. Wilson and Donnan 2012). Travels beyond a familiar "home" base always confront people with the "elsewhere" and the "other." Importantly, these practices also (re)produce socially shared meanings of (im)mobility.[2] Group distinctions are made, which feed back into the production of the social through culturally inflected notions of mobility (e.g., the categories "migrant" versus "expat"). Transnational mobility, for instance, is often seen as endemic to globalization and as one of the most powerful stratifying factors, leading to a global hierarchy of movements (Bauman 1998). In other words, the movement of people may, and often does, create or reinforce difference and immobility, as well as blending or erasing such differences (Khan 2016; Salazar 2010a).

Already in the 1980s, geographers Mansell Prothero and Murray Chapman (1985) distinguished between "migration" as permanent displacement (geographic redistribution) and "circulation" as a reciprocal flow of people.[3] From this standpoint, "circulation" (which stresses the importance of returning to the point of departure) appears as one of the dominant forms of contemporary human mobilities. In this book, I do not discuss movement as a brute fact but analyze how travels back and forth, as a sociocultural assemblage, are imagined, experienced, and valued. How are various forms of boundary-crossing movement made meaningful by both those on the move and those who are themselves not engaged in such practices? What are the sociocultural mechanisms that enable or hinder such momentous mobilities? How do people envision their "motility" (potential for mobility)? I explore these questions drawing on empirical data, secondary sources, and personal reflections.

Despite repeated claims about the importance of translocal mobilities as one of the fastest growing phenomena of our time and, increasingly, as an issue of public and political concern, no systematic studies exist on their culturally inflected meanings, values, and impacts. Moving beyond the conventional approach to human movements in clearly delineated subfields (e.g., migration and tourism studies), this book addresses the normalization of boundary-crossing movements and the relations of differential power that are generative of these mobilities, their representations, and their societal significance. I arrive at this by drawing together, in creative ways, insights and approaches from anthropology, sociology, geography, political science, media studies, and history. I aim to assess the role of momentous mobilities as an integral part of the ordinary structuring

Figure 0.1: Mobility and immobility are intertwined in multiple ways. An abandoned train car converted into an "immobile" house, somewhere along the Trans-Gabon Railway, Gabon. (Photographer: Noel B. Salazar)

of human sociability (including for those who do not participate in these practices).

The research and reflections presented here add to existing scholarship in various ways. First, I stress the complex relationship between mobility and immobility (see figure 0.1). In the 1990s, the "diaspora turn" scholars (Vertovec and Cohen 1999) denounced a categorical binary of (mainly western) civilization, whereby "stayers" are assessed positively and in a position above "movers" (seen as menace, distortion, and problem). Over the course of the last decade, many proponents of the "mobility turn" (see below) seem to claim exactly the opposite (Adey et al. 2013). This book offers empirical evidence as well as novel theoretical arguments to question and go beyond these dichotomous viewpoints. In many contexts, momentous mobilities have become a precondition for socially accepted dwelling and are considered instrumental in accruing "symbolic capital" (Bourdieu 1986). Second, in-depth research on the situated articulations between culturally inflected regimes of movement, mobility representations, and personal ideas about meaningful travels is a fruitful way for analyzing the dynamic tension between ongoing processes of mobility and fixity (Greenblatt 2009), or between the logic of places versus the logic of networks and flows (Castells 2000; 2004). Third, taking the societal implications of momentous mobilities seriously and not as a given, the research presented here helps to determine the analytical purchase of the conceptual perspective of mobility studies to normalize movement within the single category of "mobility." As such, the book builds on, but considerably expands, the conceptual framework on (im)mobility that I have been developing over the last decade (Salazar 2010b; Salazar and Coates 2017; Salazar and Glick Schiller 2014; Salazar and Jayaram 2016; Salazar and Smart 2011).

Conceptualizing (Im)Mobility

> If Enlightenment thought introduced the study of a common humankind and an anthropology of its diverse states, then it is mobility—as the traversal of boundaries—that implicitly lays the ground of a modern knowledge system.
>
> —Jessica Dubow, *The Mobility of Thought*

Human mobility—a complex assemblage of movement, social imaginaries, and experience (cf. Cresswell 2006)—is not only popular among those who talk about a "mobility turn" in social theory and who have proposed a "new mobilities paradigm" to reorient the ways in which scholars think about society.[4] Influential theorists such as Anthony Giddens, Arjun Appadurai, Ulrich Beck, Manuel Castells, Bruno Latour, and Zygmunt Bauman all conceptualize contemporary capitalism and globalization in terms of increasing numbers and varieties of mobility: the fluid, continuous (but not always seamless) movement of people, ideas, and goods through and across space. Mobility can thus be described as a key social process, "a relationship through which the world is lived and understood" (Adey 2010).

It is important to recognize various (historical) forms of mobility, because the ways people move exert strong influences on their culture and society (Casimir and Rao 1992). People across the globe have long been interconnected; populations often have been mobile; and their identities have long been fluid, multiple, and contextualized. However, considering mobility as a natural tendency in society naturalizes it as a fact of life and as a general principle that does not need further justification, making reliance on "mobility capital" the norm (Nowicka and Rovisco 2009). Any discourse used to discuss questions of mobility is inevitably value laden (Bergmann and Sager 2008; Frello 2008). In this book, I seriously question whether mobility is, in actuality, "held up as a normative ideal in popular culture and the media, and in turn mimicked by many other people" (Elliott and Urry 2010: 82). I show that the ideological values attached to human mobility are not limited to the academic or social world but also that people do not necessarily accept the dominant mobility discourse that is imposed upon them (Salazar and Jayaram 2016).

Ideas of mobility have a long history in anthropology (Salazar 2013a). While classical anthropology tended to ignore or regard boundary-crossing journeys as deviations from normative place-bound communities, cultural homogeneity, and social integration, discourses of globalization and cosmopolitanism (that became dominant since the end of the Cold War) shifted the pendulum in the opposite direction. In the 1990s, globalization—theorized in terms of transborder "flows"—was often promoted as normality, and too much place attachment a digression or resistance against globalizing forces. Mobility became a predominant characteristic of the modern globalized world (Rapport and Dawson 1998). This led to a new focus on transnational mobilities that deterritorialize identity. Arjun Appadurai's (1996) provoking notion of "ethnoscapes," for instance, privileges mobile transnational groups and individuals, such as migrants, exiles, tourists, and guest workers.[5] As Aihwa Ong (1999: 4) explains, "*Trans* denotes both moving through space or across lines, as well as changing the nature of something." While globalization studies grew in popularity, anthropologists were for a long time absent in the interdisciplinary discussion around mobility studies.[6]

The language of mobility, trendy among academics and policy makers alike, has inadvertently distracted attention from how the fluidity of global markets shapes flexibility in regimes of control (Salazar and Glick Schiller 2014). In other words, it is not because one focuses attention on the "fluid" aspects of society that societal structure disappears entirely. Barriers to border-crossing movements, for instance, typically increase after big "crises" (think of 9/11 in the United States or the more recent refugee influx and terrorist attacks in the EU), and are accompanied by the counternarrative of securitization. In fact, critically engaged anthropologists were among the first to point out that contemporary forms of mobility need not at all signify privilege (Amit 2007).

The ability to move freely is spread very unevenly within countries and across the planet.[7] For the very processes that produce movement and global linkages also promote stasis, exclusion, and disconnection (Cunningham and Heyman 2004; Salazar and Smart 2011; Söderström et al. 2013). This presents a serious criticism to the overgeneralized discourse that assumes "without any research to support it that the whole world is on the move, or at least that never have so many people, things and so on been moving across international borders" (Friedman 2002: 33).[8] Transnational traveling remains the exception rather than the norm. The boundaries people are faced with are not only related to a lack of resources (mostly economic) but can also be linked to social class, gender, age, lifestyle, ethnicity, nationality, and disability—all of which have been addressed by anthropological research in some way or other.

Meaningful Movements

> By describing the desire to have roots in one place as fundamental human need, projecting mobility as the cause of moral disorder, and equating the places of mobility with non-places, social scientists have not only entrenched a kinetophobic [fear of mobility] view towards migrants, but also underestimated the social value of mobility.
>
> —Nikos Papastergiadis, *Wars of Mobility*

Mobility, understood in the context of this book as temporary translocal travel or relocation, is almost never an end (in itself).[9] The original intention is mostly to return, "enriched," to the point of departure. As opposed to other types of mobilities (e.g., the daily home-to-work commute), the travels described here become "momentous," of great importance or significance, because of the value that people attach to them. Transnational mobilities in particular are a way in which mostly the middle classes participate in a dynamic process of reworking both their own subjectivity and the meanings of place (Amit 2007; Benson and O'Reilly 2009). Some contemporary momentous mobilities are strikingly similar to the "Grand Tour," a prescribed trip through Europe for young, educated, wealthy men in the eighteenth and nineteenth centuries, symbolizing the end of their upbringing and giving them the required social and cultural capital for a future as political leaders (Hibbert 1969; also see chapter 4 of this volume). Boundary-crossing journeys have become one of the most salient grounds for delineating middle-class standing, which itself is an important demarcation of belonging within the "mainstream" of society. This association has been further heightened by policy discourses that trumpet the importance of "international experience" within a globalizing economy (while the same practices carried out "at home" would be construed as mundane drudgery).

The importance of mobility as an indicator of social status becomes intensified during periods of life-cycle transition in which other sources of symbolic capital may be jeopardized (Amit 2007). Translocal travels are prevalent among youngsters who are "coming of age" and for whom such practices have substituted older rites of passage as a socially sanctioned strategy toward adulthood. "Traveling to gain experience" is found in student exchange and study abroad programs, the gap year after finishing studies, volunteering, and those forms of tourism that stress learning about other places and people. More surprisingly, perhaps, is that remarkably similar mobilities reappear around the time of retirement (Benson and O'Reilly 2009). In other words, boundary-crossing experiences seem to be "a vehicle for engaging with a significant life-cycle transition" (Amit 2007: 6). All these forms of mobility are believed to be "transformative" in one way or the other, offering both an escape from situations of potentially jeopardized status while providing their own source of symbolic capital.

This book, then, investigates whether momentous mobilities can be seen as expressions of a wider "traveling culture" (Clifford 1997; Rojek and Urry 1997) or a "culture of mobility" (Tarrius 2000). Culturally-inflected boundary-crossing movements, as a fundamental social and historical aspect of society, have been analyzed across the globe: in the Americas (J. Cohen 2004), Africa (de Bruijn, van Dijk, and Foeken 2001; Hahn and Klute 2007), Asia (Syed 2007), the Pacific (Connell 2008), and Europe (Fumerton 2006). In their classic analysis of studies of migration among indigenous populations in Africa and the Pacific, Chapman and Prothero (1985; also Prothero and Chapman 1985) provided evidence of the "constant ebb and flow" that constitutes a major part of life. Circular migration, as they called it, "far from being transitional or ephemeral, is a time-honored and enduring mode of behavior, deeply rooted in a great variety of cultures and found at all stages of socioeconomic change" (Chapman and Prothero 1985: 6).

Translocal mobilities are generally perceived as markers of "free" movement (Abram et al. 2017). It is a widespread idea that much of what is experienced as freedom is linked to mobility (Dean 2016; Sager 2006). It has even been suggested that this idea springs from human nature, as studies of the behavior of great apes conclude that they prefer freedom and mobility over close social ties (Maryanski and Turner 1992). Historically, mobility appeared, in romantic literature in particular, as an element of personal realization and freedom from the capitalist universe, especially from stability and from the rules imposed by the bourgeois industrial order (Gherardi 2011). Some argue that "capitalism transformed the force of the freedom of mobility into competitively organized upward social mobility" (Papadopoulos, Stephenson, and Tsianos 2008: 204).[10] People are required to take responsibility for their mobilities in a manner that confirms they are freely choosing individuals while, in fact, they act within clearly defined fields of opportunities (cf. Bourdieu 1984). Because valorizations of mobility are distributed socially, these can contribute to the classification of individuals according to their different social positions. However, there is very little research on why and how these values differ (apart from obvious differences in travel opportunities and resources).

Many contemporary theorists valorize, if not romanticize, ideas of travel and mobility (Bude and Dürrschmidt 2010). As mentioned before, this way of thinking destabilizes the fixed and ethnocentric categories of mainstream traditional anthropology and locate culture and identity in "radical" movement, both material and imagined, rather than in place (Latour 2005; Ong 1999). The idea of "becoming through mobility" (*moveo ergo sum*) is part and parcel of the perceived shift from inherited or acquired identities to a focus on identification, a change from relatively stable (place-based) identities to hybrid (achieved) identities characterized by flux (Easthope 2009). This "recasting of identity in terms of flexibility, adaptability and instant transformation" (Elliott and Urry 2010: 7) poses important challenges to issues of social belonging and cultural rootedness (Geschiere 2009; Hannerz 2002; Lien and Melhuus 2007).

General rationales for boundary-crossing mobilities must be distinguished from personal reasons: the former are formulated by external observers; the latter are given by people themselves (and even the motivations reported by "movers" do not necessarily reflect their actual behavior). From an etic perspective, the imperative to be mobile is interpreted as the individual's need for mobility to accomplish personal plans and projects (Canzler, Kaufmann, and Kesselring 2008). I argue, however, that ideas concerning perceived "benefits" of mobility are part of a wider value system that is socially shared. Mobility is believed to play an increasingly important role in the construction of people's social position (Canzler, Kaufmann, and Kesselring 2008). The more society valorizes mobility (or, at least, specific types of mobility), the greater the significance of "mobility capital"—the resources, knowledge, or abilities gained by having lived "elsewhere" among "others" (Jayaram 2016).

Mobilities become momentous because the accumulated symbolic capital can be deployed over the subsequent life course for personal, social, or career enhancement in two major ways. First, it can facilitate future boundary-crossing moves by enhancing people's differential capacity and potential for mobility (Kaufmann, Bergman, and Joye 2004). Alternatively, it can be exchanged "back home" for other forms of capital, as described by Pierre Bourdieu (1986): economic (material resources), social (relational networks), and cultural (embodied dispositions and competencies of cosmopolitanism) capital. Thus, mobility capital is turning momentous mobilities into a new index of prestige, power, and symbolic status, a new marker of distinction (cf. Bourdieu 1984).

The meaning of mobilities goes further than their endpoints, and the corresponding social and cultural embedding of movement is highly contested and stratified (Ohnmacht, Maksim, and Bergman 2009). Mobility is not just good because it "equals open-mindedness, discovery, and experience" (Kaufmann 2002: 37). It is the sum total of a seemingly infinite set of promised and assumed opportunities arising from movement that counts most (Elliott and Urry 2010). A whole set of sociocultural values has developed around voluntary translocal mobilities. In contrast to traditional emigration ideology, people engaging in boundary-crossing travels are described as having a more positive attitude toward mobility, leading "cosmopolitan lives," and not seeing themselves as victims with a "myth of return" (cf. Reed-Danahay and Brettell 2008). These "cultural sojourners" are believed to be driven by highly individualized attitudes, market orientated values, consumerism, and a sense of the power of their own agency.[11] For them, it is a continuation of their individual biographies, educational opportunity, and a rite of passage into adult life or retirement.

The sociocultural valorization of boundary-crossing mobilities makes the "movers" responsible for their "becoming." This mobility ideology equates geographical movement with social fluidity, without any critical questioning. It negates the fact that social structures also contribute to mobility behavior, that mobilities are subject to social constraint, and that opportunities of upward socioeconomic movement to which the individual responds by being physically mobile are as much "freely" wanted and realized opportunities as choices by default (with the legal structures regulating who can and cannot move being crucial). Many scholars argue that transnational mobility is a highly differentiated and differentiating activity (Bauman 1998; Beck 2000; Castells 2000), no longer the realm of the exceptional and exotic but, rather, a normal and sometimes necessary part of life, particularly for the middle classes (e.g., Larsen, Urry, and Axhausen 2006).

Additionally, I want to stress in this book the contingencies of significance: the various economic, discursive, and institutional processes that are involved in the normalization, prioritization, or insidious valorization of translocal mobilities. In other words, "mobility must have social meanings by which the effects of physical movements can be cast on others" (Liu 1997: 99). Neither "stayers" nor "movers" consume the innate significance of translocal mobilities; instead, they co-construct it in dynamic relations of exchange and interaction (Salazar and Glick Schiller 2014).

Imaginaries of Migrancy

While the reasons and motivations to cross borders and boundaries are usually multiple, they are linked to the ability of those traveling (and their social networks) to imagine the "elsewhere." In other words, "movement is not just the experience of shifting from place to place, it is also linked to our ability to imagine an alternative" (Papastergiadis 2000: 11). People seldom travel to *terrae incognitae* these days, but instead journey to places they already "know" through the imaginaries that circulate about them (Salazar 2013b). While traveling "elsewhere" may mean different things to different people, the meaning and valuation of mobility is constantly (re)negotiated on the basis of social imaginaries and cultural values (Glick Schiller and Salazar 2013a).

People's mobility "choices" are normalized within the dominant ideologies with which they engage. Julie Chu (2010: 13) calls this the "normative sense of mobility at the heart of contemporary social imaginations and embodiments." It is hard to decode these normative visions because "mobility itself is coded sometimes as adventure, an initiatory journey intended to shape the self, a dys-placement (moving in/out of place); it builds on a commitment to change …. Leaving, moving, going 'away' means following a dream, a desire, the design of a better or new life" (Teampău and Van Assche 2009: 150). Imaginaries, as socially shared patterns of meaning rather than as private cognition, can both endorse the normality or historicity of stasis or of mobility. This points to the controlling role of mobility imaginaries (cf. Castoriadis 1987; Taylor 2004). The imaginary has been conceptualized as a culture's ethos or a society's shared, unifying core conceptions, a fantasy or illusion created in response to a psychological need, and a cultural model or widely shared implicit cognitive schema (Strauss 2006).[12] I conceptualize imaginaries as socially shared and transmitted representational assemblages that interact with people's personal imaginings and are used as meaning-making and world-shaping devices (Salazar 2011a).

Empowered by mass-mediated images and discourses, imaginaries circulate globally and change the way in which people collectively envision the world and their place and mobility within it. Imaginaries travel through a multitude of channels, including people, and provide the cultural material to be drawn upon and used for the creation of translocal connections (Römhild 2003). Even when a person is place-bound, his or her imagination can be in motion, traveling to other places and other times (Rapport and Dawson 1998). By extension, it could be argued that even when one is in movement, one's imagination can be focused on a singular place (e.g., diasporic people recreating their imagined "homeland") and that these imaginaries of fixity can influence one's experience of mobility (Easthope 2009). Previous research on mobility tended to separate the imagination as being an impact external to local practice. Yet, imagination is a practice of transcending physical and sociocultural distance (Appadurai 1996). John Urry (2007: 41) called it "imaginative travel" because "much movement involves experiencing or anticipating in one's imagination the 'authentic atmosphere' of another place or places."

The various chapters of this book serve to illustrate how the meanings attached to mobility imaginaries are materialized in a variety of sociocultural practices. The imaginary (thoughts, fantasies, and desires) is a fertile source of different types of mobility that can prefigure, albeit incoherently, different discourses, power relations, social relations, institutional structures, and material practices. Studying and questioning these imaginaries of (im)mobility offers a novel way in which to grasp the ongoing global transformations of the human condition. The focus on imaginaries as a major source of relating people across territorial boundaries also productively challenges basic assumptions of, and the divisions between, previously separated fields such as tourism and migration studies.[13]

The concept of imaginaries has been particularly popular among scholars studying Chinese mobility patterns. Xin Liu (1997: 110) writes, "From the point of view of ordinary people, travel and its associated imaginings are becoming an important condition of everyday life." In a similar vein, Aihwa Ong (1999: 19) notes in her research among transnational Chinese how "flexibility, migration, and relocations, instead of being coerced or resisted, have become practices to strive for rather than stability." Pál Nyíri (2010) also describes how mobility has become one of the most important means in China through which to produce symbolic capital. Julie Chu

(2010: 10) ethnographically details how mobility in post-Mao China functions as a "condition of everyday life" and as "practices to strive for." The analysis of Xin Liu (1997: 110) has a broader resonance:

> Even though people experience differential mobility, a conceptual shift in Leaving, moving, going 'away' means following a dream .... Social differentiation is increasingly produced or reproduced by differential access to mobility .... Travel and movement have reordered the power relations between different groups of people, and their identities are reworked according to the shifting images of various kinds of selves and others.

The Way of the Method

This monograph is the result of an eclectic process of data collection, analysis of secondary sources, and personal experience and reflection. It draws on a multisited and multimethod research design, which involved strategically combining various research methods. The methodology follows a current in social research that emphasizes "constructing the object of research" as a key empirical step, and never taking the empirical object as "given" or immediately "readable" from given preconceptions (cf. Favell and Recchi 2011). The transdisciplinary design was inspired by a wide body of scholarship and is theoretically informed by the previously outlined ideas on (im)mobility.[14] Since the study is deeply grounded in anthropology, the discipline in which I have been trained academically, it was guided by the dialectic between the deductive and the inductive, between the concept and the concrete, between the objectives and the subjects.

The characteristics of (momentous) mobilities, namely their duration, frequency, and seasonality, present many methodological challenges (Elliot, Norum, and Salazar 2017). How to select and delineate a workable field of study and how to identify and approach appropriate informants? I dealt with these issues by initially relying on the least structured data collection techniques and then moving to include more structured data. Relying on "serendipity," the primary data (of sufficient quantity and depth) were reinterpreted from a theoretical perspective different from the one that produced them, leading to a revisit of the original research questions and design (Salazar and Rivoal 2013). Throughout the iterative process of data gathering and analysis, I used analytic memos to focus on emergent themes, initial interpretations, and inductively derived explanatory theories.

As Charles Briggs (2013: 228) rightly notes, "Scholars have no privileged or disinterested position here; when we construct cartographies of circulation and mobility, we are just as caught up in these processes as anyone else, just as much at the mercy of our own models of mobility and techniques of (im)mobilization." My own positionality as a young, privileged, European male (see preface) certainly affected the way I experience and attribute meaning to the mobilities I describe in this book, and the way the people I encountered and questioned on the topic positioned themselves vis-à-vis me as a researcher. Being aware of the role of gender in travel and mobility (Benhabib and Resnik 2009; Elliot 2016; Uteng and Cresswell 2008), I chose to collaborate with female local research assistants whenever possible.

The "sites" chosen for the case studies partially drew on earlier research (Indonesia and Tanzania) or on a personal affinity and familiarity (Chile and the EU). Although some readers familiar with anthropological writings undoubtedly would have preferred it, this book is not an "ethnography" (understood as the written outcome of extended ethnographic fieldwork). Because not all the studies presented here were, or could be, properly planned beforehand, short periods of fieldwork were enriched with autoethnographic elements, including my own experiences as a foreign student, mobile academic, international volunteer, pilgrim, and avid tourist. In this way, I could fill some of the gaps caused by situations where research ethics prevented me from conducting standard ethnographic fieldwork with long-term participant observation. This happened, for instance, when I met people while being "on the road" but did not have enough time to explain to them about the research and to ask them whether they would like to participate. Asking for informed consent was not always possible, and, in some instances, it would have been out of place. In such cases, I decided to focus more on my own observations and experiences. This also explains why the voices of research participants are not always as present in this book as I would have wished they were.

Autoethnography is a well-known method in anthropology, as a form of self-narrative that "places the self within a social context" (Reed-Danahay 1997: 9). It is particularly useful in contexts where traditional ethnographic methods are more difficult to implement. In *"Illegal" Traveller* (2010), for example, Shahram Khosravi interjects personal experiences about his journey from Iran to Europe as an "illegal" refugee into ethnographic writing about difficult border crossings. His work provides an important contrast to the types of momentous mobilities presented in this book. Autoethnography in general blurs the distinction between researcher and "informants." This is also the case here. Many of the meaningful travels discussed in this book are ones that I have experienced or am closely familiar with. Moreover, I extensively draw on research by other scholars to corroborate my own findings and interpretations. No matter which kinds of data were gathered and analyzed, the anthropological focus is always on how the various movements under study are made meaningful and how those meanings are circulated.

I decided to leave out so-called involuntary forms of mobility, which are driven by necessity rather than "free" choice, including the ones I was confronted with (but did not experience myself) as a refugee aid worker. This is not to deny the crucial importance of "forced" forms of mobility in coming to a general understanding of what it means to be (im)mobile. Involuntary or forced mobilities are also momentous for those experiencing them. However, they do not receive the same sociocultural recognition as the mobility forms described in this book. Elaborating on why this is the case would have required much more additional research. While this may be a topic for future research, I have paid attention to existing inequalities in mobility regimes elsewhere (Salazar and Glick Schiller 2014; Salazar and Smart 2011).[15]

Generous research funding from the EU and the Research Foundation Flanders, together with my position as an executive board member of the European Association of Social Anthropologists (2010–14), the International Union of Anthropological and Ethnological Sciences (2013–18), and the Young Academy of Belgium (2013–15), facilitated my "moves" across borders and boundaries. This led to many small side projects that are directly relevant to the core of the research presented here. I made sure to observe and, wherever possible, to experience as many types of momentous mobilities and temporary relocation as possible. In terms of my own transport and accommodation, I chose low-budget options (e.g., Eurolines buses, Ryanair flights, youth hostels, campgrounds, and guest families) as well as the high end of the market (e.g., staying at five-star hotels or traveling by Thalys and Eurostar trains). Becoming a frequent flyer of Star Alliance gave me access to the world of lounges and, occasionally, to traveling in business class. The mobile part of the fieldwork was complemented by substantial "immobility" (particularly when I was analyzing data and writing up the findings).

En Route …

> Why do you go away? So that you can come back. So that you can see the place you came from with new eyes and extra colors. And the people there see you differently, too. Coming back to where you started is not the same as never leaving.
>
> —Terry Pratchett, *A Hat Full of Sky*

The first part of this monograph, titled "Imagining Mobility," focuses specifically on how societies and cultures other than my own imagine boundary-crossing travels "elsewhere." Chapter 1, for example, describes how Chile's geographical remoteness has defined the imaginaries people share about the mobilities to and from this Latin American country. Despite its historical image as *finis terrae* (the end of the world), people from all corners found their way to these isolated peripheral lands. Based on a combination of archival research and (auto)ethnographic fieldwork, the chapter traces how old (and originally foreign) imaginaries about Chile as an inaccessible island continue to influence how contemporary Chileans, including political exiles, participate in, and frame their perceived exclusion from, a plethora of contemporary transnational mobilities, whether or not they have the means and freedom to cross imaginary boundaries and physical borders. Interestingly, the value of (relative) immobility, which is increasingly under external pressure, remains at the core of the Chilean social imaginary, geopolitics, and cultural as well as family life.

In chapter 2, I turn my attention to the widespread occurrence of various forms of mobilities in and around the Indonesian archipelago. It is important to place these movements in the context of a long tradition of exchange, facilitated by network-creating and network-dependent relationships. While migration studies scholars have paid considerable attention to internal movements within Indonesia, as well as to international (labor) migration flows from Indonesia, they have rarely considered the intersections between these two processes, which are mutually constitutive. Modern mobility practices are not simply understood through the lens of the relatively young Indonesian nation-state, administrative borders, or other categories, but as described, imagined, and experienced by those "on the move" or those personally affected by others moving. Boundary-crossing movements among people with limited mobility resources appear to be highly mediated, not only by regulations and brokers but also by "modern" technologies. I discuss how translocal travels are not generally undertaken by Indonesians with the express intention of uprooting people but are increasingly becoming one-way journeys of (more permanent) migration.

Chapter 3 narrates the mobility story of the Maasai, a widely-dispersed group of seminomadic pastoralists and small-scale subsistence agriculturists who occupy semiarid rangelands in southern Kenya and northern Tanzania. Through stereotyped (mis)representations since the colonial era, they have become icons of African traditionalism and unwitting symbols of resistance to modernist values. The sight of virile Maasai warriors, dressed in colorful red blankets and beaded jewelry, evokes the romantic image of a modern "nomad"—a priceless tourism attraction. Ironically, it is the creation of tourism activities that have pushed many Maasai to lead a more sedentary life. Based on long-term research in and on Tanzania, this chapter contrasts the stereotypical way in which Maasai (im)mobilities have been imagined with contemporary mobility practices among Maasai. I describe how mobile Maasai culture is simultaneously both reproduced and subtly contested. Maasai are "on the move" in ways that diverge widely from their image as obstinate semipastoralists.

The second part of the book, "Enacting Mobility," revisits many of the themes encountered in the first part, but situates them in the lifeworld that I know best: my own. The autoethnographic elements are more present here, because I focus on boundary-crossing mobilities by Europeans (including myself) in the fields of education, labor, and "quality of life." Chapter 4 zooms in on transnational educational mobility, the transitory movement of students in higher education to institutions outside their own country. These temporary and mostly circular movements, variously called "mobility," "exchange," or "study abroad," are widely praised, sometimes even fetishized, by policymakers, corporate culture, and the academic world alike. I take issue with many misrepresentations by discussing the EU Lifelong Learning Program (including Erasmus), the most extensive academic mobility program to date. While the numbers are rising, most students are, and will remain, extremely geographically "immobile" during their studies or careers. I reflect on the discrepancy between the political rhetoric of student mobility and the reality on the ground.

In chapter 5, I zoom in on specific types of labor mobilities. There is relatively little research on the mobility of highly skilled expatriates, mainly because it is often assumed that this social phenomenon is problem-free. I offer a critical reflection on contemporary "expat" practices. Life and work abroad, even under privileged expat conditions, is often less rosy than imagined. Highly skilled knowledge workers and managers do not necessarily enjoy more "freedom" in their transborder lives and mobilities than their lower-skilled migrant counterparts do. These days, the expected accumulation of economic and symbolic capital is less obvious than it used to be. I discuss how, with some nuances, the processes at work are remarkably similar to those usually attributed to lower-skilled migrants.

Chapter 6 reminds us that people cross boundaries not only in search for knowledge or job opportunities; spiritual quests and the search for a better quality of life have also brought people to the most remote corners of the world. Based on my personal experience and observations of pilgrimage and various types of "enlightening" tourism, I disentangle in this chapter how these forms of boundary-crossing are "transformative," offering both an escape from situations of potentially jeopardized status (e.g., around retirement) and providing their own source of symbolic capital (e.g., cosmopolitanism). Such rites of passage are a means through which people can sustain meaning and values, and (re)create themselves. This raises further ontological questions about our understanding of "identity," "home," and "belonging." I compare traditional examples of spiritual pilgrimage with contemporary practices.

In the conclusion, I summarize the most important ideas that this monograph offers while pointing out directions for future studies. Mobility research addresses new questions toward traditional social science topics. People are moving all the time, but not all movements are equally meaningful and life-shaping (both for those who move and those who stay put). Mobility becomes momentous through its embeddedness within societies, culture, politics, and histories (which are themselves, to a certain extent, mobile). As the chapters in this book illustrate, translocal mobility may have become the key difference- and otherness-producing machine of our age, involving significant inequalities of speed, risk, rights, and status, with both "movers" and "stayers" being engaged in the construction of complex politics of belonging and becoming, location, and movement.

NOTES

1. People in movement have, for a long time, been used as one of the preferred concept-metaphors for social descriptions of both self and other in the social sciences and the humanities (J. Peters 2006). Many of the concepts commonly used are marked by gender, class, ethnicity, and culture (Benhabib and Resnik 2009; Braidotti 1994; Kaplan 1996). Popular examples from social theory include Walter Benjamin's "flaneur," Michel de Certeau's "pedestrian," Edward Said's "(forced) migrant," and Gilles Deleuze's "nomad" (Salazar and Coates 2017).

2. In the words of Anna Tsing (2004: 6), various "kinds of 'friction' inflect motion, offering it different meanings. Coercion and frustration join freedom as motion is socially informed." Nikos Papastergiadis (2000: 4) uses a similar metaphor when talking about "turbulence" as "the best formulation for the mobile processes of complex self-organization that are now occurring."

3. Despite some attention to actual migratory movement, however, most research on migration has privileged the study of issues related to settlement in place (Hui 2016).

4. The term "mobility turn" has been used to indicate a perceived transformation of the social sciences in response to the increasing importance of various forms of movement (Urry 2000; 2007). The "new mobilities paradigm," then, incorporates new ways of theorizing how people, objects, and ideas move around by looking at social phenomena through the lens of movement (Hannam, Sheller, and Urry 2006). It is a critique of both theories of sedent(ar)ism and deterritorialization. In general, mobility has become a widely used perspective that takes many forms. In

other words, not everybody studying mobility necessarily agrees with the mobility turn or the new mobilities paradigm.

5. Relevant in this context is that Appadurai (1996) proposes that globalization fundamentally alters the "movement" of individuals, technology, money, media, and ideas.

6. As a reaction to this perceived gap, I founded, in 2009, the Cultural Mobilities Research (CuMoRe) cluster at the University of Leuven. This coincided with the start of the Open Anthropology Cooperative Anthropology and Mobility group, which was institutionalized in 2010 as the EASA Anthropology and Mobility Network (known as "AnthroMob").

7. Geographers such as Doreen Massey (1993: 62) have long pointed to the "politics of mobility and access" and how "the mobility and control of some groups can actively weaken other people."

8. The argument of a general increase in human mobility across time is contested. At the same time, it is undeniable that patterns of mobility are changing, whereby some types of movement may lose ground to others.

9. It is doubtful, for instance, whether there are many "existential migrants" (Madison 2010), people who freely move, not in search of a better life or to expand their options, but only for the sake of moving. Importantly, people's "intentions often change after living for a time in a new location, so that what begins as a temporary sojourn becomes a permanent stay or what begins as a permanent move turns into a temporary one" (Hamilton 1985: 405).

10. The link between geographical and social mobility is one that was made in the United States at the beginning of the twentieth century by the influential Chicago School of urbanism (Gallez and Kaufmann 2015). Think of the idea of the "American Dream," whereby mobility, or the willingness to move (with each move being a source of freedom and opportunity), is inextricably related to this dream. Such imaginaries persist today, even though very few U.S. citizens undergo (upward) status changes in their lifetimes.

11. Uriely (1994) identified a continuum of migrants from sojourners (temporary migrants) to settlers (permanent migrants), with "permanent sojourners" taking the middle ground between the two. Permanent sojourners are those who maintain a general wish to return to their homeland, and their orientation toward their new place of residence represents a compromise between the sojourner and the settler.

12. For an overview of the intellectual history and contemporary uses of the imaginary in anthropology, see Claudia Strauss (2006). Despite their frequent references to the imaginary, contemporary anthropologists have been less concerned with imaginative processes than with the products of the imagination (e.g., Appadurai 1996).

13. See Benson and O'Reilly 2009; Coles and Timothy 2004; and Hall and Williams 2002.

14. I was methodologically inspired by a wide range of sources (see Bernard 2006; Burawoy 2000; Büscher, Urry, and Witchger 2011; Elliot, Norum, and Salazar 2017; Gingrich and Fox 2002; Marcus 1998).

15. For those interested, there is increasing ethnographic research on refugee and (forced) migration journeys. See, among others, the work of Andersson (2014), Khosravi (2010), and Schapendonk (2011).

PART I

IMAGINING MOBILITY

Chile

Traveling to and from the End of the World

I spent the very end of the previous millennium in the Southern Hemisphere. My Chilean partner and I traveled to Patagonia, at the southern tip of the Americas. We landed in Punta Arenas, a city that had functioned as an important refueling port for the steamships that traveled between the Atlantic and Pacific Oceans through the Strait of Magellan, until the opening of the Panama Canal in 1914. Today, it is used mostly by tourism cruises and as a jumping-off point for scientific expeditions to Antarctica. Having just read Adrien de Gerlache's *Fifteen Months in the Antarctic* ([1902] 1998), I thought about the Belgian Antarctic expedition that had departed from Punta Arenas one century earlier. The legendary research ship *Belgica* had had on board, among others, the anthropologist-explorer Frederick Cook (whose later claim of having reached the geographic North Pole earlier than Robert Peary is disputed still today). The *Belgica* became trapped by surrounding pack ice and was the first vessel to stay over the winter months in the Antarctic, after which it safely returned to Punta Arenas for repairs. Numerous testimonies of explorers and traders alike helped to create the image of Chile as a "cold" place (as opposed to the stereotypical representation of South America as "tropical").

Like most people visiting Patagonia nowadays, my partner and I were there as tourists. We traveled along the Chilean shore, inspired by Michael Palin's voyage around the rim of the Pacific Ocean (aired as the 1997 BBC documentary television series *Full Circle*). We boarded a cargo ship in Puerto Montt for a four-day trip down south to Puerto Natales. Like Palin, we hiked through the Torres del Paine National Park. The desolate landscapes along the coastline reinforced my own image of Chile as being at the "end of the world." However, this interpretation had to be qualified when on the second day of the boat journey somebody tapped on my shoulder as we were queuing in the galley to have breakfast. I could not believe my eyes when I saw one of my Belgian classmates from university. She was also touring the region. Chile immediately became much less "end of the world"-ish for me.

***

As my own travel experience in Patagonia illustrates, people seldom journey to *terrae incognitae* anymore, but to places they already virtually "know" through the widely circulating imaginaries that exist about them (Salazar 2010a; 2012). According to Edward Said (1994), "imagined geographies" refer to how places are imagined, how meanings are ascribed to physical spaces, how knowledge about these places is produced, and how these representations make various courses of action possible. Historically laden imaginaries—socially shared and transmitted representational assemblages that are used as meaning-making devices—are the "energetic source" (M. Baeza 2008: 24) that inspires social life, including physical travels to distant destinations. One of the central characteristics of such imaginaries is the lack of correspondence between the projected ideals and aspirations on the one hand and the perceived and experienced reality on the other (e.g., the "American dream").

In this chapter, I discuss historical as well as contemporary examples to illustrate the power of imaginaries in shaping people's (im)mobility. I carried out fieldwork and archival research in Chile in December 2009–January 2010 (supplemented with data and experiences from previous visits to the country since 1998, including the one reported above). The method used involved various types of free-flowing interviews with key informants and other significant actors in the broad field of transnational mobility. Ancillary data gathered include secondary sources, audiovisual data, news media, documents, archives, websites, etcetera. In addition, I took exhaustive notes and made personal diary entries to record all my findings. A female Chilean graduate student in anthropology from the University of Chile helped as my local research assistant, both in the phase of data gathering (e.g., conducting interviews) and data analysis (e.g., coding interviews).

Chile is a long (2,670 miles/4,300 kilometers) and narrow (on average 108 miles/175 kilometers) strip of land between the Andes Mountains to the east and the Pacific Ocean to the west, the Atacama Desert in the north and the icebergs of Patagonia in the south. This "crazy geography" (Subercaseaux 1973) has not only determined its territorial borders, but also influenced the imaginaries that people, Chileans and foreigners alike, have about this Latin American country and the mobilities to and from it (Salazar 2013b). My findings reveal the remarkable influence that dated outsider imaginaries of Chile as "the end of the world" have on how contemporary Chileans participate in and frame their perceived exclusion from a plethora of contemporary mobilities, regardless of whether they have the actual means and freedom to cross imaginary boundaries and physical borders or not. The recent historical episode of Chileans in exile further complicates the story.

The End of the World (as People Know It)

> Ours is a land far away, the farthest of the Western Hemisphere, a real Finisterrae. This remoteness … turned our land a long time ago into a fertile ground for legends in the eyes of Europeans.
>
> —Luis Oyarzún, in Cecilia García-Huidobro Mac Auliffe,
> *Tics De Los Chilenos*

Prior to the arrival of the Spanish colonizers in the sixteenth century, northern Chile was under Inca rule, while various Mapuche groups inhabited the central lands and southern islands. The origin of the word *Chile* is contested. One among many possible linguistic genealogies is the Aymara concept *chilli* (where the world ends). For the Aymara, an indigenous group living in the Andes and the Altiplano, it made sense to denote the lands southwest of theirs as the end of their lifeworld. The Spanish had done the same in Europe, calling the westernmost point of the Iberian Peninsula Cabo Fisterra (Cape Finisterre). However, these geographical imaginaries drastically changed when Iberians discovered in the fifteenth century that, far beyond their western "edge of the world," there was another land: America. From that moment onward, the so-called New World became one of the most popular places onto which Europeans could project their wildest images and ideas of paradise on earth (Fernández Herrero 1994; Scott 2010).

In the age of these discoveries, the whole of the Americas fulfilled the legendary role of the "end of the world." As the conquest progressed, North and Central America gradually lost their mythical qualities, and the European imaginary of the end of the world moved from the "Far West" to the "Far South" (Franz 2000). The Captaincy General of Chile (part of the Viceroyalty of Peru), established by Spanish conquistadors in the 1540s, developed as a small and neglected agrarian colony on the fringe of the Spanish American empire (Collier and Sater 2004) (see figure 1.1). As Ana Maria Stuven (2007: 47) writes, "For the Spanish Empire, Chile was one of the least important colonies; it was extremely far from the centers of power and it was a region of intermittent warfare. Who wanted to go to Chile? Very few. And this inevitably influenced and still influences the Chilean character."

The Spanish conquistadors were among the first migrants arriving in Chile, but they are not usually acknowledged and named as such (Cano and Soffia 2009). During the sixteenth and seventeenth centuries, Chile received many Spanish migrants, together with a small group of slaves of African descent. British and French traders only started arriving in the eighteenth century. Most scholars, however, start employing the concept of migration only when Chile gains independence and starts welcoming European soldiers and maritime traders, which in turn facilitated the spontaneous arrival of other Europeans. Many European governments sponsored permanent relocation to Chile. The waves of migrants who left Europe between 1850 and World War I helped to reinvigorate the "foundational spirit" of the Promised Land.

Despite these historical mobilities, Chile developed as a socially and culturally insular country unaccustomed to the presence of large numbers of "foreigners." Many of the descriptions of Chile refer to the extreme south for the simple reason that, prior to the opening of the Panama Canal in 1914, the Strait of Magellan was the main route for steam ships traveling

Figure 1.1: The beginning of the "end of the world." An Andean border crossing between Bolivia and Chile. (Photographer: Noel B. Salazar)

from the Atlantic Ocean to the Pacific. The first Chilean governments had two main motives in attracting European migrants: the colonization of the inhospitable south of the country (finishing the task that the Spanish colonizers had begun) and the widespread belief that Europeans, as hard workers, would automatically bring development in tow (including "improving the race" and modernization). The years between the 1907 and 1952 censuses are notable for the growth of a migrant population of Arabs (fleeing conflicts in the Ottoman Empire, which then included Syria, Palestine, and Lebanon) and Asians, arriving more spontaneously. Responding to a changed context—the industrialization of the 1940s and the end of World War II—Chile no longer needed colonizers but sought specific types of economic migrants. Politics, however, would drastically change the course of the country.

The (Im)Mobility of Exile

In my luggage from exile, I bring fraternal friendship from other lands.
I leave behind sorrow and sleepless nights. I return to live wholly again.

—*Vuelvo para Vivir* (Illapu, 1991)

Through the relatives and acquaintances of my Chilean spouse, I have been confronted directly with Chile's issue of political exile. Señora Consuelo, for example, was leading a quiet life in the southern city of Concepción, without any interest in what was happening outside her geographically limited lifeworld. At the age of twenty, she got married to Jorge, who was very engaged locally as a member of the Communist Party. In 1974, a year after the military coup, Consuelo and Jorge came to know that Jorge was on a black list and at risk of being thrown in jail, so the family decided to escape. Their children, Patricio and Elizabet, were respectively one and three years old at the time. The family spent three years in Argentina, but as state violence was on the rise there too, they had to move again. After spending a short time in Venezuela, they finally arrived in Canada. They felt very welcomed by both the Canadian people and the government and settled down. The contact with family and friends in Chile was minimal because phone calls were very expensive and snail mail was not very trustworthy. In 1983, with the Chilean borders opening a little again, they traveled back to their native country. What officially looked like a holiday was in practice a trip to check whether it was at all feasible for them to return permanently. They hesitated, but felt the time was not ripe yet.

In 1989, the year that democracy was reinstalled in Chile, Consuelo regained her personal freedom and was granted a divorce from Jorge. A year later, when Patricio and Elizabet had both finished high school, the three of them returned to Chile. Elizabet could not settle emotionally and almost immediately returned to Canada; Patricio stayed with an uncle in Santiago while studying at university; and Consuelo moved back to her beloved Concepción. Patricio never finished his studies and stayed with his mother in Concepción for a couple of years before moving back to Canada. Consuelo felt torn between two worlds: the one in Canada that was inhabited by her children (and, as time passed, grandchildren) and the one occupied by her family and friends in Chile. She tried to move her permanent residence once more to Canada but felt socially isolated and too dependent on Patricio and Elizabet. Today, Consuelo leads an "international" lifestyle: she officially lives in Chile but keeps on shuttling back and forth regularly between the two countries. I met her or her children on various occasions in both countries.

***

The dramatic political changes of the early 1970s turned Chile from an immigrant to an emigrant nation. During the economic and political crisis that followed the 1973 coup, hundreds of thousands of Chileans chose to flee the repressive political regime of General Augusto Pinochet or were forced into leaving.[1] In fact, Chile became known internationally not for the flow of people into its borders (never more than two per cent of the total population) but in relation to the many Chileans who left (Martínez Pizarro 2003).

During the first years, thousands of people sought refuge nearby (in Argentina and Peru, but also in Paraguay and Uruguay), expecting to be able to return before long. The passage of time erased the illusion of a brief dictatorship, but even in former times, neighboring countries proved unsuitable for most Chileans (Wright and Oñate Zúñiga 2007). For those forced to leave, the main determinant of their exile destination was chance: international agencies paired these refugees with willing host countries, some of them real *terrae incognitae* about which the exiles knew little or nothing. Exiles were sent to over a hundred countries, spread over every continent. Many ended up in Canada, Sweden, Italy, France, Australia, and the United States. During the period 1973–85, between 500,000 and 1,000,000 Chileans, around 10 per cent of the population, left the country (Jedlicki 2001). While around 250,000 people were forced to move, others left voluntarily.[2] This diaspora radically changed the relation Chile developed with the wider world "out there" (see below).

While even as early as 1983 lists were published with Chileans who could return, forced exile officially ended only in 1988. Until that time, exile was characterized by a double flow of people entering and leaving the country. Exiles kept the dream of return alive and, as the period of exile was extended, Chile became a mythical "homeland." For the first generation, living abroad involved drastic shifts in status, often in the form of down-ward social mobility. The inability to return progressively changed the experience of temporary asylum to a state of prolonged exile. As Chilean exiles in Brussels and elsewhere told me, the feeling of displacement, as a hallmark of exile, has both spatial and temporal dimensions. During the military regime, they felt uprooted, as if they were living between two places simultaneously: "here" (the country of exile) and "there" (the imagined homeland). At the same time, they had the sensation that time had been suspended and exile was just a liminal phase they had to undergo prior to their returning home. Most Chileans, like other people in exile, had their suitcases ready to make the return trip at a moment's notice (Rebolledo and Acuña 2001).[3]

From a mobility perspective, exiles are a special case. They are mostly forced to leave their country ("involuntary mobility") and are not allowed to return ("involuntary immobility"). However, if the period of exile lasts long enough, many opt for not returning ("voluntary immobility") or for moving on to new destinations ("voluntary mobility").[4] Although envisioned as highly desirable, the (attempted) return often leads to a clash between the imagined "homeland" and the transformed reality on the ground. Many *retornados*, for instance, upheld the image of the mythical Chile after their return, despite their knowledge that the country had changed during their absence (cf. Allende 2003). Virtually all returnees found their reception in Chile "icy": years of government propaganda against them had suc-ceeded in rooting a generalized idea that Chileans abroad had enjoyed a "golden exile" ("la dolce vita"), described by one *retornado* as the idea of "people enjoying a long vacation and a trip around the world" (Wright and Oñate Zúñiga 1998: 207).[5] The exiles were also suspected of having lost their "culture of origin," embodying the paradoxical figure of "foreign nationals" (Jedlicki 2007). They were certainly perceived as "foreigners" (Pizarro 2003: 110) or, as street graffiti in the capital city of Santiago in the beginning of the 1990s stated, "The returnee is a stranger" (del Pozo Artigas 2006).

While some *retornados* could rebuild a stable existence in Chile after several years, others failed. Many of the returnees faced countless difficul-ties in Chile and decided to move back to their exile host country (Jedlicki 2007). Several, including Consuelo and her children, found themselves caught up in a constant circulation between the two countries (or even ended up in a third country). This illustrates that exile and migrant catego-ries are not fixed, since the former can easily transform into the latter (cf. Schuster 2005). As Erik Olsson (2010: 2) argues, "Return migration does not end the 'refugee-cycle' but represents a dimension in a transnational way of living." Indeed, as the story of Consuelo shows, repeated moves back and forth can become perceived as "normal." In other words, "sustainable return" may involve continued mobility within and across borders. Sustainability in this context is thus not necessarily the same as immobility, since "continued mobility may be the predominant avenue for integration and development of the economies of the retuning population" (Stepputat 2004: 13). The majority of exiles did not go back to Chile as "return migrants," as they are officially called (C. Baeza 2010). In sum, the process of *retorno* (return) often turns out to be much more complex than the mere act of *volver* (going back).

Exiles were not the only mobile group whose movements were a consequence of the military regime in Chile. Important parts of General Pinochet's economic and military policies were a direct outcome of targeted forms of transnational mobility. The Chicago Boys, for example, were a group of Chilean economists trained at the University of Chicago or by its professors who taught at the Universidad Católica in Santiago (as part of the "Chile Project," which started already in 1956). The government junta heavily relied on the advice of this economic team to set forth a policy of economic liberalization, privatization of state-owned companies, and stabilization of inflation (Valdés 1995). As far as the military was concerned, many low-ranking Chilean officers received training at the infamous School of the Americas.[6] According to Lesley Gill (2004: 80), "One thousand five hundred and sixty Chilean soldiers attended the SOA between 1970 and 1975, but the majority (58 percent) came in the two years following the coup, when the military ruled and repression in Chile was most intense."

While there were also more "ordinary" transnational mobilities taking place under the dictatorship (e.g., Chileans who went to study abroad or who traveled as tourists), it is very hard to obtain reliable data; they can be politicized in different ways, depending on the source. Most people who could engage in these practices belonged to the upper classes (and the relative numbers are lower than the transnational mobilities Chile is witnessing today). These voluntary momentous mobilities, which are socioculturally valued and underpinned by historically informed imaginaries, are similar to the ones described in other chapters of this book. They stand in marked contrast with the necessity-driven mobilities by the exiles.

Chile's Islandness

The Chilean, because of his islander complex and his feeling of belonging to an isolated world, has tended a little to think that the world is the map: here is Chile and the rest is the map. Thus, in reference to the map, Chile always wins: we are the biggest, the most able .... Because, if one faces the map, one is much better than the map. We have not experienced what the world is. In one way or the other, we have invented the world and it has not interested us.

—Manuel Montt, in Ana María Stuven, *Chile Disperso*

In 1992, countries on both sides of the Atlantic Ocean were celebrating the fifth centenary of the "discovery" of the Americas by Christopher Columbus. I was a first-year student at university and, together with a friend of mine, I had planned to join, for a couple of weeks, the "Walk Across America for Mother Earth" (the story of which was retold later in a US avant-garde theater production with the same name). This marathon protest march, from New York City to the Western Shoshone Reservation in Nevada (used as a test site for nuclear weapons), was aimed at bringing public attention to five hundred years of indigenous oppression and exploitation. Unfortunately, my friend failed some of his exams, and we had to cancel our summer plans. Ironically, I ended up spending my holidays in Spain, the home of the colonizing *conquistadores*.

Spain celebrated 1992 in grandeur, with the Olympic Games in Barcelona and the Universal Exposition in Seville, which had as its theme "The Age of Discovery." My knowledge about Chile was very limited at the time. I knew how the country had been ruled for many years by a military junta and that democracy had been restored only recently. In this respect, Expo '92 was a real revelation for me. The wooden pavilion representing Chile stood out in its architectural simplicity. The building had only one major attraction, namely a sixty-ton iceberg standing in an indoor pond. The iceberg had been shipped, in ten pieces, from Antarctica (and was also transported back there once the Expo was over). Apart from the welcome cooling inside the pavilion (the outside temperature easily reached 100 degrees Fahrenheit/40 degrees Celsius), the display made me think: Why bring an iceberg from the "end of the world" to Europe?

***

The way in which Chile took it upon itself, after the return to democracy in 1989, to rejoin the global community was partly influenced by rising mobilities across South America, the majority of immigrants (around sixty per cent) coming from neighboring countries, especially from Peru and Argentina.[7] Probably the most emblematic example of Chile's strategy of "opening up" to the world was the enormous chunk of iceberg that was towed from the Antarctic sea to the 1992 World Fair in Seville, Spain (cf. Dorfman 1999) (see figure 1.2). The iceberg symbolized a country that "started to jump on the train [of modernity], eager for closer contact with the developed world …. The culture of Chilean 'cosmo' began—the aware and travelled Chilean—which was first advanced by the returnees but, over the years, took off on its own" (Contardo 2008: 272).

The policy of engaging with the world was reflected in a radical change in the social imaginary of expatriate Chileans, from political exiles over economic migrants to diasporic citizens. Cecilia Baeza (2010) takes the national television program *Patiperros* (globe-trotters), launched in 1996, as emblematic of the changed perception in Chile about transnational mobility. This popular program lasted five seasons and was entirely dedicated to Chileans abroad. It illustrates the emergence of the popular image of mobile travelers or adventurers discovering other cultures and ways of life. According to Baeza (2010), the vagrancy of these new nomads recalls a characteristic of the *roto chileno*, the figure of the half-breed (descendant of Spanish and indigenous people), symbol of the national identity since the end of the nineteenth century (Oyarzún 1967).[8] The *roto*, stemming from the working classes, is depicted as wandering in search of adventures and work. In this sense, the contemporary reinvestment of the term

Figure 1.2: The wooden Chilean pavilion built for the 1992 World Fair in Seville, Spain, in which a sixty-ton iceberg was exhibited. (Photographer: Noel B. Salazar)

patiperro is not accidental: the word is a Chilean creolism associated with the figure of the *roto*—also qualified as *caminante* (walker), *de aquí y de allá* (from here and there), and *andariego* or *callejero* (vagabond). The *patiperro* symbolically embodies Chile's openness to globalization.

A first sign of a changing political structure in Chile in relation to expatriates was the creation, in 2000, of the Dirección para la Comunidad de Chilenos en el Exterior (DICOEX, Directorate for Overseas Chilean Communities).[9] DICOEX identifies, coordinates, and develops public policies that aim to connect Chileans residing abroad with their home country (DICOEX 2005). DICOEX focuses on the economic character of Chilean emigration, the latest wave of which took place in the period 1990–2000 (C. Baeza 2010). In a similar vein, CONICYT, Chile's National Commission for Scientific and Technological Research, launched in 2005 the web portal ChileGlobal with the help of the World Bank's diaspora program (Kuznetsov 2006).[10] The aim was to create a platform to connect expatriate entrepreneurs and professionals with Chilean investors. ChileGlobal is now fully integrated in MarcaChile, Chile's nation-branding website.

At the beginning of the new millennium, the Culture Division of the Ministry of Education launched the idea of a project designed to address the demands of inclusion and social and political participation that many associations of Chileans living abroad were making. At that time, Chile was officially made up of thirteen regions, but President Ricardo Lagos adopted the informally used concept of "Region XIV," also referred to as *Región del Exterior* (foreign region) or *Región del Reencuentro* (reencounter region).[11] This virtual administrative region, a "deterritorialized national territory" almost becoming an imaginary island, meant to represent and ensure the continued loyalty and identification of Chileans living abroad (C. Baeza 2010). This was seen as an innovative migration policy, not only because it drew on new information and communication technologies, but because it gave a name to the Chilean community abroad and recognized it to be an integral part of Chilean society (cf. del Pozo Artigas 2006).

In addition, Chileans are much more connected to the world than ever before.[12] In other words, "modernity no longer allows using one's geographical condition as an excuse [for not engaging in mobilities]. Chile is in constant contact with the world" (Stuven 2007: 47). As some argue, "Chile keeps on being an isolated country, but it has been globalizing through communications and, in this sense, the isolation of Chile has become less dramatic, but it keeps on being a relative reality. The isolation expresses itself in that, in general, all references are made towards Chile, inwards" (Emile Duhart, cited in Stuven 2007: 49). Indeed, Chileans keep on thinking that their country is an island in almost every possible sense (Universidad Católica 2008). The metaphor of Chile being an island is often used to distinguish the country from its geographical neighbors and, by extension, from the wider world. Despite their inclusion in the world and the current priority being given to the relationship with the neighboring countries, the myth of insularity among Chileans has grown.

Critical observers have argued that Chile needs even more outside influence (Gonzalo Rojas, cited in Stuven 2007: 56). Research conducted by the United Nations Development Program at the beginning of the new millennium revealed that over a third of Chile's youth was not very receptive to what is foreign and had never considered temporarily relocating abroad (PNUD 2003: 13–14). Another third, however, was highly open to what is foreign (PNUD 2003: 14–15). Youngsters living in the capital displayed the most "cosmopolitan" attitude, and here socioeconomic differences were not at play. The researchers explained these findings by pointing out that younger people do not have family duties and can still fantasize about going abroad. They also have access to very different resources the moment they imagine their future horizon (Salazar 2011b).

Many Chileans stress that they are homebound, and will often draw on the metaphor of their country as an inaccessible island as a justification for that fact. The people I talked to in Chile about this stress strong family bonds as a reason to stay put: "I wouldn't leave; in my case I'm rooted in my family and I'm not desperate to leave the country." Of course, many people in Chile do not have the means to travel abroad; at the same time, there are many scholarships these days and other opportunities created to facilitate transnational mobility. Juan, a young history student from a wealthy Chilean family I interviewed has many travel opportunities but no concrete plans.[13] He likes to think about it, but seems afraid to realize the trip. One of the reasons Juan gave me for this was that he is afraid that "seeing Chile from the outside can be a disenchanting experience" (referring to the fact that there is a danger of no longer recognizing one's own lifeworld or frame of reference anymore if one stays abroad for too long). Even if he acknowledges how valuable the experience abroad can be, Juan prefers to stay in Chile out of compliance. As Isabel, a young, middle-class woman living in a small Chilean coastal town frames it, "I have always believed that I won't stay in Chile my entire life. I have thought about living abroad in the near future, but I've never really planned anything."

These type of comments are not surprising given the long history of imaginaries depicting Chile as a paradise on earth (Pizarro 2003). Fernando Aínsa's (1986: 28) description of the Golden Age, where immobility was conceived of as a guarantee of paradise, may enlighten us here:

> It was simply a matter of being born and dying within the narrow limits
> of one's own shores, of being satisfied throughout one's life with the

products of one's native soil and, above all, of not knowing about or having the curiosity to know about what was outside the precincts of daily life. The felicity of the Golden Age was guaranteed by isolation and self-sufficiency but also by that lack of curiosity toward what might exist beyond the limits of one's own immediate world. The rationalization is simple. If primary needs were satisfied on one's own shore there was no reason to look for new worlds outside the native plot of ground.

The difference now is that Chileans (like people in other countries) do not need to physically travel abroad to know what is going on outside their country. If they do not go to the world, the world comes to them, either in the form of foreigners (be they migrants or visitors) or global media and consumer products.

Since the 1990s, the percentages of Chileans traveling abroad and the influx of foreigners into the country have increased substantially. More Chileans temporarily leave the country to study, work, or simply travel abroad, convinced that, in the words of Carolina, a middle-aged mother of three, "travelling opens your eyes and enables you to look at things from a more global perspective." However, as Manuel Montt argued, "when Chileans travel, they do not particularly strive to know; Chileans arrive abroad and start contacting other Chileans" (cited in Stuven 2007: 58). Moreover, not all Chilean travelers are able to handle distance from the Chileanness that they carry deep in their hearts and minds.[14] In sum, to quote Emile Duhart, "the self-referential world is typically Chilean. It does much good for Chileans to leave, but they are afraid of doing so. Not of physically leaving, but of leaving their environment, their frame of reference. The independent type or drifter is not very Chilean" (cited in Stuven 2007: 55).

Chileans abroad play an important role in all of this, as is given voice to in the influential literary work of Isabel Allende (2003) and Ariel Dorfman (2011). Officially, they number around one million, or about 6 percent of the Chilean population (DICOEX 2005), and many of them maintain strong ties with Chile and have helped many Chileans get rid of the provincialism they were bound to by trivializing the idea of traveling abroad and by showing that the geographical boundedness can be overcome by technical and economic means (Castillo Sandoval 2005). Travel has become one of the elements relatively easy to access by that segment of the population just below the Chilean upper class. For this class of "cosmopolitan mobile" people, who like to show off, the model is not the Chilean *cuico* (upper-class, wealthy, or snobbish people), but the global high society that travels, uses the latest technological gadgets, eats out in restaurants, and knows about wines.

Career-builders look up to the United States, while Europe sounds "chic" (but is a second option or an ideological first choice). For vacations, many travel within Chile, as it is generally believed that "we have everything in Chile, except tropical beaches" (interview with Solange Fuster, regional director of Sernatur, Chile's national tourism service). If people travel outside the country, young Chileans typically go on beach or carnival holidays to Brazil, the Caribbean, and Mexico; families with kids go to Miami; couples traveling alone go on round trips to Europe; and elderly people tend to go on international cruises. The latest trend is no longer going on vacations to rest, but to gather radically different experiences (for example, travels to the Amazonian rainforest, India, or the Middle East).

Arguments against the pursuit of transnational mobilities abound. Although Chile portrays itself as being cosmopolitan, the knowledge of foreign languages is very limited. This in turn limits job and study opportunities abroad. After 9/11, it has also become harder to obtain visas and other official documents. While these are technical barriers to transnational travel, there is also a mental barrier: the idea that everything is very far (cf. Pizarro 2003) and consequently expensive (although Chileans have gotten used to using their credit cards). The dangers of venturing abroad were also accentuated in televised programs such as Mega-TV's *Sin Retorno* (No Return). The 2013 series focused on "the shocking stories of Chileans pursuing their dream and ending up being stranded in a foreign jail" (and not just criminals but ordinary people who took the wrong decision or simply had back luck).[15]

Interesting, in this context, is the discourse about the so-called *negritos de Harvard* (dark-skinned people who studied at Harvard). This derogatory term, more Chilean than from the United States, is used to denote those middle- or working-class Chileans who got the opportunity to study at prestigious foreign institutions but are perceived of as being undeserving of being there—the idea being that they got the opportunity not because of their excellence but because of political correctness (Castillo Sandoval 2008).[16] Sociologist Fernando Villegas (2008: 44) nicely describes how those who studied abroad fare when back in Chile: "the lower-level manager ... who is waiting for the traffic light to change while trotting at an intersection .... Stationary jogging, without moving, is a wonderful and insuperable metaphor for the meaning of their restless and ceaseless toil." Thus, although studying abroad is generally considered as being something positive in Chilean society, the concept of the *negrito* shows that if one does not fit within the stereotypic profile of those entitled to study abroad, to do so is (discursively) punished.

A more recent argument to stay put is that the countries that have traditionally attracted many Chileans (e.g., the United States and Spain) have been facing socioeconomic crises. In fact, the mobility pendulum marking the relation between Chile and Spain, for instance, has shifted in the opposite direction once again. Highly qualified youths have been forced to leave Spain because of a severe job shortage in the under-twenty-five age bracket, and Chile has become a popular destination due to its stable economy, where skilled, energetic young people are in demand. Ironically, Chile is now being compared to the United States of the past (in terms of the potential to realize one's "American dream") and with Australia (for those seeking the combination of a good climate and job prospects). "Welcome to a better world," is how Chile's President Sebastian Piñera greeted his Spanish counterpart Mariano Rajoy in 2013. As this chapter illustrates, this tongue-in-cheek phrase resonates for people moving back and forth between both regions of the world.

Imagining New "Ends of the World"

> Chileans are not always aware of how out-of-the-way their country is, both on a map and in the world. They forget that this is Chile's most distinguishing feature, which has determined its history .… It is debatable whether Chile is beautiful or ugly, rich or poor, orderly or chaotic, whether its dominant gene is Araucanian or Spanish, but the enormous distance that separates it from the centers of thought and future events is its primary characteristic. So it was yesterday, so it is today. And tomorrow?
>
> —Horacio Serrano, in Cecilia García-Huidobro Mac Auliffe,
> *Tics De Los Chilenos*

The findings described in this chapter illustrate how both practices and imaginaries of (im)mobility emerge as sources constitutive of cultural meanings beyond being a mere extension or transfer of them. Imagining is an embodied practice of transcending both physical and sociocultural distance. Imaginaries are signified and resignified, indicating both sociocultural continuities and rupture. In the words of M. Baeza (2008: 288), "Social imaginaries are never definitive and, for this reason, the construction of today's reality, for sure, is not the same than the one we will have tomorrow." Anthropological analyses of mobility are thus best combined with complementary studies of the institutional locus of power over the domains that promote and constrain it (Glick Schiller and Salazar 2013b; Salazar and Smart 2011).

In the cultural logics of mobility, imaginaries play a predominant role in envisioning both the world "out there" and the (often mythologized) memory of the homeland (Jackson 2008). Mobility is as much about these imaginaries as it is about the actual physical movement from one locality to another (Salazar 2013b). The images and ideas of other places—often (mis)represented through popular media—circulate in a very unequal global space and are filtered through people's personal aspirations. Although global market flows may accelerate flexible mobility, imaginaries of these kinds of movements play out in uneven and even contradictory ways in people's desires (Glick Schiller and Salazar 2013b). What remains important is "access to economic resources and powers of symbolic legitimation, neither of which are distributed equitably .... In this respect certain individuals are much better placed to be successful 'authors' of their own lives than others" (Smith 2006: 54).

In the case of Chile, the constant recycling of old (and originally foreign) imaginaries of immobility and isolation, a play upon the nostalgic longing for rootedness (cf. Castillo Sandoval 2005), serves as cultural protection. While the transportation of the iceberg across the globe shows that Chile wants to show the world that it can move the unmovable, the dominant domestic discourse in Chile stresses that not being on the move (transnationally) is the quintessential characteristic of what it means to be a "real" Chilean. As Rogers Brubaker (2010: 70) argues more generally, "The politics of belonging are generated not by the movement of people across borders, or by the movement of borders across people, but by the *absence*

Figure 1.3: Imagining the "elsewhere." Neighborhood with Belgian street names at La Florida, outskirts of the Santiago Metropolitan Region, Chile. (Photographer: Noel B. Salazar)

of movement or mobility—in social space, not geographical space." An extremely high proportion of the national Chilean income is concentrated within the elites, and is characterized by what Florencia Torche (2005) calls an "elite closure"—a significant barrier to long-range upward social mobility. That the overall social mobility is relatively high in Chile is thus largely inconsequential because it takes place among classes that share similar positions in the social hierarchy of resources and rewards (Núñez and Risco 2004). Social mobility is still largely determined by surname, education, and chosen profession (Núñez 2004).

The national imaginary, linking perceived geographical distance from the rest of the world to imagined difference of others (in the first instance South American neighbors), discourages outgoing transnational mobilities. Such mobility reduces "distance" and thus has the potential of threatening the imagined Chilean cultural unity. A provocative 2015 blog post by a young American entrepreneur living in Santiago, titled "The Best Thing a Chilean Can Do is to Leave Chile," generated a lively online discussion between Chileans who have left and others who prefer to stay put (with various contributors using the island metaphor).[17] The debate illustrates how "immobility" is at the core of the Chilean social imaginary, geopolitics, and cultural and family life (see figure 1.3). The difficulty Chilean returnees have faced when trying to reintegrate after their exile abroad only proves this point. The Andes and other physical boundaries serve as a real barrier for those who stay, a horizon for those who choose to leave. However, in a global context in which geographical mobility becomes almost normative for any form of achievement, be it economic, educational, or personal mobility, it will become harder and harder to keep Chileans from moving.

***

The life history of my Chilean spouse confirms that, despite the dominant imaginaries, some Chileans are transnationally mobile. She herself lived in France, Ghana, Italy, Cameroon, Belgium, the United States, Indonesia, and Tanzania. In all places, she met other Chilean expatriates—(former) exiles, students, economic migrants, businesspeople, diplomats, missionaries, sportspeople, artists, volunteers, and retirees. While most of her family remained in Chile, some fled to Canada during the military regime, and others migrated to Brazil and Germany. Of her generation, a good number have studied abroad, mostly in Spain and the United States. In her new home, Brussels, concerts by Illapu or Inti-Illimani, Chilean bands who lived in exile during the dictatorship, attract huge crowds. For the old Chilean exiles, it is a moment of nostalgia, while for their offspring and the more recent economic migrants it provides the opportunity to (re)connect with Chilean culture.

Social media networks allow Chileans abroad to keep connected, informed, and engaged with what is happening in Chile and across the Chilean diaspora. For our family at least, the Chilean mainland is no longer a mysterious end of the world. However, we keep on being mystified by those other Chilean "ends of the world": the Polynesian Rapa Nui (Easter Island), one of the planet's most isolated inhabited islands, and Villa Las Estrellas, the first Antarctic village with its own town hall, hotel, day care center, school, scientific equipment, hospital, post office, and bank. And, of course, there is also the Juan Fernández archipelago, which served as inspiration for Daniel Defoe's Robinson Crusoe (1719) and which gained popularity a while ago because some believed it to be Apocalypse Island, from where the Mayan gods would watch the "end of the world" in 2012.

NOTES

This chapter is an entirely reworked and expanded version of an earlier article published in 2013 in *History and Anthropology* 24(2): 233–52.

1. Exile began and ended on foreign soil for a sizable contingent of Chileans. Thousands of Chileans were traveling or living abroad at the time of the 1973 coup: tourists, delegates to international conferences, embassy personnel, students, and professionals and workers employed outside the country (Wright and Oñate Zúñiga 1998: 28). In addition to foreign exile, the military regime also used *relegación* (internal exile) to punish "enemies" who were not considered to be dangerous enough to require expatriation. *Relegados* were normally sent to remote parts of the country where they had no ties (Wright and Oñate Zúñiga 2007: 35).

2. After the 1982–83 economic crisis, there were many economic emigrants from the middle classes (C. Baeza 2010). These groups facilitated the arrival of larger groups of economic migrants in the 1990s and later (Yépez del Castillo and Herrera 2007).

3. Hamid Naficy (2001: 261) reminds us that the suitcase is actually "a contradictory and multilayered key symbol of exilic subjectivity: it contains souvenirs from the homeland; it connotes wanderlust, freedom to roam, and a provisional life; and it symbolizes profound deprivation and diminution of one's possibilities in the world."

4. There can be several reasons for not returning. For those who have married nationals from the host country and have had children, bringing their families to a country with a different language and culture can be difficult. Some have adapted well to their new environment.

5. In response to the anti-Pinochet political activity in which many exiles engaged after settling into their host countries, the regime attempted to discredit them by concocting the image of a "golden exile"—a comfortable, even luxurious, existence that contrasted harshly with the economic hardship faced by many Chileans at home. Exiles were further denounced as subversives, foreign agents, and anti-Chil-

ean turncoats responsible for a campaign of calumny not against the regime but against the country (Wright and Oñate Zúñiga 1998: 7).

6. The School of the Americas was established in 1946 as the US Army Caribbean Training Center in Panama. In 1963, the center was renamed the School of the Americas. In 1984, the school was forced to move from Panama to Georgia, USA. The institute is believed to have trained more than sixty thousand soldiers and police, mostly from Latin America, in counterinsurgency and combat-related skills (Gill 2004). In 2001, the school officially changed its name to the Western Hemisphere Institute for Security Cooperation.

7. Chile has become a magnet for migrants from neighboring Argentina, Bolivia, and Peru. According to the 2002 national census, Chile's foreign-born population increased by 75 percent since 1992. The Migration and Foreign Residency Department estimates that almost 320,000 foreigners were living in Chile as of 2008.

8. "The *roto* is a tramp ... who does not fit in any established place or any corner of the country, and who wanders across the land or who leaves it for foreign lands. The *roto* who goes to war or enters a guerilla fight as a mercenary, or intruder, or simply an adventure seeker who travels in a ship's hold without specific itinerary, who gets lost across the Americas or anywhere else, the Chilean dog's paw, *patiperro*. This incarnates a representative image of part of the Chileans, in their different contexts and functions" (Oyarzún 1967: 16–17).

9. In 2010, the DICOEX web portal was taken over by Fundación Imagen de Chile, which rebranded it as a network for the transfer of knowledge and the generation of new business opportunities. Chile Somos Todos (website), accessed 28 February 2018, http://www.chilesomostodos.gov.cl/.

10. Chile Global: Red de Talentos (website), accessed 28 February 2018, http://www2.marcachile.cl/chileglobal/.

11. The metaphor had to be adapted to "sixteenth region" in 2007, in response to the creation of two new Chilean regions: Los Ríos in the south (Region XIV), and Arica y Parinacota in the north (Region XV).

12. International flight connections have existed for a long time. PANAGRA (now defunct) and Air France started flying to Santiago in 1929, followed by Condor in 1935 and the British Overseas Airways Corporation (now British Airways) and KLM in the 1940s. In 1946, LAN-Chile started with international flights to Buenos Aires, in 1956 to Lima, and in 1958 to Miami (Canihuante 2006: 64). As far as international business is concerned, Chile became a member of APEC in 1994 and of OECD in 2010, and currently has many bilateral free-trade agreements—including with the EU (2002), United States (2003), South Korea (2004), China (2006), Japan (2007), and India (2007). The country also has a state-of-the-art telecom infrastructure and regulatory system, and the highest mobile telephone and Internet penetration rates in Latin America.

13. One of these opportunities is Becas Chile (Scholarships Chile), a program of the Ministry of Education that aims to develop a long-term strategy of capacity building abroad by increasing the opportunities for training and specialization abroad

and promoting international networking and collaboration. See "Becas Chile," Ministerio de Educación, accessed 28 February 2018, http://www.becaschile. cl/. Young Chileans had been sponsored by the French monarchy to study in France even as early as 1824 (Canihuante 2006: 45). Personalities such as Ignacio Domeyko, a Polish migrant who became rector of the Universidad de Chile in 1852, stimulated Chilean students to study in Europe.

14. This is an idea I have borrowed from Roberto Castillo Sandoval, a Chilean author and professor of Spanish and comparative literature at Haverford College in Haverford, PA, USA.

15. "Descripción del programa," Red Televisiva Megavision S.A., 22 March 2013. Accessed 28 February 2018 via Wayback Machine Internet Archive, http://web. archive.org/web/20130511151209/; http://www.mega.cl/programas/sin-retorno/ descripcion/descripcion-del-programa.html.

16. Of course, this type of discourse sounded even more offensive when Barack Obama was president of the United States, because he could also be classified as a *negrito de Harvard* (Obama is a graduate of the Harvard Law School, where he was the president of the prestigious *Harvard Law Review*).

17. Nathan Lustig, "The Best Thing a Chilean Can Do is to Leave Chile," personal blog, 26 November 2015. Accessed 28 February 2018, http://www.nathanlustig. com/2015/11/26/the-best-thing-a-chilean-can-do-is-to-leave-chile/.

Indonesia
Merantau and Modernity

In 1997, while I was volunteering in France, I became close friends with Budi, a colleague from Indonesia. We kept in touch, and our friendship influenced the decision to choose Indonesia as a honeymoon destination. In 2000, my wife and I visited Budi and his family in Yogyakarta as part of our overland trip across the islands of Bali and Java. This journey in turn led to the idea of Yogyakarta as a potential site for my doctoral research. I returned in 2003 for three months of exploratory fieldwork and ended up spending an entire year in Yogyakarta in 2006, conducting research on tourism. While mobility was not the focus of my investigation at the time, human movement was evident all around me. I noted, for instance, the seasonal flows of tourists and how local tourism service providers were looking for short-term employment abroad during the low season—work on cruise ships or in large hotels—in Europe or in the United States being popular options. Yogyakarta, apart from being the country's second most important tourist destination (after Bali), is also a major center of higher education, attracting students from all over the archipelago and beyond. Throughout my stay, I met with many Indonesian students and with exchange students from Africa and Latin America. In addition, I witnessed how the city had attracted internally displaced people from conflict zones on other Indonesian islands.

One of the people I met in Yogyakarta was Samuel, a student in tourism from West Papua (a province of Indonesia). After his graduation, he invited me to visit him in Fak-Fak, the first Dutch colonial settlement in Papua. I gladly accepted the invitation. However, getting there was trickier than I had originally thought. I flew from Yogyakarta (Java) to Makassar (Sulawesi). After an unexpected landing on the airfield that services the notorious Grasberg copper and gold mine (a subsidiary of the American company Freeport-McMoRan), I landed in Jayapura (Papua). From there I caught yet another plane to Sorong, where I was told that there were no planes to Fak-Fak that day. Fortunately, all was not lost. Despite the availability of air travel since the 1950s, transport over sea remains a popular means of travel by which to get around the Indonesian archipelago, especially for low-income travelers. PT Pelni, the state-owned shipping company, has almost thirty passenger ships, each accommodating ten to fifteen hundred passengers (although the capacity can easily double during holidays). I was lucky enough to find a Pelni vessel at the port of Sorong that was about to leave for Fak-Fak.

The trip along West Papua's resource-rich shores lasted many hours. The ship's economy class did not offer much, apart from some basic food, cheesy adolescent movies, and sleeping dorms that looked more suitable to the keeping of cattle. However, these circumstances did create a perfect setting in which to meet people and listen to their mobility stories. My main interlocutors were four spirited young women who were studying at the State University of Papua in Manokwari, the capital of the province of West Papua. They were on their way home for a break. Two of the young women were indigenous Papuans; a second was of Javanese descent (her parents having participated in the transmigration program under Indonesia's first president, Sukarno); and the third was of "mixed descent." All four hoped to be working in tourism and were very interested in chatting to the only *bule* (white person) on board: Their (hi)stories illustrate how mobility brings people together. Their situation also confirmed the changing opportunities Indonesian women have when it comes to mobility, both in the geographical and the social sense.

* * *

Indonesia is an archipelago of more than six thousand inhabited islands in Asia Pacific, at the crossroads of Southeast Asia and Oceania. Its scattered geography has been very conducive to mobility between and beyond the islands, including complex systems of circular movements and various forms of migration and cross-cultural mixing (as the ethnographic vignette above illustrates; see figure 2.1). The long history of regional travel supports Epeli Hau'ofa's (2008: 35) claim about islanders that "it is in their blood to be mobile."[1] While local mobilities are indigenous rather than being a result of foreign contact (Bedford 1973; Chapman and Prothero 1985), the abundance of valuable natural resources meant that the Indonesian archipelago has been an important long-distance trade hub from at least the seventh century BCE. The Riau Islands, between Borneo and Peninsular Malaysia, acted as a "bottleneck for the movement of culture and trade" (Sopher 1977: 365) between India, Southeast Asia, and China. The ancient Cinnamon Route developed after 600 BCE (LaBianca and Scham 2004). Daring seafarers brought spices and the living shoots of banana and coconut trees, rice plants, and various types of yams along this route to East Africa and then to Egypt and Europe. They returned with ivory and rhinoceros horn, tortoise shells, animal skins, and African slaves. People escaping conflicts, in search of work, or following their loved one(s) or religious beliefs, as well as traders and itinerant merchants, traveled along these routes.

In this chapter, I explore the widespread occurrence of mobility between and beyond the Indonesian islands. Today, many Indonesians are engaged in a combination of short and temporary as well as long-term and long-distance travels, driven by both sociocultural and economic motivations. It is important to place these contemporary flows in the context of a long history of human movement that is facilitated by network-creating and network-dependent relationships. Some of these mobilities have been explained as a cultural characteristic (Tirtosudarmo 2009).[2] In this chapter, however, it becomes clear that the factors determining a "culture of mobility" are highly complex and variable. It takes several forms, both over time and in different places, including internal, regional, and transnational movements. It cuts across gender, class, and skill boundaries, and exists in widely different demographic contexts. I discuss how border-crossing

Figure 2.1: Four students from the State University of Papua in Manokwari traveling on a PT Pelni ship to Fak-Fak in West Papua, Indonesia. (Photographer: Noel B. Salazar)

movements among people with limited mobility resources are highly mediated, not only by regulations and brokers but also by "modern" technologies.

The main research for this chapter took place in 2011 (with short follow-up visits in 2016 and 2017). I collected archival resources in the Netherlands (the Royal Netherlands Institute of Southeast Asian and Caribbean Studies) and, drawing on earlier contacts in the region, I interviewed various mobility-related stakeholders on the islands of Java and Bali. On Java, I could count on the help of a female research assistant, a graduate student in anthropology from Gadjah Mada University in Yogyakarta. In addition, I had informal talks with (mostly female) Indonesian migrants in Singapore and Hong Kong in 2013. For complimentary data and the analysis of the findings, I also drew on earlier visits to various parts of Indonesia since the year 2000. The first drafts of the chapter were presented to Indonesian graduate students at my university, and I am very grateful for their constructive feedback.

Moving Histories

Mobility is part of people's lifeworld across much of the Indonesian archipelago (Tirtosudarmo 2009).[3] The original populations of the islands were sparse and geographically mobile. In the precolonial period, trade and other interactions were conducted via inter-island routes. Not all movement was long distance or by sea. Shifting cultivators, too, were accustomed to resettling in search of new land, which was abundant (Vickers 2004). The wider region, with its lack of territorial boundaries and fluid political allegiances to rulers (who themselves were mobile), was characterized by relatively disorganized forms of migration. A certain "wanderlust" has been ascribed to ethnic groups such as the Bugis, Minangkabau, Boyanese, and Banjarese. Even those groups usually regarded as being more sedentary have histories of migration and movement.[4] As Adrian Vickers (2004: 305–6) notes, "In the Eastern part of the archipelago almost every ethnic group documented by anthropologists has tales of origin elsewhere, of travel by boat and ship to the place they are now …. Even supposedly sedentary islands such as Bali have similar genealogies full of movement."

The arrival of foreign traders further expanded the mobility in the region. The different patterns, directions, and motivations of movement became severely affected by colonialism. Mobilities intensified and new forms were introduced, particularly state-sponsored migration and contract work. For the Dutch colonial administration, however, sedentary communities were a political, economic, and social ideal. From the nineteenth century onward, the household, the village, the land survey, the census, the map, and the school were among the technologies of rule and regimes of mobility used to control people's movements (Lowe 2003). The free and unrestricted (semi)nomadic wanderings of peoples posed serious problems to the colonizers. These movements subverted the controlling mechanisms of the state that had been erected to mediate contacts and commerce among locals.[5] Nevertheless, some groups in the region chose to remain mobile and nonterritorial because this had significant economic, social, and political advantages.

There are strong mobility traditions throughout the archipelago that pattern contemporary movements and form the basis of more recent labor mobilities. The travels of the Bugis and Makassar peoples of South Sulawesi are among the best-known examples (Tagliacozzo 2009) (see figure 2.2). For the Bugis, long-term absence from their native villages in favor of voyages to far-flung regions of the archipelago is considered a basic cultural trait. The Bugis took to the sea in the fifteenth and sixteenth centuries to escape the dominance of the Dutch East India Company in their homeland. In so doing, they became one of the most important maritime communities in the region, "roaming the archipelago in search of trade in accordance with the direction of the prevailing

Figure 2.2: Indonesians have a long history of transarchipelagic mobilities. Vessel at Kupa Beach, South Sulawesi, Indonesia. (Photographer: Noel B. Salazar)

monsoon, returning to Sulawesi only for a few months of each year to refit and repair their *praus* (sailing boats)" (Lineton 1975: 174). Bugis ships even sailed to the northern coast of Australia, where cave paintings, Aboriginal loanwords, and archaeological waste attest to their presence today (Tagliacozzo 2009). In the eighteenth century, they began establishing pioneer settlements around the archipelago, enabling more or less permanent migration of Bugis settlers (while retaining political ties to the community of origin) but also serving as bases from which to engage in circular migration (Hugo 1982). According to Jacqueline Lineton (1975: 196), "A *pasompe* (migrant, wanderer [literally 'he who sets sail']) is seen by romantically inclined Bugis—and these are not rare—to possess many of the characteristics considered most admirable in the Bugis personality: notably, bravery, cunning and a spirit of adventure." Over several decades, even well into the eighteenth century, these adventurers were known and depicted throughout the archipelago as aggressive migrants, pirates, and mercenaries.

The culture of mobile boat-dwelling people across the archipelago, comprising diverse congeries of variously named groups known as *orang suku laut* (sea nomads), also dates back many centuries. The existence of their far-reaching maritime networks reflects the almost unhampered movement these people enjoyed historically. As Cynthia Chou (2003) points out, it was the rise of the nation-state that led to the progressive peripheralization and impoverishment of the sea nomads. Still today they roam the seas of the archipelago, challenging the idea of citizenship as defined by bounded territories and guaranteed by a sovereign state (Lowe 2003). They are looked down upon by other Indonesians because they are too mobile (i.e., without a land-based "home") or because they do not engage in the "right" types of mobility (according to the currently dominant mobility ideology; see Introduction).

Merantau

> In Minangkabau culture, there comes a day that every boy must leave his family behind and face the many challenges in life ... challenges that will guide him towards becoming a man. This journey is known as *merantau*.
>
> —Gareth Evans, *Merantau*

The most widespread mobility tradition across the Indonesian archipelago is called *merantau*—"leaving one's cultural territory voluntarily whether for a short or long time, with the aim of earning a living or seeking further knowledge or experience, normally with the intention of returning home" (Naim 1976: 150).[6] As Johan Lindquist (2009) observes, the explicit demand to return indicates that *merantau* is actually about the relationship with "home" (see also Conclusion). Kinship and locality are the principal sources of identification for those who enter the *rantau* (Naim 1974: 292; Siegel 2000: 56), and it is very bad for the *perantau*, the one who temporarily moves in order to expand both his (or, increasingly, her) horizons and opportunities, to become "destitute in *rantau*" (*melarat di rantau*), to be lost in *rantau*, forgotten by those staying home (Mrázek 1994: 10-11).

This culturally inflected mobility pattern has a long tradition in (western) Sumatra, particularly among the Minangkabau people, who are considered to be among the most mobile of all ethnic groups in Indonesia (Naim 1974). Their matrilineal social structure makes males (who live as guests in the houses of their wives) marginal within society, which led to *merantau* becoming the norm for young men, with social disapprobation being incurred if they did not conform to this pattern. Unmarried Minangkabau men traveled on the *rantau*, as part of the *adat* (customary law), to make their fortunes and feed their spirits, sometimes for long periods. In other words, "young single men could situate themselves within the state-sanctioned role of *perantau*, or migratory breadwinner, whether or not they actually provided remittances for their families" (Silvey 2000b: 149). Men living off in the *rantau* who were already established as promising merchants were traditionally considered much more attractive as husbands than young men who were "left behind."[7] They typically received dowries from their new in-laws, adding wealth to their bride's family line. The usual length of a *merantau* was anywhere between six months and a year, after which the young men would return to the village with earnings, prestige, and tales of the outside world. The stock of experience gained elsewhere helped the village to understand and adapt to the outside world, and the now-wiser young men, presumably having gotten the spirit of adventure out of their systems, could settle down into marriage and village life.

To a married man, *merantau* meant a temporary release from two families' conflicting expectations that weighed upon him as a husband and a member of the maternal family. Historically, the *rantau* thus became a space in which the man gained more power than he could have in the matrilineal heartland (Mrázek 1994: 10-11). Among the Minangkabau, *merantau* is best described as a traditional "rite of passage" for becoming a man (Kato 1982: 196). Having been in the *rantau* was not only about gaining experience and a form of education, but was also a criterion by which to increase social status—not unlike the historical "Grand Tour" in Europe (see chapter 4). Importantly, "*merantau* as a means to avoid being fixed to a particular social location is only possible with on-going exchanges between people separated by physical space" (Ali 1996: 14). The *rantau* thus connotes a realm of imagined familiarity, despite the fact that many who speak of it may never themselves venture into it (cf. Salazar 2011b). This points, once again, to the important role undertaken by socially shared cultural imaginaries in making sense of boundary-crossing movements (see Introduction). The *rantau* is about "foreign spaces that are, at once, unknown and to be discovered yet known, because others, ethnically connected to you, have enabled such spaces to be imagined" (Ali 1996: 428).

Among the Minangkabau, *merantau* functions as an institutionalized cultural complex of circular wandering. However, as Graeme Hugo (1982: 68) rightly points out, "the institutionalization of a particular form of mobility, whether non-permanent or permanent, operates not only on the scale of the ethnic group but also on a regional and local scale." At the same time, *merantau* is culturally dependent. This is illustrated by the fact that it has had a historically different meaning in the matrilocal system in Aceh (the far north of Sumatra). Acehnese men were usually without resources until their parents died. This served as a strong incentive to go on the *rantau* (Siegel 2000: 54). According to Acehnese *adat*, however, men were not allowed to travel too far from their family. While *merantau* certainly did not have the "rite of passage" characteristics it has elsewhere, it did not necessarily lead to a change in status either. It was merely a way of earning a livelihood. If a man could make a satisfactory independent income, he would simply stay.

For the Boyanese, from the tiny island of Bawean, two hundred kilometers off the northeast coast of Java, *merantau* is a "cultural ideal" (Vredenbregt 1964: 109). Bawean is known as the "Island of Women" because almost every household has men working in either Malaysia or Singapore. This labor mobility is a societal rite of passage for young men, dating back to the seventeenth century. The Banjarese people of South Kalimantan also have a long history of journeying outside their homelands (Hugo 1982). Their concept of *madam* traditionally meant leaving one's natal village and crossing the sea with the aim of increasing one's wealth within a period that is not fixed (but is usually more than one year). *Madam* is used more broadly in contemporary South Kalimantan, encompassing both permanent and impermanent moves. Many Banjarese engage in circular seasonal mobility associated with trading, especially downriver to the provincial capital of Banjarmasin.

The Iban, or Sea Dayak, of Borneo (who are spread across the Malaysian-Indonesian border) have been particularly noted for their mobility. The most important traditional form of Iban mobility was restricted to groups of young men in an institution called *bejalai*. Historically, *bejalai*, "to go on journeys with the view of acquiring wealth, material goods and social prestige" (Kedit 1993: 3), was an important rite of passage for young men in Iban communities; "Iban values of valor, equality and individualism support *bejalai* and have made it a viable institution throughout Iban history" (Kedit 1993: 3). These (often adventurous) journeys frequently lasted for several years on end, and often extended to the remotest corners of Borneo, and even to Peninsular Malaysia and other islands of Indonesia. The idea was to work, to "see the world," to have noteworthy experiences, and, hopefully, to return with many gifts as well as other visible signs of wealth (to add to the family's collection of heirlooms). This was such an important cultural institution that boys were socialized early in life, through stories, to be predisposed to going away for a few years on *bejalai* as part of their initiation into adulthood.

Peter Kedit (1993: 11), himself Iban, recounts how "cultural heroes in Iban mythology performed triumphant *bejalai*, undertaking feats which provide both inspiration for and a model of conduct for *bejalai* aspirants." The success of activities achieved while traveling on *bejalai* journeys, usually in small groups and under the guidance of recognized leaders, contributed to a bachelor's status (and was exhibited through tattoos). Although primarily for the purposes of headhunting, the acquisition of trophy heads as evidence of bravery, these activities led to other rewards that enhanced a man's status and his capabilities to acquire a spouse. *Bejalai* has been transformed from headhunting raids into today's labor mobility. Iban people still go abroad to work, as mentioned, but now do so to acquire cash more than for the accrual of social prestige. In the 1970s, rural men temporarily migrated to work in logging camps. Construction work in oil palm plantations and in the petrochemical industry came later in the 1980s. *Bejalai* for many Iban became *pindah* (permanent migration) when workers stopped returning home. *Bejalai* has gradually turned into rural-urban migration, as is characteristic in most developing countries (UNDP 2009), and, as such, it is no longer restricted to men. For rural women, it was the economic boom of the late 1980s and early 1990s that caused them to move to urban centers.

In the nineteenth century, the expansion of capitalist markets throughout the Indonesian archipelago facilitated the *rantau* but continued to be associated with certain ethnic groups. By the early twentieth century, however, "the *rantau* became a way to learn about the world; for others it was a way of engaging with progressive political forces; and for still others it was an escape from the burden of culture in a matrilineal society in which men were guests" (Lindquist 2009: 29-30). According to Lindquist (2009), *merantau* has become homogenized as a national cultural form, as increasing numbers of Indonesians have been transformed into temporary migrants in search of new forms of life and labor. After independence, mobility increased exponentially across Indonesia, and in this process "*merantau* was unmoored from particular ethnic groups, becoming widely used throughout Indonesia and associated primarily with the new underclass rather than the country's elite" (Lindquist 2009: 30).[8] The vicissitudes of economics and modernity have changed the practice of *merantau*. It no longer implies a return to the village and a sharing of experience, but an escape from the limited possibilities of village life. In other words, the mobile practice of *merantau* has increasingly become a one-way journey of migration. Returnees undergo a strict mobility regime, setting them apart from other people (Kloppenburg and Peters 2012).[9]

Analyzing the situation on the island of Sumba, Jill Forshee (2000: 24) observes how a haunting tension between moving about and staying put disturbs people who leave the island:

> Although travel marks male privilege and a growing worldliness has become a Sumbanese prestige symbol, attachment to ancestral place creates a tension in the wanderings motivated by trade and status seeking. Travel entails tremendous risks, which may result in the worst sort of annihilation—the loss of body and soul .... As long-distance travel has become a regular practice for many (and a symbol of modern mobility), serious perils threaten these ventures. For those removed from their families and protective spirits, potential misfortunes (*hanggamar*) are causes for anxiety.

Better employment opportunities and wages in neighboring countries, and a perceived similarity to countries with a Muslim tradition in the case of the Middle East and with shared cultural values and languages in the case of Malaysia, Brunei, and Singapore, contributed to the establishment of so-called "traditional mobility networks" (Spaan 1994: 93). Today, Indonesians are still following these customary circuits of mobility. Outside influences may have altered the patterns of circulation, but circulation itself has endured. At the same time, "the notion of timeless movement obscures the political-economic dynamic that produces historically specific dislocations in life chances that motivate international migration, and it accounts for neither increased mobility over the last three decades or so, nor the specificity of flows" (Goss and Lindquist 2000: 398). As Graeme Hugo (2005: 95) rightfully remarks, "Any close observer of Asia over the last two decades cannot fail to have noticed how international mobility of one kind or another has entered the calculus of choice" for a large number of people. Contemporary transnational mobility in Indonesia, as in areas elsewhere, is thus the outcome of a combination of factors: traditional cultures of mobility, expanding capitalist markets, and interventions by the nation-state.

The last two decades has seen an increase not only in the numbers of Indonesians on the move but also in the types of mobility that have themselves become more complex and less selective. The forces responsible for this are associated with "globalization, increased levels of education, proliferation of international media, improved transport systems, and the internationalization of business and labor markets" (Hugo 2005: 94). *Merantau* certainly remains important, as is witnessed by the fact that is it a recurrent theme in literature, popular music (Barendregt 2002), and film (Evans 2009). For young adults, the distant *rantau* contains a future that will bring personal and public liberation from the shackles of "unthinking traditionalism" (Rodgers 1995). Narratives about mobility, however, have moved to the center of political discourse and claims over historical or contemporary mobilities have turned into a pretext for exclusion. Increasingly, Indonesians are staying in the *rantau* because of the better opportunities afforded elsewhere, and the *rantau* is coming to span the entire planet. Or, as Indonesian anthropologist Irwan Tjitradjaja pointed out to me in a conversation, "There is a continuum between internal and transnational migration."

Brokering Movement and Gender

In 2006, my spouse and I had the opportunity to visit the island of Sumba in east Indonesia. We were invited by Nuri, an Indonesian friend with whom we had studied anthropology in Belgium. The trip to Sumba had to be carefully planned because there were only two flights per week. Nuri, whose family had been a long-term object of anthropological study, gave us an ethnographic tour of the island. On the day of our departure, we experienced firsthand what it meant to be "involuntary immobile," stuck on an island. The Tambolaka airfield was full of agitated people because the plane had been canceled and nobody could tell when the next one would come. We were among a handful of foreigners, along with a French film crew and some lost tourists, who were all annoyed with the fact that our travel plans had been changed.

The others were mostly Sumbanese women who work as domestic servants abroad. Like Nuri, who led a comfortable "cosmopolitan" life in Jakarta at the time, they had visited relatives in their native villages. However, for these poor women, the cancellation of the flight had potentially catastrophic consequences. Arriving a couple of days late for work in Malaysia or Singapore could mean the termination of their contract. Their freedom of movement was thus structurally limited. Nuri's geographical and social mobility, in contrast, seemed "borderless." While her great-grandfather had fallen prey to head-hunters and her grandfather had been enslaved on Sumba, her father had become a businessperson in Jakarta, and she herself became a successful writer and academic with European degrees while living in the United States and Europe and being married to a *bule*.

I recalled the encounter with the Sumbanese women when I interviewed Wulan in 2013. It was a late Sunday afternoon, and we were seated inside the Hong Kong Central Library, just across the street from Victoria Park, where my interviewee spent the afternoon picnicking with her Indonesian friends. Wulan was twenty-seven years old but had already spent over five years working as a domestic servant for a local family in Hong Kong. Her husband and three-year-old son (who is staying with her parents) live in a small Indonesian village near Blora, Central Java. Wulan remembered that it was not very complicated making the necessary arrangements to start working abroad. Ari, an older man from her native village who himself had worked abroad for many years, had taken care of the paperwork and all other practicalities. Besides, Wulan was not the first to leave. There were a least a dozen women from her region working in Hong Kong (and some older women at work in Saudi Arabia). Unfortunately, it took her a long time to repay Ari for his services. Wulan is now saving money to build a nice big house back home, just like her neighbor did. She misses her family and laments that the relation with her son is not good. On the other hand, Wulan truly enjoys the freedom she experiences in Hong Kong, particularly on Sundays, when she has a day off.

* * *

The privileged and seemingly unhampered mobilities of Nuri (see above) are rather exceptional (cf. Amit 2007). As I noted in the Introduction, most contemporary border-crossings, particularly those related to labor, are closely guarded by nation-states (Nyíri 2010). In Indonesia, for example,

> for physical mobility to be possible, state bureaucracies have to be approached, evaded or manipulated through links with insiders¾the various *oknums* and *calur* (terms for linkages into bureaucratic offices). Various guards such as *pengawal* and *tai kong* assist in crossing boundaries. Many of them have come to play this role by attempting to move out of enclosing spaces themselves, and in the process, acquired the skills to deal with borders, boundaries, categories, documents and policing agents. (Ali 1996: III)[10]

In the case of travels to Saudi Arabia, there is a clear linkage with the religious institution and the Islamic pilgrimage or Hajj (see chapter 6).[11] Through their pilgrimages to Mecca, people from the Indonesian archipelago historically established contacts with networks of pilgrim bro-kers (Arab sheikhs), who made work and travel arrangements for them for employment in Malaya and Sabah via Singapore (Spaan 1994). In other words, the religious routes formed the basis for labor mobility. Singapore was the regional center for Hajj labor brokers who organized Hajj labor mobilities.

In general, translocal labor mobility in Indonesia has been dependent upon supposedly traditional, informal patron-client networks (Rudnyckyj 2004). Brokers usually are (or have been) mobile themselves, and the dif-ferent networks to which they have access are made available in exchange for a fee. The brokers' essential attribute, to the agencies for which they recruit prospective workers, is their potential to recruit in their own local environment (to which the agencies have no access at all). To the workers, they represent the agency and have contacts with the "big bosses" far away in Jakarta or abroad, hence the promise of the big, wide world (which is fed by social imaginaries circulating through old and new media). Yet these brokers remain part of the prospective workers' social networks and are usually trusted by both the "movers" and their families. Given changes to the global labor market, the relation between broker and worker has become increasingly marked by gender. Female workers experience various forms of control over, and restrictions to, their mobility (Killias 2010).

Multiple gendered social differences are reflected in mobility (Elliot 2016).[12] Apart from labor mobility, the gendering of movement in general is very deeply engrained in archipelagic culture(s). As Jill Forshee (2000: 23–24) writes about the island of Sumba,

> The movement of men and women of eastern Sumba reflects social and ideological boundaries and various flows between existential realms …. There is potential power in mobility, in securing or altering one's place in the world by extending influence within it. Yet there is also power in resisting unwanted shifts in location and controlling limits that others might not violate. Adventure threatens to bring pol-lution or destruction, and human mobility challenges the stability of social life in Sumba.

Women's mobility throughout the Indonesian archipelago was tradition-ally associated with family or marital migration (C. Williams 2007).

Nowadays, the mobility of women is often viewed as a disturbance, con-taining tensions and contradictions that require legitimation (see figure 2.3). While *merantau* is culturally considered to be a normal (or even nor-mative) behavior for men, and constitutive of Indonesian masculine iden-tities, women doing exactly the same are just *main-main* (drifting; literally:

playing) (Silvey 2000a). Thus, the association of men and mobility versus women and immobility and the domestic sphere has a long tradition. However, through time *merantau* has become something that is of value for (unmarried) young women too. This has much to do with the feminization of labor in the *rantau*, beginning in the late 1960s and 1970s. Women now comprise most of the migrant workforce, partly because demands from the global labor market tend to channel young, rural Indonesian women into overseas work (e.g., contract domestic work), while preventing men from doing so. The whole machinery involved in organizing Tenaga Kerja Wanita (TKW, or overseas female labor force) has also led to the expansion of human trafficking and prostitution (Lindquist 2009).

The recruitment of female workers for overseas labor is largely in the hands of men—sually the husbands, brothers, or sons of women who have traveled overseas (Spaan 1994: 103). I interviewed Nina Mariani Noor, an Indonesian scholar in religious studies who conducts research on the gender relationships of migrant workers, about this topic. She explained that the social inappropriateness of a woman traveling unescorted into

Figure 2.3: Women have been hindered in their mobilities in many ways. Indonesian girl from a small village in Bantul Regency who studied English literature and ended up working as a tour guide for foreign tourists. Yogyakarta, Indonesia. (Photographer: Noel B. Salazar)

the unknown, along with the cost of travel, prevents women from leaving their villages alone. From the day of their recruitment in the village of origin until their arrival at their employer's house abroad, female transnational workers are escorted by male brokers. As heads of kin and household, men across Indonesia are institutionalized in *adat* (customary law) to control women's mobility by their power over decision making. The fact that women travel thousands of kilometers because of new job opportunities in the sector of domestic service (an estimated 75 percent of domestic workers are female) does not necessarily challenge the idea that it is men who wield power in unfamiliar realms. Following several problems related to female workers overseas, in 2005 the conservative Indonesian Council of Religious Scholars (Majelis Ulama Indonesia) issued a fatwa (instruction) that prohibits women from working overseas without their *muhrim* (close male relatives with whom a Muslim woman may travel—e.g., father, uncle, husband, brother, or other male relative).[13] Such mobility regimes result in specific forms of control over and protection of female workers' mobility (cf. Baker 2016). However, producing safety through controlling their mobility can also result in immobility (Kloppenburg and Peters 2012).

Women's mobility in Indonesia does represent, at the same time, a partial break with earlier cultural traditions. The increased access to mobility by Indonesian women can be seen as a struggle for new subjectivity (Forshee 2000; C. Williams 2007). Their translocal movements contest a local femininity, transgressing the cultural association of women with the "home." The talks I had with the TKW at the airfield in Sumba and in Singapore and Hong Kong confirm that their translocal mobility is partly an embodied response to the constraints and rigidity of their subject positions and roles at home as well as to challenges and opportunities presented by globalization.[14] It is true that some women must leave their village (*terpaksa*) to provide for their family because their husband cannot earn enough money (particularly in times of economic crisis). However, "the transnationalization of Indonesian women's migration neither fits neatly into the state's vision of the ideal 'family' nor does the spatial mobility of transnational women generally help solidify old versions of national unity" (Silvey 2006: 34). Being transnationally mobile while still confined in their movement, many female migrant workers end up making journeys that have been characterized as "confined mobilities" (Kloppenburg and Peters 2012).

Ariana Marastuti, an Indonesian psychologist who conducts research on TKW, told me how migration leads to a whole range of health and reproductive issues. According to her, the mobility experiences are usually not very positive for the women themselves, but their families are happy because of the received remittances. However, working abroad does give them more prestige, particularly when the money earned can be invested in socially visible projects (e.g., the building of a big house in the home village). Ariana also criticizes religious leaders or government authorities, who keep quiet about the well-known negative effects of translocal migration (e.g., abandoned children).

In the wake of the feminization of long-distance mobility across the whole of Asia, brokerage is both increasingly gendering and gendered. An increasing number of mobility brokers are now women, even if men still appear to be predominant (Lindquist, Biao, and Yeoh 2012). Importantly, gender often structures the forms that brokerage takes, as debt, labor rights, and visa processes often vary between men and women, particularly with the increasing formalization of migration. Mobile workers are more resourceful in obtaining information through expanded social relationships and new ways of connecting. These networks are essential in empowering the workers when they face difficulties. Women use the possibility of traveling and working abroad to realize and develop ideas of how they would like to live in a modern world. The TKW, or overseas female labor worker, is seen as a "woman out of place," "a figure whose transnational mobility ... both threatens the national order and promises a way forward" (Barker and Lindquist 2009: 54).

Mobile Traditions and Modernities

In Indonesia, as elsewhere, contemporary mobilities are informed both by a long tradition (see above) and by more recent imaginaries of what it means to be "modern." While the meaning of "modernity" has been hotly debated across the scholarly spectrum as a contested concept full of ambiguities and tensions, as a social imaginary it plays a pervasive and powerful role, and it seems crucial to people's self-understanding. In Indonesia, the seductive allure of becoming *moderen* (modern) is an enticement, particularly to the young and the upwardly mobile. In a fascinating multiauthored essay titled *Figures of Indonesian Modernity*, fourteen anthropologists focus on a series of characters that are pervasive in "modern" Indonesia. The lead authors (Barker and Lindquist 2009: 38) define modernity as

> a temporary place holder for the constellation of forces that define the contemporary moment in at least one corner of the world ... this moment is characterized by the pervasive effects of capitalism and commodification, a deep ambivalence about older figures of

authority, and the emergence of new claims to authority grounded in new media.

Interestingly, some of the figures covered in the 2009 essay are directly related to border-crossing mobilities: the TKW, or overseas female labor migrant, who embodies the contradictions of class and gender mobility (Silvey); the *petugas lapangan*, or field agent, who functions as an informal labor recruiter for transnational migrants (Lindquist); and *Pak Haji*, or Mr. Hajj, who wears the white cap that proclaims he has made the pilgrimage to Mecca (Darmadi). This illustrates how modernity is linked to "moving forward" in both physical and imaginative ways (cf. Cresswell 2006).[15] The idea of modernity commonly includes two distinguishing (and almost normative) characteristics: (1) a break from an out-of-date past, and (2) progress into an improved future. The case of Indonesia illustrates the imaginary aspect of this idea because culturally inflected mobilities such as *merantau* remain important while the dream of more social mobility is unattainable for much of the population. "Modern subjects" are above all mobile urbanites, in stark contrast with the *orang kampung* (rural dwellers, understood to be "country bumpkins" or "hicks").[16]

While older people often connect modernity to orthodox Islam (as opposed to premodern spirit beliefs), the younger generations in Indonesia seem to be adhering to a more secular kind of modernity. For them there are also linkages between becoming Indonesian, increased identification with the Muslim world, becoming urban, becoming "modern," and becoming wealthy. According to research carried out by Choy Sin Hew (2003), for example, many women had migrated from their villages to large cities in order to become "modern." Although their work was repetitive, dirty, "dead-end," and frequently involved shift work, the women rarely complained: their main aim was to live in the city, to be independent, and to send money home.

In Indonesia, the idea of becoming modern has become correlated with the use of new information and communication technologies. The mobile phone, and particularly the smart phone, is not merely a tool for communication; it is also an emblematic cultural artifact infused with symbolic meaning and representational value that plays a role in the construction of "modern" subjectivities. The mobile phone has become constitutive of a "mobile modernity" (Barendregt 2008). In this (imagined) modernity, people are free to move corporeally, socioeconomically, and imaginatively. Their imaginaries draw upon (mostly) imagined mobilities in which they, too, are "flexible citizens" (Ong 1999). In other words, "modernity has become equivalent to mobility" (Barendregt 2008: 160). However, for most people this mobility should be qualified as "limited mobility" because even the mobile technologies they have access to are being constrained by time and space. This reduced technological access contextualizes and conditions their geographical and social (im)mobilities.

Archipelagic Mobilities

In 2010, I attended the Annual Meeting of the Society for Economic Anthropology in Tampa, Florida. The topic of the conference was "Contested Economies: Global Tourism and Cultural Heritage." I therefore thought it fitting to pay a visit to the Port of Tampa, a well-known cruise ship terminal. I witnessed the docking of the MS Carnival Inspiration, a fourteen-deck vessel with the capacity to carry 3,450 passengers and a crew of 920 people. I was particularly interested in the latter population. As passengers were disembarking, I observed many crew members hurrying to the local bars near the cruise port. Outside Hooters, I met several Indonesian and other Asian men. They were not really interested in what was going on inside but wanted to capture the free Wi-Fi signal to communicate with their families back home.

A year later, I was reminded of this encounter when I was interviewing a Romanian woman who founded Miami, a school for cruise ship training in Yogyakarta, and was now running a cruise crew recruitment agency. She herself had worked on a Carnival cruise ship, where she met her future Indonesian husband. She confirmed that many people she recruited were young men (including some of the tour guides I had previously studied). Their main motivation was economic (although they also liked the travel aspect of the job). Because of their limited command of English, most of them ended up doing jobs on board that required little contact with passengers. Their maritime mobility experiences seem very different from the historical ones that characterize the Indonesian archipelago.

***

Questions about mobility take on particular meanings in specific political-economic contexts that have produced those movements and discourses (Ford and Lyons 2006). Though few regions have been able to match Southeast Asia's ethnic diversity, even fewer have been able to match its histories of movement (Tagliacozzo 2009). As Adrian Vickers (2009: 70) argues,

> The study of Southeast Asia needs to take account of mobility across the region and its various cultural and material manifestations. If we assume that mobility is an inherent part of Southeast Asian states and societies, then we can first assume that people moved and brought

elements of culture backwards and forwards; and, second, that wider patterns of fluidity are built into local epistemology and ontology.

Mobility is certainly central to the lives of many people of Indonesia, the largest archipelagic state in the world by area and population. However, as described in this chapter, Indonesian patterns of human movement have undergone dynamic changes over the past century, linked with various regional political events and socioeconomic circumstances. In the past, indigenous patterns of mobility tended to revolve around trade networks and seasonal subsistence, but with the expansion of European colonialism and global capitalism, mobility has shifted to accommodate and deal with these changes. In many cases, externally generated changes reinforced traditional forms of mobility, such as *merantau*, and added new ones.

One gets a good impression of the massiveness of Indonesian inter-island mobility at the end of the Muslim fasting month, when millions of Indonesians (not exclusively Muslims) crisscross the archipelago to return "home" (*pulang kampung*). Many spend most of their money, painstakingly earned during the year, to have some quality time together with their family (particularly with their parents). This mass homecoming practice is called *mudik Lebaran*.[17] It is not merely a religious or spiritual affair, but also an economic and cultural phenomenon. Typically, it involves travel from centers of employment or education—cities—to rural villages or provincial towns where people have left their family behind. The traditional shipping routes connecting the various islands of the archipelago are still used, but the expansion of inexpensive air connections has dramatically increased the number of Indonesians traveling. *Mudik Lebaran* shows the lasting importance of family networks and returning "home," as I have discussed in the context of *merantau*. The rich tradition of *merantau*, or traveling to gain experience (at different levels), serves to illustrate that translocal boundary-crossings are not made with the intention to uproot people but are experienced by both "movers" and "stayers" as incomplete and open-ended.

As *merantau* is culturally institutionalized, it assumes an element of circularity, in that leaving and returning are equally encouraged.[18] Most Indonesians are part of this mobility, whether personally or through the back and forth movements of relatives or significant others. *Merantau* is a process that is strongly connected to cultural and kinship values. The mobility of women was hindered for a long time as cultural norms constrained their individual freedom. However, a female *rantau* emerged in the late twentieth century and continues. The traditional *merantau* experience speaks of travels that draw people closer to, rather than pushing them away from, "home." However, the locally rooted meanings of *merantau* mobility have changed in response to the rapidly changing wider economic context.

NOTES

This is a revised and expanded version of a chapter in Nataša Bon and Jaka Repič's *Moving Places: Relations, Return and Belonging*, published by Berghahn in 2016.

1. This statement stands in contrast to what is known as an "island mentality" (see chapter 1). For people living on islands, there is a tension between being geographically remote and yet being very dependent (economically) on contact with the outside world (King and Connell 1999). Remoteness is a double-edged feature. As Phillip Vannini (2011: 257) rightly points out, "islandness" goes together with the negative characteristic of isolation but also with the positive quality of insulation, comprising "feelings of protection, safety, distinction, and disconnection."

2. Scholars of the Pacific Ocean region, for example, have traditionally used both geography and culture as determining factors to distinguish mobility patterns, such that "Polynesia is characterized by international migration to metropolitan countries of the Pacific rim, Melanesia [to which the eastern part of Indonesia belongs] by internal migration, and Micronesia by both patterns, together with increasing receipt of international labor migrants" (Goss and Lindquist 2000: 397).

3. The rich vocabulary people have developed to talk about mobilities is evidence of this. Jill Forshee (2000: 210), for example, describes the different terms that exist in eastern Sumbanese to describe movement: *palaku* connotes journeying, *danggangu* applies to wide-ranging travel for the purposes of trade, whereas *mbawa* implies traveling about for pleasure, usually over short distances.

4. Conventional stereotyping depicts the Javanese, for instance, as people who are born, live, and die in the same house, scarcely traveling beyond the confines of their natal village. One of the arguments is that traditional social structure (including the very strong attachment the Javanese possess to their natal village) inhibits movements between villages (Mantra 1980). However, the peasantry of Java appears to have been quite mobile throughout history, with significant numbers moving considerable distances—not always voluntarily, but also as part of various programs of *transmigrasi* (Hoey 2003).

5. The postcolonial Indonesian state continued its policies along similar lines. Tsing (1993), for example, describes the attempts of the Indonesian state to control the nomadic Meratus hill peoples of Kalimantan.

6. The word *rantau* refers to the (often adventurous) geographical, social, and moral realm of journeying outside the ethnic "homeland." It was originally limited to the coast to which people traveled from the hinterland, but the notion acquired additional meanings of traveling upriver, studying abroad, wandering, and boundary-crossing mobility in general.

7. In this context, the idea of being left behind has two related meanings: (1) remaining in the village and (2) not "progressing" or becoming "modern."

8. At the same time, the ratio from Sulawesi remains at a higher level, suggesting that the cultural orientation to *merantau* continues to influence mobility from this area.

9. From 1999 until 2012, all Tenaga Kerja Indonesia (TKI) or "(overseas) Indonesian labor migrants" had to use the special Selapajang Terminal at Soekarno-Hatta International Airport in Jakarta. This is a separate building located some distance from the "regular" airport terminals where all other people enter the country. The return migrants are welcomed back as *pahlawan devisa* (foreign exchange hero) because of the remittances they bring. The Selapajang Terminal was originally intended to protect migrant workers from preying transportation operators or money changers offering unfair rates, but restricting their arrivals to a designated terminal only made them more vulnerable.

10. *Oknum* is a euphemism for rogue elements in the Indonesian police and the militaristic preying on migrant workers. *Calur* or *calo* are the words used to denote employment brokers, the line between informal and legal variants being difficult to draw. *Pengawal* (literally "body guard") and *tai kong* are terms for migrant brokers—like "snakeheads" (helping Chinese people across the globe) and "coyotes" (helping people across the US-Mexico border).

11. The Hajj was a form of mobility that was potentially threatening the stability of colonial states back in the nineteenth century.

12. Tsing (1993: 219), for example, has noted that in the Meratus region of Kalimantan a traveling woman is considered to be a "disorderly" woman. Forshee (2006: 142) describes how the cultural ideals of masculine and feminine mobility across Indonesia are even visible in traditional wear: "Following customary poise, women throughout Indonesia should be slow and graceful (*halus*), and clothing accentuates their movements. Most traditional wear inhibits long strides affecting a woman's poise. Some have interpreted this as constraining women's mobility in a larger sense."

13. According to Islamic law, *muhrim* (or *mahram*) indicates a degree of consanguinity that renders marriage impossible, but gives a man and a woman the right of association. Theoretically, a Muslim woman's *muhrim* forms the group of escorts with whom she is permitted to travel.

14. The fate of Indonesian domestic workers in Hong Kong is accurately depicted in Lola Amaria's (2010) documentary *Minggu Pagi di Victoria Park* (*Sunday Morning in Victoria Park*). The title refers to the Indonesians meeting every Sunday in Hong Kong's Victoria Park to spend their only leisure time available together.

15. For the multiple links scholars have made between modernity and mobility, see the work of, among others, Arjun Appadurai (1996), Marc Augé (1995), Zygmunt Bauman (2000), Walter Benjamin (1999), Tim Cresswell (2006), and Dean MacCannell (1999).

16. This becomes evident when labor migrants return to their village of origin with some savings, a new look, and, above all, "a body politics (speech and deportment) that speaks of experience of modernity and a shrugging-off of the label '*orang kampung*'" (Elmhirst 2007: 232).

17. *Lebaran* is an Indonesian word that substitutes the Arabic *Eid al-Fitr*. *Mudik* is derived from *udik*, a noun denoting someone from a remote area, as well as a humble or innocent person. By adding the consonant "m" (*mudik*), it lexically comes to mean traveling from the city to the village, from a "modern" place to a remote and less developed place.

18. Circular mobility is generally community-based and occurs within the most "customary" societies: the depth of traditional culture explains the strong linkages with the territories of origin and the cohesiveness of group structures. More recently, scholars have analyzed how the figure of the returnee energizes and redefines nationalism in an era of increasingly fluid and indeterminate national sovereignty (Xiang, Yeoh, and Toyota 2013).

Tanzania
The Maasai as Icons of Mobility

Like most people, I had heard about the Maasai long before ever setting foot on East African soil. I had read about long-striding, tall warriors, clad in red blankets, in glossy magazines and in tourism brochures, and I had seen them on television or on the big screen. Maasai are often represented as freedom-loving nomadic pastoralists who are continuously "on the move." In 2007, while conducting research in Tanzania, I had the opportunity to collaborate closely with Maasai people. My research assistant, Joseph, did not really fit the stereotype. He had grown up in an urban context and had received his secondary schooling in neighboring Kenya. He is a telling example, however, of how tradition remains important when carving one's own path. This is illustrated, for instance, by Joseph's preference to walking over any other means of transport. Walking not only is related to the herding of cattle but also plays an important role in various Maasai rites of passage. Not surprisingly, Joseph has established himself as a successful walking safari guide. Ironically, it is tourism development that has significantly altered the ways in which many Maasai people are (im)mobile.

***

The Maasai are a widely dispersed ethnic group living across southern Kenya and northern Tanzania—an area known locally as "Maasailand."[1] Despite their small numbers and marginalized position in East Africa, they have attracted enormous interest across the globe since the reports of first contact with Europeans in the nineteenth century. For foreign explorers who came across this "nomad warrior race" (Hinde and Hinde 1901: x), the virile Maasai represented the epitome of a wild and "free" (because mobile) lifestyle.[2] In part due to historical (mis)representations,

Maasai are considered to be an integral part of the African wilderness, an image that corresponds to a stereotypical idea of the primitive, sexual, violent African, or the romanticized image of the "noble savage" (Hughes 2006a).[3] Through a powerful stereotyped image, the Maasai have become true icons of an imagined indigenous "traditionalism," unwitting symbols of resistance to modern(ist) values (Galaty 2002). While I have discussed representations of the Maasai as "noble savages" elsewhere (Salazar 2009), in this chapter I focus on the (imagined) linkages between Maasai and mobility.

Maasai (im)mobilities were not the focus of my doctoral research in Tanzania, but I did collect a good amount of relevant data for this chapter in 2007. I returned to Tanzania in 2009 for a more focused data collection trip, looking for archival sources in Dar es Salaam (Tanzania National Archives) and interviewing people in Dar and in the wider region around Arusha (northern Tanzania). My former research assistant, a young Maasai man, accompanied me throughout this fieldwork. He was of invaluable help identifying potential research participants (particularly Maasai people) and discussing my interpretations. Through electronic contacts and social media exchanges with him and other informants, I continued working on this topic in the years after my stay in East Africa.

As Anatoly Khazanov (1994: 1) writes, "The myth of the nomad may be even older than the myth of the 'noble savage.' …. In modern times both myths (of the savage and of the nomad) have been revitalized, but the myth of the nomad would seem to be the more lasting one." The semiotic association between Maasai and "mobility" has been exploited shrewdly in various advertising campaigns for global brands and by some Maasai themselves.[4] In 1996, the company Swiss Masai (*sic*; now Masai Marketing and Trading) launched its Masai Barefoot Technology shoe. This innovative rolling shoe wear, which mimicked "natural instability," was supposedly developed "by observing the wonderfully agile Masai people walking barefoot on natural, uneven ground."[5] This description is not accurate, because most Maasai do not walk barefoot, certainly not for long distances. Traditionally, they walked around in footwear made from cow skin. Nowadays, many wear sandals made of tire rubber or, if they can afford it, walking boots. The rubber sandals were capitalized upon by the British fair-trade fashion store Fresh Cargo, which undertook a joint venture with Maasai to implement "fifty years of Maasai Warriors' experience in sandal making."[6] Their Maasai Treads flip flops were recycled out of denim, leather, and tires. In 2010, the Spanish shoe company Pikolinos launched a similar footwear line "designed and manufactured in Kenya by women of the Maasai tribe, one of the planet's most threatened" people.[7]

The shoes themselves are the result of transnational mobility: they are produced in Spain, decorated in Kenya, and then distributed worldwide.

Some Maasai themselves have taken advantage of their widespread image as ambassadors of "mobility." In 2008, for example, a group of six Maasai participated in the Flora London Marathon to raise money for water pumps in their village in northern Tanzania.[8] A year later, three Maasai participated in the New York City Marathon, sponsored by the athletic shoe company Puma, to raise awareness for the Maasai Wilderness Conversation Trust.[9] None of them did very well from a competitive perspective—two of the Maasai running the marathon in London actually took an extra day to reach the finish line. In 2010, two Maasai participated as the "Maasai Warriors" team in *The Amazing Race China Rush*, the first sub-Saharan participants ever on the show.[10] Unfortunately, they could not do justice to their reputation as traditional experts in mobility because they were the first team to be eliminated.

Although few Maasai possess a car, the automobile industry has also used the Maasai to advertise their products. In 2003, Land Rover launched its (bright red) Freelander Maasai vehicle. The award-winning advertisement figured a group of Maasai-looking Africans lined up in the shape of the crossover SUV, their shields representing the wheels of the car.[11] This campaign was followed up in 2011 with a Maasai windshield cleaner in an ad promoting the Land Rover Defender off-road utility vehicle.[12] Masai is also the name of a UK-based company selling accessories and parts for Land Rover vehicles.[13] In France, Masai is the brand name for quads, all-terrain vehicles with four wheels (some models being available in—yes— bright red).[14] In these cases, the Maasai are being associated semiotically with ruggedness and freedom of movement—an image that works well for vehicles associated with safari and other adventurous environments.

Maasai also seem to inspire the promotion of another type of mobility, namely mobile telephony (cf. Nilsson and Salazar 2017). In 2011, an Indian advertising agency used a Maasai-inspired image to promote the local language translator of Samsung's Galaxy smartphone series.[15] Two years earlier, the Bank of Chile had used a Maasai-looking African in a campaign to promote Pin Pass, an electronic retail payment system.[16] They probably were unaware of the fact that, since 2007, the "real" Maasai have access to one of the most developed mobile payment systems in the world—M-Pesa, a mobile phone–based money-transfer and microfinancing service for Safaricom (Kenya) and Vodacom (Tanzania).[17] For the price of less than a single goat, mobile phones have become an affordable way for Maasai to take advantage of the latest communication technologies (Rutten and Mwangi 2012).

More rarely (because not really fitting the primitive image), Maasai have figured as transnational travelers. In 2010, Brussels Business Flats, a company offering temporary accommodation for expatriates in the "capital of Europe," ran a remarkable promotional campaign. In one of the ads, the real estate company depicted a smiling young Maasai-looking (Samburu) man standing in front of the Brussels Stock Exchange, with the accompanying slogan "Just arrived in Brussels?" A year earlier, the remarkable Chinese-Tanzanian coproduced movie *From China with Love* had told the unlikely tale about a Maasai businessman who falls in love with a Chinese girl he meets on a business trip to Hong Kong. He brings the girl back home to marry her, but the couple faces numerous problems, many of which are related to cross-cultural communication difficulties.

In this chapter, I contrast these stereotypical ways in which Maasai mobilities have been imagined with contemporary practices of mobility among Maasai people. What role does translocal mobility play in their lives? While the widely circulating cultural representations of Maasai may remain limited to herding-related mobilities, the Maasai themselves are on the move, and they move in ways that diverge widely from their image as obstinate semipastoralists. To contextualize the current developments, I start by discussing briefly the history of Maasai mobilities and their representations.

When "Pasture" Became "Land"

> When we study the history of nomadism we are always studying (at least) two things—the socioeconomic activities of the pastoralist economies that were using the territories into which the European imperialist nations expanded, and the way the western cultures that invented nomadism as a scientific field of study and a social problem related not only to pastoralism but also to their own mobility.
>
> —John K. Noyes, *Nomadic Fantasies*

Nomads, as an archetype of human mobility, have fired people's imaginations over the centuries, either as a contemptuous case of backward barbarism or as a romanticized example of freedom (Ure 2003). Think of the Bedouin of Arabia, the Tuareg of the Sahara, the Mongol-descended horsemen of the Central Asian steppes, and the Maasai of East Africa. As Peter Kabachnik (2010: 205) argues, "Nomads are the Other of the sedentarist system." The scholarship on nomadism is not immune to its own bias: "anthropologists have often perpetuated a stereotype by deliberately seeking out the most conservative of the nomads for study. Rather than representing the norm, such ideal 'pure nomads' are exceptional" (Barfield 1993: 214). According to the romantic view, nomads move because it is natural to do so and they like being on the move. In fact, nomadic peoples tend to be marginalized, primarily because of the harsh and precarious conditions and high mobility of their way of life.[18]

Up to as recently as the end of the twentieth century, the prevailing view was that nomads presented a preliminary evolutionary stage before becoming agriculturalists.[19] However, mixed farming with stock keeping (the domestication of herd animals) was the historical prerequisite for nomadism. Presumably, nomads did not exist in North Africa before about 5500 BCE, when the Sahara was grassland that was increasingly occupied by pastoral people. Similarly, livestock-keeping communities would not have occurred in East Africa prior to about 500 CE (Scholz and Schlee 2015). Although they have been described and imagined as "pure pastoralists" (e.g., Jacobs 1965), it is the interplay between nature and society, between alternating climatic conditions and sociopolitical changes, that forced peoples such as the Maasai to adopt a peripatetic way of life in order to survive.

Speakers of the Eastern Nilotic Maa tonal language, the ancestors of the Maasai came from southern Sudan sometime during the first millennium CE to "settle" in Kenya and, later, in northern Tanzania (now constituting a population of approximately 1.7 million). Like the Fulani in West Africa or the Nuer in Sudan, they were a herding group, raising cattle but also small stock such as goats and sheep. Younger boys herd the calves (or may go out with their older brothers), while the older boys, from about the age of nine or ten, spend most of their time herding the cows long distances away.[20] As the time for warriorhood approaches, the focus of the attention shifts from herding to spending time roaming the countryside in small bands (see Knowles 1993). Accompanied by a group of elders, adolescent boys visit other settlements to gain support for their cause, namely the introduction of a new period of circumcision. This also serves as preparation for their time as warriors. Warriors carry the long walking stick (*eng'udi*) that typifies the pastoralist. Mobility of the human and livestock population is essential for the wellbeing of both.[21] During warriorhood, men spend much of their time away, wandering through the territory visiting friends.

During their time as "warriors" (which lasts for anything from five to fifteen years), males are in a liminal state, outside normal social practice. In this sense, the mobility Maasai warriors engage in is very similar to rites of passage in other cultures (see chapter 2).[22] In later age groups, they keep on traveling together in small groups, usually based on the friendships they formed as *ilmurran* (junior warrior), for instance to cattle markets (Knowles 1993). Men also travel long distances to attend the rituals of their age-mates and their age-mates' children. Women, too, spend time together when they are traveling to a ceremony (it is often customary for the women to depart and to arrive earlier than men so that they can set up and prepare things).

Much of the founding ethnography in anthropology is about nomadic peoples (Engebrigtsen 2017). John Noyes (2000: 47) describes how in nineteenth-century Europe "nomadism" was used as a general description of "a propensity to wander, an inconstancy and hence an obstacle to civilization. This was not confined to anthropological and ethnographic discourse. It also influenced policymaking in the colonies, particularly in discussions of land rights and land utilization." This label influenced the colonial administration's view of pastoralists. In the case of the Maasai, Joseph Thomson's (1885) travelogue *Through Masai Land* played a major role in disseminating their iconic image. In his book, which was translated into various languages, Thomson declared large areas of Maasailand were uninhabited, ignoring seasonal transhumance by the Maasai, migrating with their livestock. Thomson and others condemned the Maasai for their apparently aimless wandering (while the Maasai themselves rightly saw the explorers as aimless rovers).[23] However, far from being independent "wanderers," pastoral nomads rely heavily on trading relationships with settled communities to obtain the goods that they themselves do not produce. Historically, the Maasai traded with agricultural neighbors or took up agriculture themselves (Spear and Waller 1993).

According to Noyes (2000: 48), "The conceptual location of nomadism at the sloppy intersection of pastoralism and spatial mobility is not accidental. It is an intellectual construction that responded to conflicting rationalizations of human society." The response was a European one to the mobility of capital and labor in the expansion of Western capitalism: "As settler economies expanded in the colonies, discourses on nomadism became a channel for articulating the perceived limits to European mobility, for projecting these limits onto other societies and for adopting the socioeconomic forms of mobility that had been perfected by the very same societies that were so openly denigrated" (Noyes 2000: 52).

While modernist social and cultural thought consistently mobilized the nomad as a figure of threat, geographer Tim Cresswell (1997) presents an interesting analysis of the romanticization of the nomad in poststructural and postmodern social theory, where the figure of the nomad is used metaphorically to posit new freedoms and movements (e.g., the figure of the "global nomad"; see chapter 5). Indeed, scholars in the social sciences and humanities have been flirting with the romance of the nomadic lifestyle to incarnate the mobile, the homeless, and the diasporic subject.[24] This is hard to do without turning nomadism into a metaphor for a pure nomadic mobility that, as was argued before, never existed in the first place. In their "nomadology," Gilles Deleuze and Félix Guattari (1986) maintain that nomads move at the same time that they remain still. They take the "nomadic" to be that which is peripatetic, set adrift, and in this regard their social model seems to be that of all individuals, groups, and societies in a constant state of movement. They do not seem troubled by the frequent observation that "no mobile populations wander randomly, since every population manifests a mixture of sedentary and nomadic qualities" (Bogue 2004: 169).

Sedentary State Control

> The placelessness ascribed to nomads is a result of their having been constructed as mobile wanderers with no interest in place coupled with various strategies used to disrupt the places that are important for nomads and facilitate the nomadic way of life.
>
> —Peter Kabachnik, *Nomads and Mobile Places*

Back in 2009, I interviewed Koinet over lunch in Maasai Café, just across the street from the Arusha International Conference Centre, where he was working at one of the court cases of the UN International Criminal Tribunal for Rwanda. After Maasai chef Leboo (who worked nine years in Italy and even had a cooking program on television there) had come to greet us and take our orders, Koinet shared his own story with me. He grew up in a *boma* (settlement) at Selela (nearby Ol Doinyo Lengai, the Maasai "Mountain of God"), but went to school in neighboring Kenya. During that time, he won an exchange scholarship and spent three months in Germany (including a little excursion to Spain to participate in a cross-country race). Back in Tanzania, he continued his studies in Dar es Salaam and obtained a master of laws (LL.M.) degree from one of the country's new public universities.

While he works as a lawyer and assistant lecturer at a local university, he spends most of his free time advocating for Maasai land rights. Thanks to his smart phone, Koinet is extremely active on multiple social media channels related to this ongoing battle. He posts under various names because this allows him to position himself differently toward fellow Maasai and other stakeholders. As he explained to me, it is a matter of strategically using various aspects of his Maasai identity. His phone also comes in handy to keep track of the cattle he owns. While Koinet has outsourced the daily management of the herd to younger relatives, he wants to keep an eye on the buying and selling of cows. In contrast to his busy transnational life as a lawyer and activist, he uses his holidays to "reconnect," by walking all the way from Arusha to Selela, visiting relatives and age-set friends, and then walking back.

***

Avinoam Meir (1997) distinguishes the centrifugal ideology of nomads seeking autonomy and mobility from the centripetal ideology of the sedentary state that strives for dominance and encapsulation.[25] Freedom of movement over large tracts of land is essential to pastoralist production. Various colonial (Hodgson 2000) and postcolonial (Schneider 2006) policies, however, have made it very difficult for people such as the Maasai to continue nomadic practices.[26] Colonialism deprived them of freedom of movement by enveloping them within the boundaries of states (i.e., Tanganyika and Kenya). Mobility was constrained by district boundaries, game parks, nature reserves, quarantine zones, and tribal grazing zones. Despite persisting images that heavily romanticize the Maasai's perceived freedom from authority, they have been forcibly relocated a number of times by colonial powers, thereby losing a considerable part of their pastures (Hughes 2006b). This was easily justified because "by equating nomadism with any movement, forced movement gets subsumed under the expected practices of these groups. Thus, intolerance and exclusionary practices are ignored" (Kabachnik 2012: 223).

Independence did not halt the decline of pastoralism; it accelerated it. The governments of both Kenya and Tanzania retained the colonial mentality against pastoralism. The so-called national interest disarmed the Maasai of their land. The Maasai in Tanzania lost grazing rights to large areas of pasture because of policies that supported private and state wheat farms, and forced villagization (in *ujamaa* ranches under Tanzania's first president, Julius Nyerere) and the demarcation of national parks and conservation areas.[27] This forced many pastoralists to combine livestock keeping with agriculture.

According to Terrence McCabe (2003), some Maasai engaged in agriculture to avoid selling off their stock to purchase grain. In the 1990s, for many the pastoral Maasai lifestyle and the transhumant pastoral system changed toward a sedentary agropastoralism.[28] Maasai are growing in numbers and increasingly moving to urban centers to seek work (to be discussed). At the same time, some authors have argued that "while these trends may be significant, an historical precedence of ebbs and surges in mobility indicates they may not be new or unidirectional" (Fernandez-Gimenez and Le Febre 2006: 341). In general, the population of Tanzania disrespects Maasai people (Salazar 2009), influenced by colonial as well as postcolonial policies based on a metaphysics of sedentarism, where nomadism (imagined or real) is equated with backwardness—very similar to how the Romani and other Traveler people are treated in Europe or the Fulbe, Fulani, or Peul in West Africa.[29] The admiration Maasai generally receive from foreign tourists have made the relation with other ethnic groups only more complex.

Nevertheless, mobility remains at the core of Maasai identity. Jessika Nilsson (2016) recently explored how their culture of mobility is constructed with respect to a mobile conception of land and of indigeneity.[30] Interestingly, she not only discusses traditional elements such as cattle herding or marriage mobilities (of women), but also mentions *arere nkejek*, the practice of walking for pleasure. The latter also figures centrally in Maasai storytelling, inherited narratives passed down by senior elders, the "walking encyclopedias" of Maasai culture. As I could observe by spending time with Joseph, my Maasai research assistant, engaging in such walking activity is not only enjoyable for the walker (giving a sense of freedom); it is also a way of keeping Maasai culture alive (and, as with other mobilities discussed in this book, the walkers receive social credit and status from their peers and wider sociocultural network for doing so).

Relational (Im)Mobility

> The word was passed round that the Masai had come .... Passing through the forest, we soon set our eyes upon the dreaded warriors that had been so long the subject of my waking dreams, and I could not but involuntarily exclaim, 'What splendid fellows!' as I surveyed a band of the most peculiar race of men to be found in all Africa.
>
> —Joseph Thomson, *Through Masailand*

While the iconic image of free-roaming Maasai warriors is widespread, few people would associate Maasai nomadism with camels. Nevertheless, in the much-visited northern tourism circuit of Tanzania, tourists can go on a Maasai camel safari. The camels were left abandoned after a failed international development project (aiming to replace cattle with camels) until a clever entrepreneur came up with the idea to use them for touristic purposes. In 2007, Joseph and I joined a group of American tourists on one of these trips. At the start, the tour guide (not Maasai but Meru) introduced all the camels by name. The accompanying Maasai men (one per camel and all dressed up like proper "warriors"), on the contrary, were never mentioned, let alone properly introduced. Since the guide spoke no Maa and the Maasai spoke little Swahili, a dialogue was hardly possible. The pattern of not treating Maasai as individuals is common practice among other ethnic groups in Tanzania. For the tourists, the lack of communication possibilities meant that they could develop the "wildest" ideas about Maasai as camel nomads (and the combination certainly made for original pictures). It added yet another "exotic" layer to how Maasai mobilities are imagined.

* * *

The majority of foreign tourists visiting Tanzania (mainly from Europe and North America) come to witness a unique form of transborder mobility, namely the cyclical Great Migration of millions of wildebeests and other grazing herbivores across the Serengeti-Mara ecosystem (Salazar 2010a). As mentioned previously, the same protected areas that draw tourists were often created by removing Maasai (and other) people from previously inhabited lands (R. Neumann 1998). Few tourists would be aware of the problems that tourism has caused, and continues to cause, for the Maasai.[31] The appeal of game viewing appears to be in the autonomy and mobility of wild animals, two elements that are believed to be characteristic of Maasai people too: they have always distrusted state authorities, and their nomadic existence has been compared to the migration of wildebeests and zebras.

Apart from restrictive (post)colonial policies that constrained Maasai movements, tourism has (economically) pushed many Maasai to lead a more sedentary life (and this is in sharp contrast with wildlife, which can roam around freely in protected areas).[32] At the same time, Maasai mobilities are likened to those of the wildlife (Salazar 2010a). Safari guides jokingly say that foreign visitors do not come to see the Big Five—a hunting term historically used to denote the five most dangerous African animals: lion, leopard, rhinoceros, elephant, and buffalo—but the Big Six: the big five plus the Maasai. A new development within *bomas* (settlements) along heavily trodden touristic circuits is the permanent presence of the junior warrior age group. The *ilmurran* play an important role in performing dances, whereas traditional customary practice stipulated that they should live together in their own *manyatta*, a temporary camp in surrounding bush areas—a liminal phase of life allowing them to detach themselves from their family and to become independent, mature individuals.

Young Maasai men hang around the *bomas* and show off their recently gained social mobility by wearing socks and shoes (preferably trekking boots), smoking cigarettes with filters, putting on watches, or, through the ultimate symbol of mobility, using cell phones. It is noteworthy that these consumer items are technologies of mobility or of mobile communication that Maasai use to update their customary forms of mobility (Nilsson and Salazar 2017). These examples illustrate the changing and hybrid nature of Maasai identity markers. What nostalgic outsiders consider to be authentic Maasai culture is the natural result of many decades of external influences (see figure 3.1). Paradoxically, Maasai aspirations of moving upward socially can only materialize if they represent to tourists the life-world in which they live as developing little or not at all (Salazar 2006).

Despite recent changes, tourism business still capitalizes on the widely circulating colonial imaginaries of nomadic Maasai. Quite a few cultural tours to villages around Arusha, Tanzania's safari capital, are marketed and sold as visits to Maasai *bomas*, while the settlements are, at best, ethnically mixed (as living proof of their mobile histories). At the same time, the Maasai are perceived as "immobile" locals—true "natives" (living in the place in which they were born)—and, therefore, authentic. This mental connection between immobility and authenticity fits the generally accepted characteristic of mobility as involving change. Consequently, many Maasai project themselves into relatively immobile (and, by association, more authentically local) roles. This makes them complicit in the perpetuation of biased global tourism imaginaries of time-frozen social identities and cultural traditions (Salazar 2010a). These "imagined stagnant locals are excluded from the new circulating globality, which leaves them outside, just as progress and modernity were imagined as leaving so many behind" (Tsing 2000: 346). The way in which (im)mobility in the context of transnational tourism is enacted and given meaning is intimately tied to widely circulating imaginaries of (assumed) sameness and difference.

Figure 3.1: Not exactly what tourists imagine when they think of Maasai. A multiday Maasai camel safari near Mt. Kilimanjaro, Tanzania. (Photographer: Noel B. Salazar)

Maasai on the Move

> A colonial story in Kenya told among expatriates and repeated to modern tourists is of the Englishman who asks directions from a primitive-looking red-robed Maasai standing on one leg, who answers in English with a perfect Oxford accent. The surprised Englishman learns that the Maasai was indeed educated at Oxford University, but gave it all up and returned to his people because of his preference for the Maasai life. What is interesting here is that educated Maasai can comfortably move back and forth between urban Nairobi and their village compound in the bush. Yet the story assumes the Maasai is only and completely a pastoralist. The third ending is that it can't last; it becomes a narrative of the disappearing primitive, of a doomed and defeated people, the last remnants of the Old Africa, relics of a bygone era.
>
> —Edward M. Bruner, *The Representation of African Pastoralists*

In 2009, I interviewed Naisiae, a young, entrepreneurial Maasai woman. She was born in Maputo, Mozambique, where she spent the first three years of her life. As a child, she spoke Portuguese, and only learned Maa and Swahili at a later age. Naisiae's grandparents were most informative in teaching her about Maasai culture. Her father was an art teacher, which inspired her to study fine arts. Naisiae won a prestigious scholarship to spend three months at a specialized institute in London. A couple of years later, Naisiae exhibited some of her artwork in Norway. The people she meets during her trips abroad sometimes seem surprised to hear that she is Maasai, saying things like "You seem a civilized one." She is annoyed by the misconceptions people have, but very proud of being Maasai (and this even though not everybody within her own clan necessarily appreciates her "modern" way of life). Naisiae herself rarely wears traditional attire but keeps the "inner part" of her culture alive. She now works as an artist-in-residence at a luxury safari lodge close to the Ngorongoro Crater. Her story, while certainly not the most common one, shows the diversity that characterizes contemporary Maasai society.

***

Depending on the circumstances, the Maasai have historically shifted between nomadic pastoralism and seasonal transhumance (more fixed patterns of movement). While there is now extreme variation among Maasai regarding their degree of sedentarism (Coast 2000), the image that sticks in one's mind is the one described by the first European explorers. The Maasai that have settled have done so for a variety of reasons. Already by the nineteenth and early twentieth century, new market opportunities (e.g., cattle markets) led to sedentarization, while the main reasons for becoming sedentary in the later twentieth century were population pressure, land crowding, and ecological decline. Other reasons for the increasing sedentarization include individual land tenure (which is incompatible with transhumance), the erection of fences, and increased use of education services.

Schooling fixes nomadic groups into a more static setting geographically (tying families, or at least mothers and children, to a homestead near the school), and education itself influences the schooled in ways the community cannot control because it influences the ways in which knowledge is transmitted and how bonds to Maasailand are traditionally formed. Historically, Maasai have shunned formal education, partly due to their mobile lifestyle and partly because the relevance of it for pastoralism was not evident. Many Maasai blame the recent decline in economic circumstances on their generation's lack of schooling. They now see the need for their children to be educated so they can protect the Maasai community from the forces seeking to destroy it. However, secondary schooling shortens the rite of passage for junior warriors of living together, thereby weakening the bond to their age-set and their role (as warriors) in Maasai society.

While herd mobility did not traditionally imply household mobility necessarily, entire Maasai families are now exploring new horizons (as the story of Naisiae above illustrates). Contemporary migration patterns are affected by environmental conditions, government policies, new technologies, and public services. While some Maasai head south, going as far as Zambia, where they try to sell their medicines and their services as traditional healers, many more travel toward the big urban centers. There are many young Maasai in the coastal town of Dar es Salaam and on the beaches of Zanzibar, the places where most of the package tourists stay. Attracted by potential employment opportunities, unemployed up-country Maasai have journeyed to these coastal areas to find risky, poorly paid, unskilled, casual work. Benefiting from their colonial image as fearless and warrior-like people, they take up jobs as night guards or security guards, sell artifacts and adornments along the beach or in towns, and perform traditional dances in hotels.

In Zanzibar's Stone Town, for example, there are plenty of Maasai tourist art traders. They have all migrated from the northern districts of Arusha and Kilimanjaro, following the tourist movements. Many of them were first employed as *walinzi* (guardians) in hotels. However, being extremely popular with tourists who tour the national parks, they became an attraction themselves and now perform for tourists. Most of them work in the souvenir trade and travel regularly between the mainland and Zanzibar. Quite a few Maasai got into tourism in the mid-1990s, impelled by livestock losses from disease, severe drought, and land alienation. Interestingly, most of

Stone Town's Maasai or Maasai-style tourist art is made by Zanzibari people (and imports from China are on the rise). The Maasai men who produce beaded jewelry are a cultural oddity, because beading is a woman's task in Maasai culture. Tanzanian Maasai women have also started migrating from Maasailand to Dar es Salaam and other cities, even as far as Zanzibar, Kampala, and Nairobi, producing and selling beads and traditional medicines for cash to support their families (see figure 3.2).

The new phenomenon of long-distance and border-crossing migration is indicative of an overall intensification of impoverishment of the Maasai (Coast 2002). Young Maasai men who travel to the coast to become "beach boys" may expand the sense of roaming adventure long associated with their age group, but elders are concerned about their moral decline from encounters with Western tourists (Hodgson 2001). They are often seen by other Maasai as deviants, likely to stay in town and become "lost" to the more traditional Maasai community (May 2003: 17). The new migrants usually profess little knowledge of, or interest in, the government's doings, a profound dislike for life in the city, and an expressed desire to earn enough to replenish their shrunken livestock herds and return "home"—a wish to remain pastoralists and politically, as well as

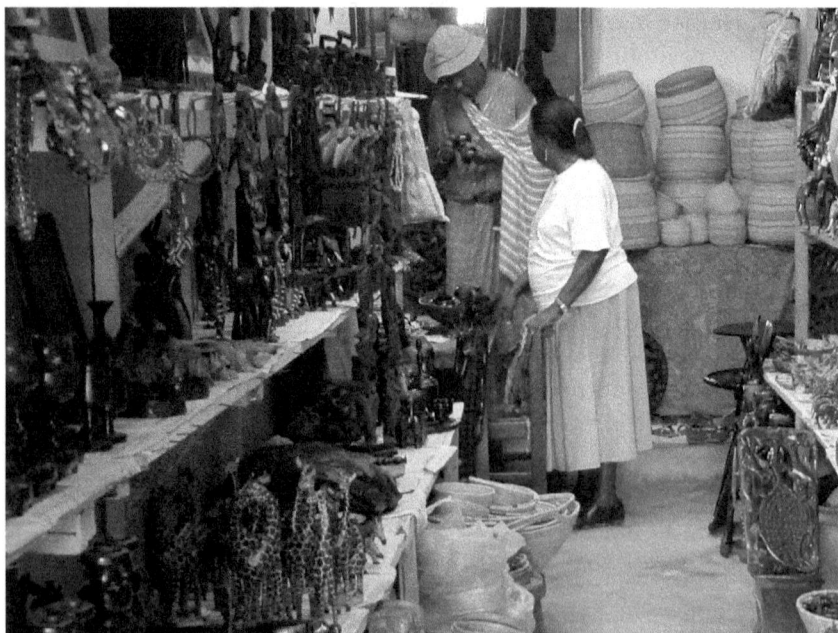

Figure 3.2: Maasai in search of better "pastures." My Maasai assistant visiting a Maasai woman running a souvenir stall in Dar es Salaam, Tanzania. (Photographer: Noel B. Salazar)

socioculturally, independent.[33] Despite the strong Maasai cultural identity, they may cease to be pastoralists, at least in economic terms. Perceptions of shame by others, as well as a lack of opportunities, may constrain unsuccessful migrants from returning.

Other Tanzanians express condescending views of Maasai migrants, typifying them as "unmodern" and as people who are lazy, naive, drunk, and dirty (May and Ole Ikayo 2007).[34] In Tanzania, as well as elsewhere (see Introduction), different categories of mobile people are clearly valued differently (cf. Salazar and Coates 2017). Although various policies have been developed over the last century to try to "develop" and settle the Maasai (Schneider 2006), their nomadic image is widely used as part of an instrumentalist agenda (including tourism advertising). Their marginalization has been enacted at once through the carrying out of material and discursive efforts by elites to disenfranchise Maasai and label them as "second-class citizens"—efforts that have been buttressed by disparaging stereotypes of "the Maasai" as backwards, "traditional," and culturally conservative (Hodgson 2001).

Lacking political or social capital, many Maasai themselves manipulate and reinforce their ethnic identity by continuing to wear traditional garments and by engaging in practices that emphasize their difference from other Tanzanians. While retaining its distinctiveness in stressful circumstances (e.g., by creating new forms of old "traditions" in urban settings), Maasai culture thus exhibits a multiple as well as flexible nature. It is simultaneously both reproduced and contested, going against the lingering representations of immutable and unreasoning Maasai "rigidity." Mirroring patterns of other migrant or subaltern groups throughout the world, Maasai are intermarrying, adopting the languages and livelihoods of neighboring communities, and participating in various national and international development activities. There is a rapidly growing group of well-educated urban(ized) Maasai, although there is still a very clear gender bias (Coast 2002). In sum, if mobility in the past was pastoral and seasonal, mobility today is driven by the need for "greener pastures" of another kind (Salazar 2011b).

Where to Go Next?

> To the modernist imagination the figure of the nomad is one of threat .... It was in this guise that the nomad took his/her place right at the birth of the modern social sciences and cultural studies .... Just as the postmodern theorists enjoy the disruption of boundaries that the nomad necessitates, the modernists feel nausea at such a threat.
>
> —Tim Cresswell, *Imagining the Nomad*

When I returned to Tanzania in 2009, after an absence of two years, I met up with Joseph, my research assistant. He had finished his studies as a tour guide and had landed his first job working for a small walking safari company. I was surprised when we got together because I had never seen him dressed like a Maasai warrior. He told me that he was doing this more regularly now, also while taking clients out on safari (because he noticed how differently tourists respond depending on how he is dressed). It was quite a sight when we walked around Dar es Salaam. People were wondering what this *mzungu* (white guy) and "his" Maasai warrior were up to. Joseph seemed to know many people in Dar. A good number of young Maasai from north Tanzania had migrated to the coastal area in search of job opportunities. We saw them, dressed in the usual "red," working as guards and selling souvenirs and, occasionally, as white-collar workers. Being schooled and being bright, Joseph's future can develop in many directions. He is fortunate enough to be able to convert his passion for walking in nature (and, more recently, photography) into a well-paying tour-guide job for an international safari company. I am extremely proud every time I see him appear in a nature documentary from one or the other international television channel.

***

Many Maasai have discovered their mobile culture's capacity to make its impact upon the global scene. Paradoxically, in the case of tourism, this has partially resulted in the loss of some of its traditional mobile characteristics, mainly because the development of tourism is so deeply embedded in Maasai cultural factors. When people occupy a contested space that they are striving to legitimize, they reproduce their identity through the confirmation of cultural representations that speak to their conceptions of themselves and their interpretation of what they perceive to be outsiders' perceptions of them. As I have argued in this chapter, tourism is far from being the only factor influencing Maasai culture and identity. History, politics, and indigenous rights are all closely intertwined. These elements combined prove to be an integral part of the Maasai cultural process and provide institutionalized and prestigious forms through which cultural and ideological processes, including those related to mobility, can be mediated.

Everybody seems to "know" the Maasai (warriors)—with spears and shields, dancing or charging across the open plains—at a time their communities are faced with political marginalization and are often being dispossessed of their "homeland." There may be a monolithic romanticized, distorted, and exoticized outsider image of Maasai (im)mobilities, but what is crucial for an understanding of Maasai culture and identity is to examine the reality on the ground to determine how those iconic discourses and images are locally enacted and contested. Moreover, also within Maasai culture there have been multiple changes, and Maasai society is much more heterogeneous than outsiders imagine. This translates, among other things, into valorizing mobilities other than the ones traditionally related to herding (see figure 3.3).

As this chapter has illustrated, human mobility is molded by personal and cultural knowledge, skills, technological and financial means, and positions within larger sociocultural networks. The case of the Maasai reminds us that mobility needs to be framed in relation to the political system of nation-states, which set and control the parameters of (trans) national movements and prefer relatively immobilized subject populations (Salazar and Glick Schiller 2014).[35] Nation-states have always preoccupied themselves with the ordering and disciplining of (mostly lower socioeconomic status) mobile peoples, viewing them as a threat to their sovereignty and security, a disorder in the system, a thing to control—be they nomads or pastoralists, runaway slaves, gypsies and exiles, drifters and hobos, tramps and bums, homeless people, hippies and dropouts, or labor migrants. In sum, the case of the Maasai sadly confirms that "there

Figure 3.3: Maasai warriors where one would not directly expect them. Maasai activist, in full gear, visiting Skansen museum in Stockholm, Sweden. (Photographer: Noel B. Salazar)

are severe negative repercussions when people are labeled as nomads" (Kabachnik 2012: 2011). It also shows the need to disentangle nomadism as an economic mode of production, an exoticist system of representation, an archetype of mobility, and a problematic critical concept.

While the Maasai outsider image remains relatively "immobile" (and this can be observed across the globe), the Maasai themselves are increasingly "on the move" in ways that go far beyond their stereotypical representations of mobility as nomadic pastoralists. It is the tension between these processes and the reactions Maasai develop toward them that determines the range of possible (im)mobilities and their cultural value. The stories of Joseph, Koinet, and Naisiae illustrate how younger Maasai no longer depend solely on their own culture for recognition and to carve their own path. Rather, they have become enmeshed in complex local-to-global networks that facilitate their translocal mobilities. At the same time, they remain strongly attached to their Maasai sociocultural base. For the Maasai, as for many other peoples, mobility is hugely important for identity-building (see Introduction). In the current circumstances, it is a matter of finding a balance between historically important ways of moving around the land (still highly valued within Maasai culture) and novel translocal and even transnational mobilities (which are better accepted by the wider society in which Maasai are necessarily embedded).

NOTES

This is an expanded and completely revised version of a chapter in Alexis Bunten and Nelson Graburn's *Indigenous Tourism Movements*, published by the University of Toronto Press in 2017.

1. Before a 2014 East African Community Agreement, a passport was needed to cross the border between Tanzania and Kenya. In the past, however, many Maasai and their cattle regularly crossed the border without the required documents. The fact that border patrol officers ignored this "illegal" practice reinforced the image of "freedom" that is often attributed to (semi)nomadic people such as the Maasai.

2. The central Maasai political and social structure is a system of age-sets. Approximately every fifteen years, the boys between twelve and twenty-five who have reached puberty and are not part of the previous age-set are circumcised and initiated as *ilmurran* (junior warrior).

3. While Maasai women occupy much less of the spotlight than their male counterparts, they do share some of the warrior-like characteristics (Barfield 1993). Like other nomadic women, they are thought of as being more autonomous and virtuous than sedentary ones.

4. While the focus here is on mobility, the Maasai have also been used to promote products as diverse as clothing, jewelry, perfume, food, or coffee.

5. MBT website, accessed 28 February 2018, http://us.shop.mbt.com/index.php/about-us.

6. Fresh Cargo website, 13 October 2014. Accessed 28 February 2018 via Wayback Machine Internet Archive, http://web.archive.org/web/20141013235808/; http://www.freshcargo.co.uk/shoes.

7. Pikolinos website, accessed 28 February 2018, http://maasai.pikolinos.com/.

8. "Maasai warriors finish Flora London Marathon," accessed 28 February 2018, http://www.telegraph.co.uk/sport/othersports/athletics/2297414/Maasai-warriors-finish-Flora-London-Marathon.html.

9. Maasai marathon website, 23 January 2010. Accessed 28 February 2018 via Wayback Machine Internet Archive, http://web.archive.org/web/20100123101625/; http://www.maasaimarathon.com/.

10. *The Amazing Race* is a reality TV game show in which teams of two people race around the world (or, in this case, a country) in competition with other teams. The original series aired in the United States in 2001, and the concept has since been copied across the globe. See The Amazing Race website, accessed 28 February 2018 via Wayback Machine Internet Archive, http://web.archive.org/web/20150906084722/; http://www.chinarush.cn/season1/en/team/2012-04-05/74.html.

11. Land Rover "Maasai" ad, accessed 28 February 2018, http://www.adforum.com/creative-work/ad/player/32133/sxi:3134711.

12. Land Rover Defender ad, 7 November 2015. Accessed 28 February 2018 via Wayback Machine Internet Archive, http://web.archive.org/web/20151107103911/; http://adsoftheworld.com/media/print/land_rover_defender_landscapes_masai.

13. Masai Land Rover Accessories & Upgrades website, accessed 28 February 2018, http://www.masai4x4.com/.

14. Masai Quads website, accessed 28 February 2018, http://www.deltamics.com/masai.php.

15. Samsung Galaxy Masai ad, accessed 28 February 2018, http://www.adsoftheworld.com/media/print/samsung_masai (Samsung Electronics itself is a South Korean company).

16. Banco de Chile Pinpass Masai ad, accessed 28 February 2018, http://www.youtube.com/watch?v=yRG_R_P8lsk.

17. Safaricom Kenya m-pesa website, accessed 28 February 2018, http://www.safaricom.co.ke/personal/m-pesa and Vodacom Tanzania m-pesa website, accessed 28 February 2018, http://vodacom.co.tz/en/.

18. In a similar vein, Anthony D'Andrea (2007: 23) points out that "hypermobility tends to be more explicitly embodied in formations that combine mobility and marginality." While this combination has been historically found among pastoral nomads, it is now reappearing in novel forms that have been termed "neo-nomadism" (see chapter 5).

19. Worth mentioning here also are the influential ideas of Ibn Khaldūn (1967) on the dichotomous relation between "Bedouin civilization" (nomadic life) and "sedentary people."

20. Younger girls may also help the young boys in the herding of the sheep and goats if they are near home, and older girls may also herd the calves (Knowles 1993).

21. It is a common misconception that the mobility of nomadic groups such as the Maasai is purely functional (e.g., only in search of cattle grazing grounds), excluding leisurely diversion and sociability (Nilsson 2016).

22. There are, for instance, remarkable similarities with the walkabout rite of passage in Australia, whereby male Aborigines would undergo a journey during adolescence and live in the wilderness for a period of up to six months.

23. The roots of the word "nomad" (from the Greek νομή, "pasture") relates to the necessarily ambulant practice of pastoral husbandry, which has nothing to do with aimless wandering. Neal Sobania (2002) gives a nice example of the stereotypical image of pastoral nomads in the nineteenth century by analyzing a trade card produced by Liebig's meat extract, entitled "Masai on the move." As he writes, "The image, including women, children, a sheep, cattle, and a donkey loaded with household goods, is part of a recognizable pastoralist identity" (Sobania 2002: 315).

24. For excellent summaries of the problems inherent in using the nomad as a critical figure, see Noyes 2004 and Engebrigtsen 2017.

25. According to Gilles Deleuze and Félix Guattari (1986), sedentary states have always sought to control the nomadic flows of labor. Cresswell (1997: 364) notes, "It is not that the State opposes mobility but that it wishes to control flows, to make them run through conduits. It wants to create fixed and well-directed paths for movement to flow through."

26. The first forceful alienation of pastoral lands in Maasailand was carried out by the Germans (1885–1919), followed by more systematic large-scale alienations by the British (1919–61). The trend in favor of agriculture increased under the independent government (1961–present).

27. Villagization is a well-known strategy used by government or military authorities to resettle people (usually forcefully) into designated villages to facilitate control (particularly when the people are believed to harbor disloyal or rebel elements). In Tanzania, villagization was also used as part of a program of collectivization of farming and other economic activity, under the socialist Ujamaa policy set out by Nyerere (Scott 1998).

28. Transhumance here refers to periodic (normally seasonal) movement with livestock to obtain water and grazing, but also includes movement with livestock to sell animals. Among the Maasai, the land-use pattern involves regular seasonal movements between low-lying plains and highland pastures. The pastures in the cool highlands are used for grazing during the dry season. Here the settlements are larger and more permanent than the wet-season settlements in the plains, to which the Maasai move with their cattle during the rainy season (Århem 1985).

29. In contrast, mobile minority ethnic groups such as the Chaga (Mt. Kilimanjaro area) and the Haya (area west of Lake Victoria) are looked up to for their lucrative trading networks across the country.

30. The concept of indigeneity is traditionally understood as "belonging to the land" (before "others" arrived). The Maasai originally migrated from more northern countries in Africa and appropriated what is now known as "Maasailand" through displacing and assimilating other ethnic groups. However, because of their global visibility tourists only think of them as "local people," and Maasai activists have become ambassadors of the worldwide indigenous movement (Hodgson 2011). In fact, the Maasai were the first African indigenous group to attend the United Nations Working Group on Indigenous Populations in 1989. Their point has been to convince human rights activists and policy makers alike that also nomadic people have profound ties to the territories within which they move. The case of the Maasai has figured prominently in the campaigns of Survival International, an organization working for tribal peoples' rights worldwide.

31. Stop Thomson Safaris website, 22 November 2012. Accessed 28 February 2018 via Wayback Machine Internet Archive, http://web.archive.org/web/20121122103119/; http://stopthomsonsafaris.weebly.com/ Tourism Concern, an independent, non-industry-based UK charity regularly advocates for the plight of the Maasai. See "Maasai land conflict in Tanzania sparks online campaign against Thomson Safaris," accessed 28 February 2018, http://www.tourismconcern.org.uk/index.php/news/33/154/Maasai-land-conflict-in-Tanzania-sparks-online-campaign-against-Thomson-Safaris.html.

32. In 1959, with the establishment of Serengeti National Park, the Maasai who lived there were evicted and moved to the Ngorongoro Conservation Area. In 1974, they were forced to evacuate some parts of Ngorongoro as well, because their presence was believed to be detrimental to wildlife and landscape. In the 1980s, they faced further restrictions as the conservationist attitude of the government stiffened. In 2006, the Tanzanian government even gave an ultimatum to Maasai communities living inside Ngorongoro, around sixty thousand people, to vacate the area by the end of the year. Similar stories can be told in Kenya about Amboseli, Mara Masai, Tsavo, and Samburu.

33. Also (semi)nomads intend to return to a "home" base, usually a part of their total, exploitable habitat that is essential to their livelihood and sense of identity.

34. The problematic nature of the binary "tradition" versus "modernity" has been noted elsewhere too (Germond-Duret 2016; Nilsson 2016).

35. Human mobilities do not necessarily involve crossing the borders of independent states, though they may involve the crossing of perceived national boundaries; and people crossing a state border may see the border as dividing a single nation (Olwig 2003).

PART II

ENACTING MOBILITY

CHAPTER

4

Education
Leaving to Learn

To be educated is not to arrive at a destination, it is to travel with a different view.

—Richard Stanley Peters, *The Philosophy of Education*

Educational Mobilities

I spent most of my formative years in Belgium, in the coastal province of West Flanders. Compared to the multicultural context in which my children are growing up now, my school in the 1980s was very homogeneous in terms of ethnicity and nationality (apart from some kids with a foreign background who had been adopted by Flemish parents at a young age). At the same time, I had plenty of contact with "others." Living in Bruges, a renowned cultural heritage destination, gave me the opportunity to meet people from across the globe. My secondary school did welcome a couple of foreign exchange students, who spent a year in Belgium and then returned home. I remember Marc, a Canadian who had come to Bruges in the hope of enhancing his knowledge of French. He soon realized that he was in the "wrong" part of the country. Since learning Dutch was not on his agenda, we benefited from his presence to enhance our English. In the last years of secondary school, we had educational visits to neighboring countries, but during those trips contact with "locals" was always extremely limited.

The first "serious" mobility experience of many Flemish youngsters is linked to their enrollment at an institution of higher education elsewhere in the country. This leads to a curious phenomenon: the students who stay in rented accommodation in the town in which they study travel back home every weekend. This not only yields practical advantages (from having your parents wash and iron your clothes to even preparing meals for the week to come), but also allows students to remain firmly networked to relatives and old friends "back home." After having finished their studies, most return to their region of origin. Even if they have found a job elsewhere, they prefer the daily commute over living closer to the place where they work.

As an undergraduate student at the beginning of the 1990s, I participated in the weekly train rides back and forth between Bruges and Leuven. However, after a while I started diverging from the typical pattern. Stimulated by the international students with whom I shared housing and who were left alone during the weekends in Leuven, I decided to regularly spend Saturdays and Sundays away from my family. Some of the Europeans were part of Erasmus, the student exchange program that had been launched a couple years earlier. However, at that time the curricula across Europe were so unequal that there were few study-abroad options, and many Flemish professors discouraged students from going anywhere (by embracing the motto "it's much better here than elsewhere"). Stubborn as I was to have an experience abroad, I became a "free mover" after my graduation and enrolled in a master's program in the U.K. This step was the first one in a long row of transnational (and even trans-continental) academic mobilities. I had learned how to leave.

***

This chapter disentangles the role of boundary-crossing mobilities in the context of education, broadly conceived but with a focus on university education. Educational mobilities refer to the myriad ways in which people are on the move in pursuit of educational opportunities (Waters 2015).[1] These temporary and mostly circular movements, variously called "mobility," "exchange," or "study abroad," are widely praised, sometimes even fetishized, by both policymakers and the educational sector alike. The positive valuation of education-related mobilities goes hand in hand with a number of fashionable falsehoods (Welch 2008)—for instance, that they are (1) a recent phenomenon (linked to globalization); (2) oriented towards the West; (3) a matter of free choice; (4) limited to students; (5) gendered; (6) culturally, economically, and politically neutral; (7) the cause of brain drain; and (8) automatically leading to cosmopolitanism.

Focusing on Europe, I will take issue with many of these assumptions. The core of this chapter draws on my own experience, as a foreign student in the United Kingdom and the United States, as a professor in Leuven, as a visiting professor in Bergamo, and as a guest lecturer at various universities across Europe and beyond. In all these places, I observed practices related to educational mobility, and I also talked with students and teaching staff, both informally and formally (the latter mostly in the period 2010–15). Exchanges with scholars of the Young Academy of Belgium, the Royal Flemish Academy of Belgium for Science and the Arts, and the Network of European Young Academies further deepened my insights. Because of the autoethnographic elements and my own academic embedding in Belgium, I decided to limit the analysis mostly to the European context (but I do, of course, acknowledge the importance of educational mobilities elsewhere, particularly in Asia).

Few studies question the meanings people attribute to educational mobilities (R. Thomson and Taylor 2005). As I discuss elsewhere in this book, the value placed on mobility (in the sense of "leaving home" with the intention of returning "enriched") is often intimately bound up with the process of constructing a new and individual identity (see chapters 1 and 2). Indeed, apart from a physical, social, and symbolic transition from one "world" to another, educational mobility can also be conceived of as a resource in the transition from youth to adulthood (see figure 4.1). Education intensifies the movement and change associated with acquiring new experiences, new perspectives, self-development, and freedom.[2] As geographer Clare Holdsworth (2009: 1850) notes, "Scholarship on youth transitions, while not ignoring mobility, has tended to treat mobility as part of the process of transition and, as such, has focused on the empirical significance of mobility rather than exploring the meanings of mobility as well as its outcomes."

Figure 4.1: Foreign students from various countries at a farewell party for one of their friends in Leuven, Belgium. (Photographer: Noel B. Salazar)

Interestingly, rather than embracing opportunities to move across borders, most (young) people are staying put. Educational mobility experiences relate to "motility" (Leivestad 2016), socioeconomic background, and access to resources in terms of economic, cultural, and social capital (Jones 1999). Differential experiences of mobility not only reflect access to resources, but mobility strategies can also reinforce inequalities in education experiences and outcomes. In sum, many elements surrounding educational mobility discourses and imaginaries need to be critically unpacked and put in contrast with how people respond (if at all) to this rhetoric. I start by placing educational mobilities in Europe in their broader historical context.

From Academic Pilgrimage to Virtual Educational Mobility

As with other types of mobility described elsewhere in this book, people who travel in search of educational opportunities and knowledge are not a new phenomenon. In ancient Greece, students from all over the region traveled to Athens, the intellectual capital of the Mediterranean and well connected by trade routes. A common language (Greek) and the means to travel facilitated the spreading of ideas and made it possible for itinerant scholars to move across a vast region.[3] Like the Hellenic world, the early world of Islam, too, was united by a common language (Arabic) and was characterized by vigorous trading. Many medieval Muslim scholars from the West, particularly Spain, Sicily, and southern France, traveled to the great Arabic knowledge centers, such as Baghdad, Damascus, and Cairo, and to Cordoba in Spain (Welch 2005).[4]

The concept of a "university" evolved out of these intellectual roots or, rather, "routes." Mobility, not just of people but of the institutions themselves, was a key characteristic in the founding of these establishments. The first generation of European universities had a common teaching language (Latin), a similar organizational structure, a shared curriculum with common texts, and similar admission and graduation requirements. All of these facilitated academic mobility, better known as *peregrinatio academica* (de Ridder-Symoens 1992). This historical "academic pilgrimage" was the preserve of the happy few, mainly the sons of intellectual and financial elites. Their mobility was further stimulated by an existing European "travel culture," which dated back to previous traditions of traveling for ecclesiastical reasons, medical training, or for translation.

In the Middle Ages, people in search of knowledge often had no other choice but to travel because there were so few academic resources.[5] From the fourteenth century onward, universities and local authorities, however, took various measures designed to discourage rather than to favor academic mobility. The gradual subdivision of the networks of universities, and the restriction of the competence and student population of the universities to specific territories, negatively affected the mobility of people. Sovereigns could forbid "their" students from studying abroad. The argument was always the same: foreign universities were seen as a source of religious and political contamination, and student emigration as inflicting great economic and financial losses upon their own university cities. In addition, indifference to the plight of poor students was widespread in the fifteenth century and hindered academic mobility.

In the sixteenth century, foreign travel in itself came to be considered an educational value in humanistic studies (de Ridder-Symoens 1996). Students from the north of the Alps flocked to northern Italy in search of sources of knowledge as well as culture, spending time in several universities along a well-beaten track (*iter Italicum*), either directly or after having spent time at French universities (*iter Gallicum*). The Reformation, the Counter-Reformation, and the ensuing religious wars seriously hampered international mobility in Europe. In the seventeenth and eighteenth centuries, it became fashionable among young, wealthy Europeans to attend multiple institutions during the so-called "Grand Tour" (Hibbert 1969). These educational travels abroad of the bourgeoisie served other purposes and ideals than those of the earlier *peregrinatio academica*.

The prescribed Grand Tour functioned as an almost mandatory rite of passage, giving the participants the social capital required for a future as political leaders and ambassadors (Wokler 2007). Until the rise of the "national" university in Europe, with its mission of providing legal and administrative talent for the nation-state, universities were open to students from everywhere. Aided by a common ancient language, intellectuals moved freely in search of subjects, teachers, and environments conducive to their interests. With the rise of nation-states, however, academic mobility lost most of its educational and cultural importance.

While the *peregrinatio academia* and the Grand Tour were elitist forms of European "travel culture," since the Middle Ages an elaborate parallel network of traveling apprenticeships had developed throughout Europe. This "tramping tradition" (Adler 1985)—compulsory long-term translocal travel as part of craftsmen's training with masters, called *compagnonnage* in France and *Wanderjahre* or *Wanderpflicht* in Germany—was a widespread method of education, market control, and professional network building by guilds and other craftsmen's associations throughout Europe (Böröcz 1992).[6] As Judith Adler (1985) notes, this working class travel system of fraternal ritualism involved a greater number of participants and covered a broader geographical area than its elite counterpart of the Grand Tour.[7]

Educational mobility is often provoked by external events (including wars and persecution). We should also not forget that much of the global educational mobility is shaped by the legacy of colonial relations. The intellectually fertile Weimar era (1918–33) in Germany, and more particularly its aftermath, provides another example. The restriction of intellectual life, and often outright persecution, of 1930s Nazi Germany and Austria led to the exile of intellectuals, often Jewish, to American and other universities (Welch 2005). The first study-abroad program for US undergraduate students, the Delaware Foreign Study Plan (later renamed as the Junior Year Abroad), was created in the 1920s by a World War I veteran who had fought in France and who became a French professor.[8] The boom of student exchange programs came after World War II, when the language-learning purpose of study abroad was combined with a broader social and cultural consideration. In 1945, US Senator J. William Fulbright proposed a bill to use the proceeds from selling surplus government war property to fund international exchange between the United States and other countries.

The end of World War II also led to the Cold War, a period in which mobility between the two "world order" systems of education remained highly restricted and under close official control. In addition, the growth of the university system across the globe led to a decrease in scholarly mobility. At the same time, the Cold War stimulated countries such as the United States to promote student mobility through Fulbright Scholarships and funding from the US Agency for International Development. Many of these programs, which were highly successful, were designed to showcase American-style democratic capitalism to the future elites of less-developed and nonaligned countries while at the same time enhancing foreign trade-making and intelligence-gathering (Robertson 2006).[9] The world wars also led to the development of school-based homestay programs abroad (at the level of secondary education).[10] Participants live with host families and attend a local school as a full-time student during the course of an academic year, semester, or trimester. AFS Intercultural Programs (originally the American Field Service) grew out of a service of volunteer ambulance drivers during the two wars, evolving over the years into an international youth exchange organization with a presence in over fifty countries.[11]

Educational mobilities, like other types of mobility, have been facilitated by transportation and technological advancements. At the same time, they have been provoked by rises and falls in economic conditions. Greater economic integration among Mexico and Canada and the United States through the 1994 North American Free Trade Agreement (NAFTA) is an example, giving greater impetus to the internationalization of educational institutions (Welch 2005). In 1993, the universities of the Asia-Pacific region, from Japan to Australia and including most Southeast-Asian countries, decided to develop University Mobility in Asia and the Pacific (UMAP), a mobility program very similar to the European Erasmus program (see below). The South East Asian Ministries of Education (SEAMEO) launched a pilot mobility scheme in 2009, the M-I-T Student Mobility Project, involving higher education institutions within the region, beginning with Malaysia, Indonesia, and Thailand (Robertson 2010). Despite all these initiatives, there remains a great deal of geographic inequality in existing mobility flows.

According to a report by OECD (2012: 361), the factors driving the increase in contemporary student mobility range from the

> exploding demand for higher education worldwide and the perceived value of studying at prestigious post-secondary institutions abroad, to specific policies aiming to foster student mobility within a geographic region (as is the case in Europe), and efforts by governments to support students in studying specific fields that are growing rapidly in the country of origin.

Despite all the rhetoric about personal freedom (see Introduction), the growth in educational mobility is thus clearly not the result of mere individual decisions. Host countries see it as an export activity that yields economic returns, and market their education programs internationally (Tremblay 2005). From the sending countries' perspective, educational mobility often helps address the excessive demand for higher education in the context of limited domestic offers.

Education specialist Ulrich Teichler (2012: 12), however, argues that "international learning is bound to lose its exceptionality ... as a consequence of a general internationalization of the daily life and as a consequence of increasing 'internationalization at home' of the study provisions." Indeed, the increased mobility of students and scholars allows less mobile colleagues to benefit from what has been termed "internationalization at home" (Wächter 2003). Some transnational higher education models include "flying faculty," where academics are flown in to teach for a short period in another country. Another development along similar lines is the phenomenon of international "branch campuses" and other foreign education outposts, whereby universities implant themselves in various parts of the world. The number of these kinds of campuses has mushroomed over the last decade.[12]

So far, physical mobility has been the main approach in education. New information and communication technologies allow people to participate in "virtual academic mobility," in which students from different countries study together. Virtual mobility—virtual courses, virtual student placements, and virtual support activities—can offer many benefits and be an important complement to physical mobility. However, as virtual tourism will never replace "the real thing," it is highly unlikely that virtual academic mobility will completely replace physical mobility, rather than supplementing it. MOOCs, massive open online courses (aimed at large-scale interactive participation and open access via the web), for instance, are heavily contested.

As far as the mobility of university students is concerned, it is important to distinguish between two types of student mobility. Degree mobility—studying abroad for a full degree—is mainly "vertical," from countries of a quantitatively or qualitatively lower level of educational provision into those with a higher level. Credit mobility, studying abroad mainly for a short period as an exchange student, is, in the main, "horizontal," happening between countries with a similar quality in higher education. Credit mobility is often driven by a desire for a linguistically and culturally different experience. Degree mobility, on the other hand, is fueled by the attempt to get a better education than one could get in the home country. A "cosmopolitan" dimension is an accidental by-product in degree mobility, not something actively sought.

The European Imperative: "Move or Perish"

Even though I never had a chance to be an Erasmus student myself, it is no exaggeration to say that the Erasmus Program has profoundly influenced my own academic experience. Even while being forced to stay put as a student, I had an opportunity to interact with the exchange students who came to Leuven. The old Flemish town was (and still is) known as picturesque, and reputed to offer a solid education and excellent student life. I remember how I was puzzled in the 1990s that some Erasmus students spoke so little English, let alone Dutch. How much would they benefit academically from their experience abroad? Years later, I can look at the Erasmus Program from the perspective of a lecturer. The exchange scheme has grown tremendously. Students now come from a more diverse set of countries. Apart from having exchange students in my regular courses, I have also been linked to two Erasmus Mundus programs, in which graduate students change countries, and sometimes continents, every single term. Everybody seems to assume that such experiences will a priori be positive (although the stories that students share with me paint a more complex picture).

The fact that the anthropology master programs in Leuven are taught almost exclusively in English attracts many foreign degree students. Petar, for example, is from Croatia, a country in the Balkans that only joined the EU in 2013. He decided to study in another European country because of the precarious situation in his country. In that sense, Leuven was very attractive to him, offering excellent quality for a cheap price. Since the macroeconomic circumstances had not changed after finishing his master's degree, Petar enrolled in another master's program at our university. He then moved to Denmark to start a Ph.D. program. The pattern of accumulating degrees is something we see most commonly among students from developing countries (I once met an Indian man who was completing his third doctoral degree).

Chiara is Italian and decided to study in Belgium through the intermediary of some relatives (part of her family migrated to Belgium to work in the coal mines in the 1950s). It was her first experience of living in another country. Her original plan was to return to Italy once she obtained her degree, to apply for jobs. However, due to contacts made during her stay in Leuven, she was offered a job in Switzerland that completely matched her interests. During a visit to her "old" friends in Belgium one year later, she passed by my office. She said she really liked living and working in Switzerland. Unfortunately, her contract there was only temporary. Not being a permanent resident, this meant that she will soon need to be on the move again.

Although Lotte is from Flanders, she decided to enroll in our English-speaking program. She loves traveling, and this passion of hers also became visible in her essays and the choice for the Caribbean as the location for her ethnographic fieldwork. Lotte is one of those rare M.A. students who already attend international conferences to present their research. Moreover, in her second year, she won a scholarship to spend a semester as an exchange student at a university in California. Because of these connections, her international academic network grew rapidly. This, in turn, helped her when she decided to apply for Ph.D. programs in the United States. Also in this process, she focused on institutions located in attractive locations.

***

Europe has been made, unmade, and remade over the centuries through the movements of peoples (Favell 2009). Tumultuous times such as the two world wars seriously hampered these historically inscribed mobilities. The post-1945 political process of European unification sought to reverse this. Intra-European mobility has been a key element of the EU project since its inception and one of the key indicators of its success (Shore 2000). Several initiatives have focused on enhancing and supporting intra-EU mobility, partly with the explicit aim of increasing support for the EU and to promote economic growth (Recchi and Favell 2009). Grand slogans such as "mobility for all" have become a common feature of official EU policy documents and have been promoted in recent years as nothing less than an EU-wide objective, to make mobility "the rule rather than the exception." Not surprisingly, educational mobility has received a level of attention not known anywhere else in the world. From a young age onward, Europeans participate in the EU Lifelong Learning Program (of which Erasmus is the most well-known) (see figure 4.2).

According to figures gathered by UNESCO (2012), there are over 3.5 million mobile university students. This is a mere 2 percent of the global tertiary education population. To compare, in 1975 only half a million students enrolled outside their country of citizenship (but the total enrolment at that time was smaller by about the same factor). Almost 60 percent (approximately two million) go to study in North America and Western Europe, followed by twenty percent in East Asia and the Pacific.[13] The European continent receives almost half of all mobile students. Almost 90 percent of the students moving around Europe are Europeans, and, of these, three out of four are from EU member states. Most of these student movements involve spontaneous degree mobilities (such as the examples of Petar and Chiara above). However, the numbers of EU nationals enrolled outside their country of nationality are lower than those of foreign nationals studying in the EU.

Figure 4.2: The organization of student mobility requires a whole infrastructure. A wall full of instructions for the evaluators for the Marie Skłodowska-Curie Fellowships inside a building of the European Commission, Brussels, Belgium. (Photographer: Noel B. Salazar)

EU nationals participate more in programs of credit mobility. The European Commission has played a key role in steering this. The initiative for an intra-European student exchange program was conceived in the 1970s and 1980s and eventually led to a European Community strategy with the aim of a "People's Europe" (Sigalas 2010). Erasmus, the European Community Action Scheme for the Mobility of University Students, is the EU's flagship mobility program. It is no coincidence that it is named after the medieval humanist scholar Erasmus of Rotterdam (1465–1536). As an itinerant scholar, Desiderius Erasmus Roterodamus perfectly epitomizes international academic mobility. He lived and worked in several parts of Western Europe in search of knowledge, experience, and insights that only contacts with other countries could bring. The revival of the medieval idea of European universities accessible to all students was a logical deduction from the formation of a legal and political European community. This led to a search for means through which to promote high educational mobility to serve the creation of a European identity as something complementary to a national identity.

The Erasmus program was established in 1987. That year, 3,244 students from Western Europe went to study in one of the eleven countries that initially participated in the program. Since then, the exchange program has grown quickly. Today, it has welcomed over three million participants, and thirty-three countries inside and outside Europe participate in the most visible and popular program of the EU. In 2009, the Erasmus Mundus program was launched. This enables students from outside the EU to engage in master and doctoral programs at EU higher education institutions, and encourages the outgoing mobility of EU students and scholars toward "third countries."[14] Since 2014, Erasmus has continued as Erasmus+ (the plus indicating the allocation of a larger budget to include more diverse types of educational mobilities). In its starting year, Erasmus+ offered a record number of 650 thousand individual mobility grants, including 400 thousand higher education and vocational student exchanges, and 100 thousand volunteers and young people undertaking youth work abroad. There are slightly more women participating in the programs.

Mobility is a key instrument for developing the European Higher Education Area.[15] However, 90 percent of European students never participate in mobility programs. The main barriers to an experience abroad are a lack of financial resources to compensate for the additional costs, and personal relationships (European Commission 2014). However, as the European Commission itself recognizes, funding is important, but money alone is not enough to make mobility a realistic opportunity for all. In 2009, the Council of the European Union placed mobility at the top of its strategic objectives for education and training (the latter referring to programs aimed at learning "skills," in ways that are similar to the European tradition of *compagnonnage*, mentioned above). They present mobility as "an essential element of lifelong learning and an important means of enhancing people's employability and adaptability" (Council of the European Union 2009: 3).

In 2011, EU education ministers agreed on a joint plan (in the form of Council Recommendation 2011/C 199/01) to remove administrative and institutional obstacles to studying or training abroad. This recommendation forms part of the Europe 2020 (the EU's competitive and sustainable growth strategy for the coming decade) flagship initiative Youth on the Move.[16] The document stresses that learning mobility is one of the fundamental ways in which young people can strengthen their future employability, as well as their intercultural awareness, personal development, creativity, and active citizenship. Interestingly, the document also targets "stayers." It aims to promote the added value of learning mobility not only among learners (potential candidates) but also their families, teachers, trainers, youth workers, and employers. In addition, it seeks to encourage peer exchange between mobile and not-yet-mobile learners to improve motivation and to foster a "mobility culture" (e.g., by promoting greater social recognition of the value of learning mobility).

EU mobility initiatives also cover informal learning through transnational volunteering or voluntary service.[17] The EU initiatives concerning the mobility of young volunteers date back to the mid-1990s. The European Voluntary Service, part of the Youth in Action Program (financed by the European Commission), offers young people the possibility of doing voluntary internships in European countries. The volunteers gain competences needed for mobility (either for learning or work purposes) and are believed to return more mature, more self-confident, and, potentially, as more active citizens (PPMI 2010). Note that also here the expectation is that participants will return "home."

For many European students, the Erasmus Program is their first experience of living abroad. It has thus become a widespread cultural phenomenon and the subject of many cultural productions, such as the popular French-Spanish film *L'Auberge Espagnole* (2002). This lighthearted movie tells the tale of Xavier, a French economics student who is promised a job with the French government after having gone on an Erasmus exchange to Barcelona (to gain a working knowledge of Spanish). In Spain, the young man shares a flat with a group of students hailing from all over Europe (a European melting pot in miniature). The film emphasizes the role of differential mobility in the construction and mapping of European identity (Ezra and Sánchez 2005). In the movie, student mobility is the privileged reserve of the educated upper-middle classes, with echoes of the artistic or literary Grand Tour. The film features a series of adventures that serve as an initiation to (adult) life. Studying abroad, as one of the movie's characters says, is "where a year can change a lifetime." Indeed, in the end Xavier turns down the boring office job.

In 2005, the sequel to the movie was released, entitled *Les Poupées Russes* (The Russian Dolls). This film, which programmatically addresses the need to spread a larger Europe as far east as Russia, expanding both east and south, was launched after the referendum on the European constitution was massively turned down in France. The reunion of the Barcelona team is made possible through displacement, temporary exile, and shifting back and forth between one's language and another. It makes sense that the "Erasmus generation," which is made up of "young people who have enjoyed the practical benefits of European integration, are highly mobile, think of themselves as European citizens, and consequently are a base of support for further European integration" (I. Wilson 2011: 1114). The characters cross many borders and engage in many deterritorializing journeys, which take several forms, including home-seeking journeys, journeys of homelessness, and homecoming journeys. It is a story in which many Erasmus alumni I have talked to over the years recognize themselves.

Academic Capital or Academic Capitalism?

One of the domains of university administration that has grown most exponentially over the last decades is that of "internationalization." Because of my "international profile," I had little option but to become part of our Faculty Commission for Internationalization. Over the years, I have witnessed a staggering number of agreements being signed with partner institutions in Europe and far beyond. These agreements are supposed to facilitate incoming and outgoing mobilities. In fact, it is almost impossible to find enough students (and staff) every year to fill all spots available. Some can still not afford the trip abroad (despite the provided mobility funding); others are simply not interested. Furthermore, the stress on reaching quota seems to have turned mobility itself into an end rather than a means to reach educational goals. We, the anthropologists, usually "score" very well in terms of mobility. However, that is largely because people choosing to study anthropology already have an interest in "other" people and places (and, thus, an inclination to travel "elsewhere").

***

Like other mobilities, educational mobilities are shaped by cultural traditions and social structures (Bourdieu 1988). In other words, we cannot understand them without also looking at how current socioeconomic conditions are instrumental in (re)producing inequality (see Introduction). The growth of educational mobility has accelerated during the past decade, mirroring broader processes of neoliberal globalization and the privatization of education. The suggested explanations for the marketization of education are well known and include policy rhetoric about a "global knowledge economy" (Kim 2009). According to Terri Kim (2009: 400), what makes contemporary educational mobility distinctive and differentiated from patterns of former times are the simultaneous interlocking relations of the (1) spontaneity of individual movements, (2) both national and supranational policy frameworks that facilitate and reinforce highly skilled migration, and (3) institutional networks of (increasingly corporatized) universities.

Neoliberal forms of governmentality are clearly evident in the educational sector of the European Commission (Mitchell 2006). Both the policies and the programs associated with education and training are becoming more oriented toward the formation of a mobile, flexible, multilingual, and self-governing cross-border European workforce, and less oriented toward an institutionalized affirmation of personal development and individual or group "difference." The current rhetoric is accompanied by multiple EU treaties that promote the standardization, homogenization, and international certification of educational skills, allowing and encouraging a greater mobility across international borders. Europass, the European curriculum vitae standard, also includes Europass Mobility, an extra document that records details of the contents and the results (in terms of skills and competencies or of academic achievements) of a period spent in another European country for learning purposes.[18] Because someone's "history" of translocal mobility is manifested on the CV, his or her relative acquiescence and success in the project of perpetual mobilization and self-improvement remains a permanent mark (Mitchell 2006).

The official EU discourse is mostly about credit mobility—relatively short educational journeys abroad, after which the students have little choice but to return to complete their degree. Despite the multiple efforts of democratization, Erasmus students tend to come from higher socioeconomic groups, and they represent between only 0.1 and 1.5 percent of all students enrolled (European Parliament 2010). The Erasmus program promotes student mobility within the EU largely on the assumption that mobile students will become more pro-EU (a qualified form of "cosmopolitanism," if you will). While former Erasmus students may, indeed, be more pro-EU than their peers, this is because students who choose to take part are already more pro-EU (I. Wilson 2011). Many of those who have not stayed abroad also claim that they are not interested in doing so (Eurobarometer 2011).

Top motivations to study abroad that students mention are the opportunity to live abroad and meet new people, improve foreign language proficiency, and develop transversal skills (European Commission 2014). Importantly, not everybody benefits from mobility to the same degree. In Western and Northern Europe, students are more likely to have been exposed to travel abroad earlier in their lives through school exchanges and other trips. Those who move most are predominantly young people belonging to the middle classes of Southern and Eastern Europe (like Petar). They use geographical mobility to achieve upward social mobility (although this is not always achieved because transnational mobility experiences do not, despite being valued by corporate recruiters, guarantee the achievement of democratization on the labor market).

Possible negative effects of transnational educational mobilities, such as those resulting from culture shock, have not been monitored systematically thus far (because most stakeholders simply assume that such mobilities are, a priori, positive). In practice, the outcome of educational mobility is hard to pin down, raising suspicions that it is sometimes simply undertaken for its own sake, as a means to artificially pad a CV rather than a way to expand one's knowledge base (Schiermeier 2011). Moving for the sake of moving may have little effect on one's capability or marketability (although, importantly, it may help the socialization into future mobilities). Nevertheless, mobility policies keep on depicting a rosy picture:

> Mobility is viewed as producing 'effects' that range from enhancing the quality of programs, to creating excellence in research, strengthening the academic and cultural internationalization of European higher education, promoting personal development and employability, fostering respect for diversity, encouraging linguistic pluralism, and increasing cooperation and competition between higher education institutions. From this list, mobility is conceived of as a positive force; a powerful mechanism of social change. However, statements like this are an overly romantic rendering of mobility. (Robertson 2010: 642)

With few exceptions, EU countries vaguely endorse mobility as a desirable activity and adopt a "the more the merrier" approach (Teichler, Ferencz, and Wächter 2011). They generally support mobility because they deem it contributes to the "internationalization" of their higher education system, increases the overall quality of education, helps them develop good relations with other countries, and creates graduates that can function in international work environments. Within countries, the focus of policy statements is either on outgoing temporary credit mobility (nineteen countries), or on incoming degree mobility (eighteen countries). Tellingly, outgoing degree mobility and incoming credit mobility play no role at all in official educational policy documents. Most countries remain vague about their reasons for desiring educational mobility. Those with more palpable motivations mention an increase in the quality of education and in graduate employability. For incoming degree mobility, "knowledge gains" and related economic reasons figure highly. Skilled migration, internationalization at home through more foreign students, development aid, and foreign cultural policy are further rationales (Teichler, Ferencz, and Wächter 2011).

Louise Ackers (2008) notes a tendency (in both policy circles and academic research) to conflate different forms of mobility and to equate these with notions of excellence or quality. Structural factors shape the normative meanings of educational mobility, and Pierre Bourdieu's (1984; 1988) theory of the educational trajectory of individuals is still instrumental in disentangling these factors.[19] Like other kinds of symbolic capital, "mobility capital" becomes endowed by those who have the power to construe values for it: "Those students who appeared to possess the cultural capital that could be turned into educational credentials had a clear mobility orientation; they knew they wanted to leave and that to do so they needed the mobile capital of educational credentials acquired in the 'market' of the school" (Corbett 2004: 455). The fact that the assumptions attached to educational mobilities are so credible means that those who move can rely on promoting personal qualities that are assumed to derive from their mobility experiences, whether they benefit from moving away in the ways that are popularly portrayed or not. The mobility imperative also creates a stereotyped image of the "successful" mobile student versus the unsuccessful "stuck" other.

Meanwhile, Europe's top research universities are pushing for more structured forms of student mobility (De Moor and Henderikx 2013). Instead of "exchange mobility" (where students themselves choose to have an experience abroad for a short or longer period of time), they propose to invest more in "networked mobility" (where a university joins a network with several partners and sends its students for a certain period of time to one or more partner institutions) and "embedded mobility" (where a limited number of partners form a consortium in which students "rotate" and follow parts of their educational trajectory in two or more partner institutions). This again illustrates the tension with discourses of personal freedom to choose where one goes (Dean 2016).

Learning to Leave

Most of my Flemish students (and students in general) do not participate in educational mobilities. They have several reasons to do so, but they do not need to justify themselves. They represent the majority, and their behavior is "normative" (although it is not always perceived as such). What exactly they lose out by not "leaving to learn" is a question that is rarely asked. Moreover, it is not as if these people never travel. Among my students, everybody has been on holidays to other countries, and a substantial number has been to other continents. In addition, they benefit from the mobility of others. Students attending my classes represent an eclectic mix of people. "Internationalization at home," as they call this in the literature, allows the students to experience a rich diversity in the classroom. Without leaving, the Flemish students learn a lot about "other" worlds. However, this can only work if foreign students keep coming to my university.

***

Mobility means different things in different places, and young people within the same location engage differently with mobility. Educational mobility takes many forms, both real and virtual. We should criticize the view that the decision to engage in educational mobilities is related only to personal choice and responsibility, because this obscures how such experiences are embedded in sociocultural contexts that shape both who has access to them, and how people understand and attach meaning to them. Study-abroad programs are increasingly a "globalizing project" developed at the intersection of educational institutions seeking new income sources, and the ideology that the world is comprised of a mosaic of cultures and that "intercultural experience" is valuable. Intrinsically linked to the ideology of mobility is the fact that mobility appears as a good investment, especially in future career opportunities (Brodersen 2014). Moreover, the European example of the Erasmus student exchange program nicely illustrates how experiences of transnational mobility facilitate subsequent mobilities and generate extended networks, which can in turn encourage future moves. In other words, in the process of "leaving to learn," young people are also "learning to leave." The way in which mobility functions can indeed be understood as mobility capital, "a processual category allowing us to distinguish between the capacity to be mobile and actual mobility and which influences both the unequal chances of access to and the social differentiation based on mobilities" (Brodersen 2014: 105).

Expectations of educational mobility are rarely contested. Most stakeholders take such mobility for granted rather than questioning the validity of the assumptions on which it is based. It is becoming increasingly pressing that we consider both the ethics of mobility and the ethics of place that govern education and research in a global world.

What are we to make of mobility as a social and political project for the academy, and as a way of thinking about wider transformations in the spatial, infrastructural, and institutional moorings that configure and enable mobilities? What alternative concepts and intellectual resources can we bring to bear on the study of mobilities that move our analyses beyond simple human capital accounts, on the one hand, and an overly romantic engagement with movement, on the other? What are the ethical and social justice issues which are raised when mobilities are caught up in the power geometries of everyday life? (Robertson 2010: 643)

In the case of students, the stress on mobility is linked to the sociocultural valorization of "a particular model of transition to adulthood which focuses on separation, self-reliance, and responsibility for the self, rather than one based on interdependencies, mutual support, and responsibility for others" (Holdsworth 2009: 1861). In other words, the experience of becoming educated seems to necessitate the estrangement from one's "home" base. The part that mobility plays in narratives of transition is historically and culturally specific (see also previous chapters). Moreover, "young people are torn between competing forces in relation to notions of home, tradition and fixedness on one hand and of mobility, escape and transformation on the other" (R. Thomson and Taylor 2005: 337).

Figure 4.3: Young Belgian people exploring plenty of opportunities to study or work abroad at an annual educational fair in Brussels, Belgium. (Photographer: Noel B. Salazar)

Even if educational mobility is one of privilege, the same type associated with tourism, it is thus not necessarily a "free choice." Educational mobility masks a whole range of strategies. I concur with Ackers (2008) that mobility is not an outcome in its own right and must not be treated as such (as an implicit indicator of internationalization). It should neither be specifically privileged nor "penalized." The level of diversity is significant, and each form of mobility or international engagement has its benefits and risks. Not all students and scholars will become mobile soon; it is not even desirable that they do so. Some institutions have reached a point of saturation where incoming mobility is concerned, and the carbon footprint of internationalization is another serious (and underestimated) concern. Governments and educational institutions need to adopt a more nuanced approach to educational mobility and move away from viewing it as an end (in itself). Moreover, we need more research on the discrepancy between the optimistic rhetoric of internationalization and the reality "on the ground" before, during, and after the experience abroad.

Finally, students have different credentials, interests, and motivations for moving abroad, temporarily or permanently. For some, transnational educational mobilities are an important channel of labor mobility (see figure 4.3). The term "educationally channeled international labor mobility" (Liu-Farrer 2009) has been suggested to describe the overlapping trends of international student mobility and labor mobility (see chapter 5). Although popular, the notions of brain drain and diaspora are not adequate to describe and understand contemporary educational mobility.[20] Contemporary educational mobilities are becoming much more intricate than what is conventionally seen as unidirectional movement. A story to be continued ...

NOTES

1. The measurement and classification of educational mobility depends to a large extent on national migration legislations and data constraints (West and Barham 2009). The concept of "international students," for example, refers to students who cross borders with the intention of studying (be it for a degree or as part of an exchange). However, the operational definition of this category varies from those who are not permanent residents or, alternatively, students who received their prior education in another country (regardless of citizenship). The widespread practice in Europe is to take foreign student numbers as an approximation of student mobility.

2. Interestingly, Erik Erikson, the psychologist who developed this idea as part of his well-known psychosocial development theory, eschewed college in his twenties for travel around Europe, being of the opinion that the reflective physical

journey was a more appropriate and effective higher education than the standard, formal, in-place academic version (Haines 2012).

3. According to Shigeru Nakayama (1984), the rather limited mobility of scholars isolated at the eastern end of the Eurasian landmass explains why the Chinese tradition based on the works of Confucius did not evolve into a central position in the development of global science, as the Greek philosophers had done.

4. The concept of *rihla* (travel in search of knowledge) was traditionally a primary motif in the lives of many Muslim scholars, who were an extraordinarily mobile group.

5. The autobiographical works of Pierre Abélard (1079–1142, *Historia Calamitatum*) and his pupil John of Salisbury (1120–1180, *The Letters of John of Salisbury*) vividly paint the world of students and their masters.

6. While in the past it was required to travel before becoming a skilled master, it is now voluntary and a matter of honor. In 2010, this European tradition was inscribed by UNESCO on the Representative List of Intangible Cultural Heritage of Humanity. See "Compagnonnage, Network for On-the-Job Transmission of Knowledge and Identities," UNESCO, accessed 28 February 2018, http://ich.unesco.org/en/RL/compagnonnage-network-for-on-the-job-transmission-of-knowledge-and-identities-00441.

7. In some sectors of the British working class, tramp trips appear to have become rites of passage to full male adulthood. However, the English tramping system evolved primarily as a response to the problem of unemployment, and though young men were more likely than older ones to tramp when local demand for labor diminished, tramping was not limited to youth alone (Adler 1985). These days, only the title "journeyman" itself remains as a reminder of the custom of young men traveling throughout the country.

8. The two world wars constituted conflicts in which millions of people gathered intense experiences of (voluntary and involuntary) mobility and cross-border contacts.

9. There also existed equivalent programs, such as the Commonwealth-based "Colombo Plan," which were originally aimed at battling the "communist enemy" through the construction of universities and the training of scholars and students from the partner countries (originally only seven countries belonging to the Commonwealth of Nations).

10. Such programs are different from a year out (also known as a "gap year"), in which students disengage from curricular education and undertake noncurricular activities, such as travel or work. The assumed benefits associated with this practice are inherently tied to the idea of being "cosmopolitan": mobile, engaged with the world, and eager for new experiences (Snee 2014). It is also possible to participate in international education programs that combine language study, homestays, cultural immersion, community service, and independent study.

11. Another example is Youth For Understanding. This organization began by bringing teenagers from war-torn Germany to the United States to live with a family and

attend high school for a year to heal the wounds of World War II. The organization expanded in ways similar to American Field Service and is now active in over forty countries.

12. In Brussels, Belgium, alone, there are approximately fifteen such campuses (some of them no larger than a rented room in an office building).

13. Central Asia and Sub-Saharan Africa have the most mobile students. Top destination countries are the United States, United Kingdom, Australia, France, Germany, and Japan. The top source countries of international students are China, India, and Korea. Asia is the region of growth for future international students.

14. See "Erasmus Mundus Joint Master Degrees," European Commission, accessed 28 February 2018, http://ec.europa.eu/programmes/erasmus-plus/opportunities/individuals/students/erasmus-mundus-joint-master-degrees_en.

15. Outward mobility rates of graduates from within the EHEA are very low, with a weighted average slightly below two per cent.

16. "Youth on the Move: A Europe 2020 Initiative," European Commission, accessed 28 February 2018, http://ec.europa.eu/youthonthemove/; "Europe 2020," European Commission, 20 May 2012. Accessed 28 February 2018 via Wayback Machine Internet Archive, http://web.archive.org/web/20120520171326/; http://ec.europa.eu/europe2020/reaching-the-goals/flagship-initiatives/index_en.htm.

17. Interesting in this respect is the sociological study of Anna Bagnoli (2009), in which the four most common (and often overlapping) modes of youth mobilities were compared: taking a year out, backpacking, studying a foreign language abroad, and au pairing. Despite obvious differences, all these forms were interpreted by participating young people as journeys of self-discovery leading to a (re)construction of their identities.

18. The Europass Mobility was established by decision No. 2241/2004/EC of the European Parliament and of the Council of 15 December 2004 on a single Community framework for the transparency of qualifications and competences (Europass). See "Connect with Europass," Europass website, accessed 28 February 2018, http://europass.cedefop.europa.eu.

19. Bourdieu stressed the importance of various kinds of symbolic capital and their relation to economic capital. "Symbolic capital" refers to the degree of accumulated prestige, celebrity, consecration, or honor, and is founded on a dialectic of knowledge and recognition. "Cultural capital" concerns forms of cultural knowledge, competencies, or dispositions. Cultural capital in its institutionalized state (e.g., academic credentials) can be exchanged for economic capital in the labor market.

20. The term "brain drain" was popularized in the 1950s in relation to immigration to the United States.

Labor
Capitalizing on Movement

In contrast to most people I know, my first full-time employment (back in 1998) was a job abroad. Before that, I had worked only three months in my home country as an interim for an international NGO, knowing beforehand that the contract could not be extended. When I was offered a permanent position in the organization's headquarters in Rome, I did not hesitate. It was not the first time I relocated temporarily. I had studied for over a year in the UK and had subsequently been active as a long-term volunteer in France. In a sense, the position in Italy was the continuation of a chain of mobilities, although it was the first work-related one. Based in Rome, I was given the opportunity to visit the NGO's offices in various corners of the world. After two years, I transferred to a job in a related organization in Brussels. This time, too, I was sent around the globe on short-term missions.

My current job as a university professor (since 2012) and my involvement in various international scholarly organizations also require regular traveling, at least one cross-border voyage per month and a couple of transcontinental trips per year. I often tell my friends jokingly, "When flight attendants start recognizing you, you know that you probably travel too frequently." It reminds me of the Hollywood movie *Up in the Air* (based on Walter Kirn's 2001 novel). In that movie, George Clooney plays a corporate business traveler who exists in a state of constant transit, although he dreams of a job that involves less travel. The story makes me reflect about frequent, job-related traveling. Although often admired (particularly by those who have more sedentary jobs), the lived experience of the highly mobile is much less rosy than imagined.

***

Work-related mobilities exist in many shades and colors. Just as the temporal patterns of work have been diversifying, so too have its spatial patterns. Economist Stefan Lilischkis (2003) describes various types of mobile workers: (1) "Yo-yos," who occasionally work away from a fixed location or head office (e.g., attending international meetings or conducting scientific field work); (2) "Pendulums," who alternately work at two different fixed locations (e.g., consultants working at their office and a client's premises); (3) "Nomads," who work in multiple places and are moving from one fixed location to another (e.g., performers, managers, and diplomats); and (4) "Carriers," who work while on the move (e.g., people in the transport sector).[1]

In this chapter, I am particularly interested in transnational labor practices that include temporary relocation, even if not an official change of residence (Findlay 1988). Such work-related mobilities are by no means new (Prothero and Chapman 1985).[2] However, because of processes of globalization, increased levels of education, proliferation of international media, improved transport systems, and the internationalization of business and labor markets, the nature and purpose of work-related mobilities are becoming increasingly complex (McKenna and Richardson 2007). This has led to a range of new professional roles and career paths (Cerdin and Selmer 2014). I am mostly interested here in so-called "highly skilled" mobilities because of their positive societal valuation (compared to similar mobilities by "lower-skilled" migrants that are mostly looked down upon).

The temporary to permanent character of work-related mobilities has led to terminological ambiguities. Scholars have used a multitude of denominators, partially overlapping with one another, to denote short-term mobilities. In the past, these have variously been labeled as "repeat, rotating, multiple, seasonal, cyclical, shuttling, or circuit-based modes of migration" (Vertovec 2007: 5).[3] For labor mobility between countries where there is free border movement, the terms "commuter migration" (Torre, Rodríguez Vecchini, and Burgos 1994) and "revolving-door migration" (Duany 2002) have been used. In corporate settings, notions appear such as "flexpatriates" (Mayerhofer et al. 2004), referring to short-term (less than a year), commuter (usually weekly or biweekly) or frequent flyer (business travel without relocation) assignments. Traditional expatriates, employed and sent by their country or company, are distinguished from "independent internationally mobile professionals" (McKenna and Richardson 2007), "self-initiated movers" (Thorn 2009), or "self-initiated expatriates" (Andresen, Al Ariss, and Walther 2013).

For the research that feeds this chapter, I benefitted hugely from the fact that I live in Brussels, Belgium. This facilitated access to a plethora of actors in the field of transnational labor mobilities, both policy makers (mainly at the EU level) and "practitioners." I gathered anecdotal information through my active involvement in an international organization for (highly skilled) expatriates (in the period 2008–10). Because of my own frequent travels across Europe and beyond, I talked informally to a good number of people while on the move or while waiting (in airport or train station lounges). As in the previous chapter, I sketch the wider context of career mobilities but focus my examples on Europe and Europeans, including Belgian expatriates I met and interviewed in Tanzania (2009), Chile (2010), and Indonesia (2011).

Mobile Careers and Career Mobility

Contract workers and transnational labor circulation are commonly hailed as arrangements that benefit all parties involved. They reflect a global division of labor that has been emerging since the late 1970s in the wake of other forces of globalization.[4] Jobs are moved from one location to another, or to multiple other locations. Professional careers have increasingly been linked to geographical mobility.[5] As the etymology of the concept suggests, a career involves a "journey" (cf. the age-old European tradition of *compagnonnage*, described in chapter 4). A person's professional trajectory is always in movement; it develops through different kinds of mobility: descending/ascending or horizontal occupational mobility, inside or outside the same organization.

Transnational work experience is often an accepted expectation for career professionals (M. Smith and Favell 2006). The mobility of a (disloyal) individual used to be deemed bad for a company. Now, however, employers often require their staff to be mobile, to be willing to work elsewhere, with international assignments forming an integral part of their career development. As Aihwa Ong (1999: 19) writes, "Flexibility, migration, and relocations, instead of being coerced or resisted, have become practices to strive for rather than stability." People are "often proud to explain how they repeatedly manage to obtain visas and work permits, to find work, and learn new languages. Some develop a kind of performance of cosmopolitanism in social situations, intended to portray something of their trajectory to various audiences" (Ossman 2004: 117).

While a privileged and transient population of expatriates has existed as long as nation-states have (E. Cohen 1977), more widespread transnational mobility is a more recent phenomenon. As Val Colic-Peisker (2010) notes, transnational professionals have only recently started to feature in systematic social research. "Skilled transients" (Findlay 1988) or "international itinerants" (Banai and Harry 2004) are a major feature of global mobility systems. Whereas the term "migrant" seems to imply a meaning of necessity, more than an individual, "free" choice, to travel elsewhere, the notion "expatriate" evokes imaginaries of transient globetrotters who are privileged and somehow separate from migrants (E. Cohen 1977).[6] Contrary to most other types of (lower-skilled) labor migrants, expatriates are believed to actually gain social status by their move abroad, rather than losing it (e.g., occupational downshifting).[7] They also tend to enjoy a relatively greater freedom of movement than those labeled as "migrants," who are often unwelcome and subject to immigration regimes restricting their mobility across borders (see figure 5.1).

The political and economic preference for frequent short-term/non-permanent circulation over long-term/permanent migration produces a "transient" pattern of human movement and establishes a highly mobile, cross-border transnational labor force. People moving within companies have more guaranteed jobs, so that employability for them is a qualitative issue of how the experience abroad influences their long-term employability. Ironically, for traditional expatriate jobs, the remuneration and advantage packages have become less and less interesting (Cartus 2012).

Figure 5.1: Young Belgian expat relaxing in front of a hut he built on a small plot of land he purchased in Magogoni, across the port of Dar es Salaam where he works. Mji Mwema, Tanzania. (Photographer: Noel B. Salazar)

In effect, the traditional expatriate is slowly disappearing, to be replaced by "nomadic workers" or "global nomads" whose ultimate border-crossing mobilities meet the challenges of global(ized) business (Beaverstock 2005). I noticed this trend in Indonesia, for instance, with a shift of expatriates from the typical business locations (e.g., Jakarta and other big cities) to more pleasant working environments (e.g., the island of Bali).

In human resource management, the concept of the "boundaryless career" (Arthur and Rousseau 1996) has been used to describe the (hyper) mobile professional. The term is meant to capture increased mobility patterns, whereby people move in and out of organizations and jobs. According to the authors behind the concept, it explains changes in how individuals (presumably) perceive and enact their careers in today's highly complex and fluid work world:

> Instead of relying on organizational norms and structures to provide guidance, individuals are making choices based on introspection and self-awareness that then drive them to behave in ways that reinforce their self-concept. They direct their own career development and training and specifically seek work experiences that will provide learning opportunities, increase their employability in any number of work situations, and enhance their intrinsic satisfaction. (Hartung and Subich 2011: 127)

Boundaryless career theorists stress the necessity of accumulating tradeable "career capital" in the form of values and identity ("knowing why"), skills and experience ("knowing how"), and networks and reputation ("knowing whom"). Boundaries are crossed because people have the will and the personal resources ("motility") to cross them. In this logic, (purposeful) mobility is being used as the primary proxy for boundaryless career attitudes or outcomes—"boundarylessness as mobility."

Labor mobility is positively valued—for instance, by respected international organizations such as OECD (Dayton-Johnson et al. 2007) and UNDP (UNDP 2009). As with mobility in general (see Introduction), work-related mobility is intimately intertwined with the promise of economic and symbolic mobility. This is based on the assumption that a position abroad is "a source of exceptional learning ... that allows individuals to enhance their employability over time" (A. Williams 2009: 23). As a result, "mobility itself becomes a valued measure of individual achievement; people point out the obstacles they had to overcome to make each successive move" (Ossman 2004: 117). One can see border-crossing mobility as a response to a neoliberal requirement for employment flexibility, which is believed to be a prerequisite for "success" (Sennett 1998).

Some have questioned "whether the assumption of agency in boundary-less career theory privileges educated elites and marginalizes lower-skilled workers, women and minorities for whom boundarylessness simply means unemployment, insecurity and anxiety" (Inkson et al. 2012: 328). Indeed, labor mobility may also be the result of fecklessness and/or marginalization. The neoliberal frameworks that value flexibility and mobility, and reward entrepreneurial individuals, may oppress lower-skilled workers (and migrants) by withdrawing job security and causing loss of community attachments (Sennett 1998). Widely shared imaginaries of mobility frame increasingly converging realities, for instance middle-class mobile European expats and non-European migrants, as radically different. Moreover, as Richard Sennett (1998) argues, career mobility is not simply a matter of choice. Rather, it is forced on vast populations, also highly skilled people, as a means of flexibilizing the labor force and optimizing the distribution of human resources.[8] Indeed, economic constraints turn out to be equally as or more significant than their personal preferences in propelling people abroad and in influencing their choice of destination (Kennedy 2010).

The perceived value of "mobility capital"—the resources, knowledge, or abilities gained by having lived "elsewhere"—nicely fits the definition of symbolic capital (Doherty and Dickmann 2009). In the context of labor, spatial mobility is believed to enhance occupational mobility. Mobility capital can be deployed over the subsequent life course for personal, social, or career enhancement in two major ways (see Introduction).[9] First, it can facilitate future border-crossing moves by enhancing people's differential capacity and potential for mobility (Kaufmann, Bergman, and Joye 2004). Alternatively, it can be exchanged "back home" for other forms of capital, as described by Pierre Bourdieu (1986): economic (material resources), social (relational networks), and cultural (embodied dispositions and competencies of cosmopolitanism) capital. Importantly, the value of professionals' mobility capital is not the same in all contexts (Jayaram 2016). It largely depends on individuals' capacity to transfer its components across borders (Doherty and Dickmann 2009).

Social Costs

The neighborhood in which I live in Brussels is being reconverted from an old industrial zone to a more residential area. In my street alone, there are three construction sites. Whenever I pass by, I hear several languages being spoken by the workers. The minivans on the street reveal that they hail from different European countries (Poland, Romania, Portugal, etc.). Every three months, these posted workers rotate, moving to another country and another construction site. This temporary mobility regime is very beneficial for the companies hiring them. However, I have not heard anyone envying these workers for their mobilities.

When I tell people about my own job-related journeys, many seem jealous. Very few are aware of the downside to (hyper)mobility. The fact that I am a "frequent traveler" with a major airline and some of Europe's high-speed train companies is only an indication of the quantity of movements back and forth. What about the quality? Apart from my personal experience, I have observed and talked to many other so-called "high-skilled" people who are "on the move" for their work. Very few seem to enjoy their job-related mobilities, certainly not when the frequency is (too) high. The access to more comfortable ways of traveling (e.g., lounges, first class) and accommodation compensates very little for the sense of missing things happening in their social network. I have witnessed many times how being away (particularly for longer periods) deteriorates my social relations with family members and friends. Just like with the posted construction workers, I hear no frequent travelers talk about the intrinsic value of mobility. On the contrary, most hope that their mobilities will only be temporary (linked to a short stage in their career).

***

Geographical mobility is extoled in business circles as a practice that requires no reward (because it is so "normal"). Laura Gherardi (2011: 117) rightfully points out "the problematic nature of romantic mobility in advanced capitalism, that is to say of a totally positive image of mobility as seen in management literature as an end in itself, and ... the possible relationship between the geographic mobility required in a working environment and personal fulfillment." The high social status associated with frequent mobility, specifically by air and road, is at least partly attributable to its glamorization in the media and other forms of public discourse (Thurlow and Jaworski 2006). This glamorization of hypermobility has silenced discussion of the negative personal and social costs of frequent travel (S. Cohen and Gössling 2015).

While scholars discuss the emergence of new global elites or a transnational capitalist class with unprecedented mobile and supposedly "cosmopolitan" lifestyles, they often forget that most of these people do not make their most important life decisions alone (Leinonen 2012). The term "trailing spouse" historically denotes a woman who follows her life partner elsewhere because of a work assignment.[10] The term indicates the gender bias in expatriate work, which continues to be male-dominated (this in contrast with lower-skilled jobs). The accompanying partner is not always willing to relocate—for instance, when there is a lack of support by the sponsoring employer to address her (or his) needs. Long-distance mobility has given rise to "astronaut families" (*taikong* in Hong Kong) and "geese families" (*kirýgi kajok* in South Korea). In these instances, one parent stays with the children in one country while the other parent works in another one. Related to this, there are "satellite children" or "parachute kids," who live alone or with a relative, family friend, or unrelated paid caregiver. This phenomenon of the "transnational split family" (Abelmann, Newendorp, and Lee-Chung 2014) appears to be common among East Asian (Taiwanese, Chinese, and Korean) communities (Ong 1999; Tsong and Liu 2009). In this context, Aihwa Ong (1999) invokes the notion of a family "regime," arguing that while mobility may be empowering for some, other family members are often "localized" and immobile, and their freedom significantly curtailed.

At the same time, mobile professionals are faced with figuring out how to manage mobility on their own. This explains why expatriate networking organizations (like the one I was involved in from 2008 until 2010) are so popular. Often unacknowledged is the fact that "travelling is emotionally and physically tiring, making oneself at home in a new place is difficult, real choices are severely curtailed, and technologies tether people to grueling work schedules regardless of time-zones, home, work and leisure contexts and infrastructural support" (Büscher 2014: 235). Many of those who on paper seem to belong to the global mobile elite experience problems

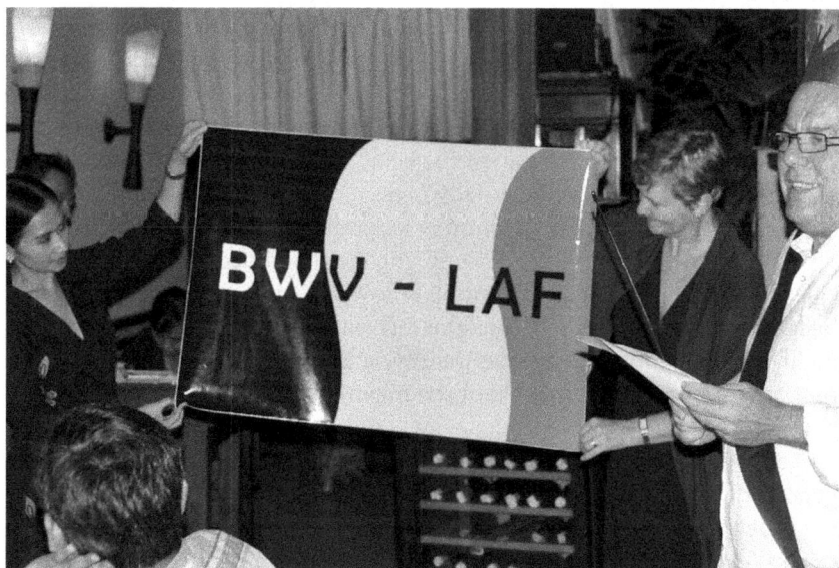

Figure 5.2: Belgians and Indonesians celebrating the Belgian national holiday in Ubud, Bali. (Photographer: Noel B. Salazar)

that are more commonly associated with migrants of lower social status (Leinonen 2012). Transnational work-related mobilities are often accompanied by a difficult transition to new jobs and new locations requiring new training. People experience many challenges: "learning multiple languages, integrating into multiple labor markets, building multiple social networks, and adapting to cultural contexts" (Main 2014: 130).

In addition, they need to work "through a variety of logistical and emotional challenges, including how to collaborate with colleagues at a distance and how to stay present (e.g., socially and emotionally involved and connected) in the lives of friends and loved ones" (Meerwarth 2008: 103). There are also downsides to global mobility in terms of having a support network (see figure 5.2). Even if people have a strong support network, they may not be able to draw on it. As Tracy Meerwarth (2008: 102) points out, "Personal conflict and tension often arise when trying to manage culturally valued concepts such as integration and mobility simultaneously." Not surprisingly, (hyper)mobile working lives often lead to depression and burnout (Gherardi 2011). Thus behind the image of global elites hide other socially differentiated realities than that of an assumed borderless world (Favell, Feldblum, and Smith 2007). The experience abroad does not always have a happy ending (Salazar 2014a).

The socioeconomic profile of those on the move does not always correspond with their actual migratory experiences. Krisztina Csedő (2008) makes an interesting distinction between "highly qualified" and "highly skilled" migrants. A person may be qualified for a highly skilled position, but only those who manage to transfer their skills to the labor market of the receiving country can be considered highly skilled. Whether the person succeeds in this or not depends, according to Csedő, on the ability to signal the value of his or her general and specific skills to potential employers in the destination labor market. However, it would be a simplification to claim that the difficulty with finding work reflects only the ability to transfer skills to the labor market. Even highly qualified people may encounter "glass ceilings" or downward mobility in their professional advancement because of their status as "foreigner" (Leinonen 2012). Many educated, highly skilled people must leave their human capital behind at the border (e.g., the stereotypical example of the migrant taxi driver who has a university degree).

Robyn Iredale (2001) notes that, ironically, a major barrier is the emergence of global standards in various industries and sectors that facilitates the globalization of some occupations and professions. She argues that existing standards enable the mobility of Western trained professionals around the world, while limiting the ability of non-Western trained professionals to move. In developing countries, Western expatriates are often resented as their presence is seen as a continuation of dependency and neoimperialism as well as blocking the avenues of occupational and social mobility for locals (Fechter and Walsh 2010). In those same countries, the question of the transnational mobility of highly qualified workers is manifested through a concern about so called "brain drain" and the loss of economic potential which could result from this (see also chapter 4).

Do work-related mobilities increase or diminish opportunities for socioeconomic mobility? I asked many mobile professionals this question, only to conclude that the relationship between temporary work abroad and occupational mobility is unclear. Some researchers suggest that the experience and money obtained does give people scope to get better jobs, either at home or in the host country. Others argue there is no positive effect at all and, in the case of some groups, the effect can even be negative (Masso, Eamets, and Mõtsmees 2013). This may particularly be the case in regulated circular migration systems, which see people returning year after year to the same job rather than trying to negotiate their way into better jobs and localities like unregulated circular migrants might do (Vertovec 2007). Work-related mobilities rarely allow for family unification because of immigration restrictions imposed by destination countries, and it is difficult to suggest that people naturally prefer to be without their families (Wickramasekara 2011: 23).

Temporary transnational working schemes have been criticized as "labor without people" (Wickramasekara 2011: 3). That is, the host society has less incentive to invest in the welfare and integration of temporary workers when those people will only reside for limited periods within the society. In other words, the workers have fewer rights and opportunities. In turn, the "sojourners" (Siu 1952) themselves have less incentive to invest in (i.e., integrate into) the host society. They intend to travel afar for economic intents, but plan to return eventually, after they have made a significant sum of money.[11] Moreover, host societies wishing to promote work-related mobilities may be less inclined to develop integration policies for temporary workers for fear that an integration strategy would encourage them to stay permanently (European Migration Network 2011). Continuous mobility can thus be very isolating, as those involved are prevented from "settling" anywhere. People may end up losing out financially, as remigration to the country of origin costs money, as do intermediary agencies that are sometimes used to find employment.

As Nina Glick Schiller (2009) shows, migration researchers are contributing to the legitimization of new forms of mobility-related exploitation by emphasizing the benefits of transnational remittances while neglecting to address the severe and permanent restriction of rights that accompanies short-term contract work and the decreasing access of temporary workers to naturalization.[12] Some migration scholars, for instance, have continued to sing the praises of circular short-term mobilities with regard to development. This reinforces the desirability of the new mobilities regime of contract labor, which makes settlement increasingly difficult. New migration laws leave foreign workers with only short-term options. Absent from the scenario of the benefits of circular migration are "the dehumanizing aspects of short-term labor contracts with their dramatic restrictions on, or denial of, rights and privileges to the individuals who are producing wealth, paying taxes, and sustaining infrastructures and services to which they have no entitlement" (Glick Schiller 2009: 27–28).

European Labor (Im)Mobilities

> Mobility is increasingly perceived in Europe as a key instrument in the quest for more and better jobs. Geographic mobility opens the door for Europe's citizens to new languages, new cultures and new working environments. Job-to-job mobility helps workers to adapt more easily to Europe's rapidly changing working environment and to cope better with the effects of globalisation.
>
> —EC, *Europeans on the Move*

Brussels is a good place to study work-related mobilities. A symbolic venue to start is the Midi train station and adjacent bus terminal. Some people arrive by train from the airport, others either by train or bus from neighboring countries. Judging from the size of the luggage, one can immediately spot who is arriving in the city for reasons other than a short visit. What is striking is the diversity of arrivers in terms of age, gender, language, or ethnic background. Some have already secured a job, while others heavily count on existing networks to rapidly find work. I live in a so-called "arrival neighborhood," welcoming a motley group of people who are looking for opportunities in the city. Many come and leave again—to another part of the city, elsewhere in Belgium, or abroad. Similar patterns can be observed in more central parts of Brussels, where people from across Europe (and beyond) try to land a job at the EU institutions. In contrast to the Eurocrats with permanent contracts, who have settled in Brussels, the people on temporary contracts come and go with high frequency.

To familiarize myself with the world of high-skilled mobile professionals in Brussels, I became actively involved in the organization of one of the many expat communities (a local branch of a global network with over two million members). As I discovered, the monthly informal gatherings are particularly attractive to newly arrived people (and those catering all kinds of services to them). Because of the more "high-class" locations where the meetings are held (often in bars of top-end hotels), the community automatically excludes those who are economically less endowed. At the same time, the real "elites" will not show up either (they have their own exclusive networks with even higher participation fees). An interview with Ann, an experienced relocation officer (who herself has lived and worked in different countries), only confirmed how socially separated all these "communities" of foreigners are. Once members of the expat network find their way around the city and start establishing their own local social networks, they tend to disappear from the radar. Others leave Brussels, ready to become active in one of the other three hundred local communities of the network. Within a period of two years, I witnessed an impressive number of people coming and going.

***

The right to move freely within Europe (predominantly work-driven) is linked to both market integration and to the rights represented by the status of EU citizenship. Citizens of the European Union have the right to work in another member state and the right to reside there for that purpose. In addition, they also have the right to equal treatment in access to employment and with respect to working conditions (Donaghey and Teague 2006). For their part, each member state is required to facilitate the full domestic integration of a worker and his or her family from another member state. Intra-EU labor mobility is a key factor for economic growth. The free movement of workers and the creation of an open European Labor Market have been the objectives of the EU since its creation, and are one of its "Four Freedoms."[13] The idea behind this is that removing barriers and reducing adjustment costs and skills mismatches will lead to "reducing pressure to migrate on those who do not wish to move while offering genuine possibilities for those who do" (EC 2001: 12).

Since its inception in the 1950s, much of the discussion about labor mobility in the EU bemoaned how little movement was taking place. Different languages, the lack of full mutual recognition of educational and professional qualifications, and the persistence of national labor market restrictive practices were identified as the main barriers preventing workers moving from one member state to another (Donaghey and Teague 2006). In other words, market imperfections and the lack of transparency and knowledge were traditionally seen as the main culprits of low cross-border mobility (Van Houtum and Van der Velde 2004). However, whether the complete removal of such barriers would lead to a dramatic increase in mobility in the EU is far from certain (because it is based, once again, on the assumption that most people desire to be mobile). While the level of geographic mobility within the EU is frequently held to be low, data show that it should have been even lower given the rise of prosperity and the decline of income differentials. Sociologist Ettore Recchi (2008) argues that pro-mobility policies and the rise of nonlabor migration have countered the diminishing appeal of intra-EU mobility that might be expected on the basis of purely economic conditions.

Only with the 2004 enlargement did cross-border labor mobility start to become a reality within the EU, with substantial numbers of East European workers seeking employment in the older member states. This was followed by much talk about a perceived massive increase in transnational labor flows inside the EU and the potential negative impact this might have on national social standards and even on national political and communal identities (Verstraete 2010). People from the new member states (e.g., Poland, Romania, and Bulgaria), indeed, show a high level of mobility and flexibility in the labor market. Not only do they work for periods of varying duration in the shadow economy, but they also adapt to market demands by changing employers, places of work, and sectors of employment frequently.

How many people are on the move across Europe? In 2010, the EU counted the movement of 3.1 million legal immigrants into one of the member states, 1.6 million of which were EU nationals, and the remaining 1.5 million coming from outside Europe (Eurostat 2013). Six hundred thousand citizens returned to their country and at least two million emigrants left one of the EU countries (there are no exact figures, but most of this is study- and work-related). Taking into account undocumented movements, the total number of migrants in Europe is estimated to be around fifty-five million, or more than 7 percent of the population (United Nations 2013). Unprecedented levels of movements from third countries and intra-EU mobility over the past decade have increased the proportion of people who do not live in their own native country or culture. At the same time, only 10 percent of Europeans have lived abroad at some point in their life. Europeans are thus relatively immobile across borders.[14] It seems reasonable, then, to conjecture that the persistent low mobility within the European Union is to a significant extent voluntary (Favell and Recchi 2011).

Since 1994, the European Employment Services (EURES), consisting of the national employment services of the member states, help potential employers and employees to find each other. Aiming to lower search costs, EURES has launched the "European Job Mobility Portal," a website that has job descriptions and professional CVs available for downloading.[15] Not surprisingly, special attention is devoted to working "abroad." Legal and institutional barriers to movement have been substantially reduced over the last two decades. Paradoxically, work itself has become more mobile, while workers have not. The perceived lack of a European "culture of mobility" prompted the European Commission to designate 2006 as the European Year of Workers' Mobility, with the subtitle "Towards a European labor market."

A small minority of (hyper)mobile Europeans lies at the heart of conceptualizations and idealizations of flexible European citizenship (see figure 5.3). They are highly symbolic of some of the ideas of a unified Europe conceived by the founding fathers of European integration (Favell 2008). They are not significant enough to alter aggregate social mobility charts, but symbolically the very emblem of the new, denationalized Europe that the EU has enabled. They embody the process, flux, and change that the EU has released, albeit around the edges of European society.

The EU is a unique regime. The cross-border mobility of workers can be considered transnational mobility, though the European legal framework meanwhile considers it domestic or internal mobility. EU institutions discursively frame the cross-border movements of EU citizens as "mobility," while "migration" refers to the movements of so-called third-country nationals (cf. Schrooten, Salazar, and Dias 2016). As Thomas Faist (2014: 211) notes, "Intra-EU labor mobility can thus be viewed as a form of first-class migration, without the time-consuming controls, visas or residence

Figure 5.3: Never a quiet moment at The Loft, one of the lounges at Brussels Airport, Belgium, where mobile Europeans and others meet, work, and rest. (Photographer: Noel B. Salazar)

restrictions characteristic of international mobility or migration, between the EU and third countries." At the same time, hierarchizations do exist among workers from EU countries. An official European Commission document from 2006, entitled "Europeans on the Move" (EC 2006: 45), contextualizes mobility as follows:

> Mobility has to start in the minds of people, it is not just the physical getting up and going. It means that people should not expect to have a career in the same place for 60 years but not everyone wants to be a modern nomad and there has to be respect for people who attach greater importance to their roots. To assume that everyone is going to become mobile is not necessary. It is not needed but worker mobility cannot be disconnected from education, language skills and so on. It has to start there.

The EU provisions for freedom of movement have been almost entirely constructed around the imaginary that transnational movements are predominantly the preserve of permanent labor migrants who are citizens of member states. This pervading imaginary gives scant recognition to the realities of globalization, nonlabor migration, and the increasing and diverse forms of clandestine and short-term movements. Gregory Feldman (2012) calls this "the fantasy of circular migration," indicating a movement toward an EU labor regime made up of circulating labor from within the European Union and new and very controlled forms of contract labor from elsewhere. Within Europe, as elsewhere, most migration is not permanent, but part of a process of mobility in which both return and serial migration are natural economic responses to a dynamic economy. Circular migration programs are the main legitimate portals for legal (temporary) entry. Interestingly, circular migration functions as a tacit compromise between nationalist conservatives (neonationalists) concerned that migrants will become permanent fixtures of society and economic conservatives (neoliberals) concerned that cheap labor will not be available for economic growth (Feldman 2012). This is because the "insistence on temporariness attempts to turn people into 'pure' economic inputs who will depart when their labour is no longer necessary" (Dauvergne and Marsden 2014: 232).

Indeed, temporary and circular mobilities are receiving increasing policy interest within the EU as forms of mobility that have the potential to satisfy labor demand while ensuring return and providing benefits to both the migrant and the country of origin (Triandafyllidou 2013). Such circular movements implement a form of "deregulating migration" and promote the right to mobility and freedom of movement (IOM 2009).[16] The mobile worker not only maintains contact with his or her country of origin, but is also portrayed as becoming a protagonist of his or her mobility.

However, the concept of temporary and circular mobility varies among EU member states (European Migration Network 2011). Paradoxically, many of the jobs filled by temporary migrant labor programs are not temporary. According to Catherine Dauvergne and Sarah Marden (2014: 231), "Temporariness, rather than leading to a 'win-win-win', embeds and normalizes a directionality in which workers' rights are limited and states' rights (to expel, to control) are expanded. A second ideological function of temporariness is that it distracts attention from inequality between regulatory regimes applied to 'high-skilled' versus 'low-skilled' workers."

Labor-related mobility is encouraged through so-called "EU Mobility Partnerships" (Parkes 2009). For example, Belgium, Bulgaria, Germany, Greece, Hungary, Lithuania, Poland, Portugal, Sweden, and the United Kingdom participate in the EU Mobility Partnerships with Georgia and Moldova. Luxembourg, Portugal, and Spain have signed the Mobility Partnership with Cape Verde. These new policies resemble the older guest workers programs (Castles 2006).[17] Bilateral cooperation with third countries is also carried out in order to promote reciprocal temporary mobility of young professionals between EU member states and third countries, usually referred to as "Youth Mobility Agreements" (European Migration Network 2011). Nine countries (Czech Republic, Estonia, France, Latvia, Lithuania, Malta, Slovak Republic, Sweden, United Kingdom) have cooperation agreements, primarily with Canada, New Zealand, and Australia but also covering other third countries, which facilitate the admission of young professionals. These have the broader aim to promote closer cooperation with the member state and the third country, as well as to increase the mobility of young people, to allow graduates to gain their first work experience and to get to know a new culture, thus improving intercultural dialogue and understanding.

The management of the EU bureaucracy itself requires substantial amounts of mobility. The seven institutions of the EU are spread across four cities in four countries: Brussels, Luxembourg, Strasbourg, and Frankfurt. Other EU agencies and bodies are based across the EU. Members of the European Parliament (MEP), where decisions about the free movement of people are made, must divide their time among locations. In an average month, an MEP has a week of committee meetings in Brussels, one week of plenary sittings debating and voting on legislation and resolutions in Strasbourg, another week of party meetings in Brussels, and one week in his or her home country addressing the concerns of constituents and local political business. There are also regular interparliamentary delegation visits to other countries. Administrative sections of the EP Secretariat are based in Luxembourg. The costs of having three addresses are high in terms of both time and money, and continue to be a contentious issue.

Most parliamentarians oppose these constant back-and-forth movements, particularly the "traveling circus" (of not only people but also thousands of documents) between Brussels and Strasbourg.[18] Every now and then, there is a campaign for a single seat of the EP (either one of the two).[19] Ironically, as the locations of the major seats have been enshrined in EU treaties, the European Parliament has no right to decide its own seat, unlike other national parliaments.

Bound to Work

Usually, it is the idea of mobility, and not the temporariness of stay, that appeals to mobile professionals. At the same time, the motives, goals, and orientations characteristic at the beginning of labor mobility—that is, the firm intention to return—cannot be regarded as static or constant. People come under the influence of conditions in the host society and the perceptions of the country of origin from abroad. As this chapter has illustrated, there are problems with mobility imaginaries that automatically couple geographical with social mobility (cf. Pajo 2007).

We should question the assumption that mobility has a positive effect on career advancement. Interestingly, the verb "to career" means to move swiftly and in an uncontrolled way in a specified direction. Global neoliberal capitalism has made many people "trapped in mobility whether they are high earning professionals with bulimic work patterns or part of a new 'precariat'" (Büscher 2014: 224). Spatial mobility in the form of freedom of movement often comes at the price of downward occupational mobility. As this chapter has shown, "mobility not only provides the opportunity for more flexibility, control and freedom to choose how, when, and where we work, but also brings with it uncertainty, ambiguity, and challenges as boundaries blur and space–time compresses" (Gluesing, Meerwarth, and Jordan 2008: 154). The intersection of mediating influences, such as the changing social divisions of labor, regulation, and institutions, and issues of social identities, social recognition, and discrimination determines whether transnational mobility leads to labor market entrapment or stepping-stones for individuals. In this context, the real meaning of boundarylessness is not the actual extinction of older boundaries, but making these boundaries more permeable.

As Nina Glick Schiller (2009: 30) rightly points out, "Migration studies too rarely address the global system that is reducing the opportunity for social and economic equality and justice around the world and the human costs of new short-term labor contracts." Short-term contracts resurrect older forms of indenture, with limited rights and mobility. Despite this, some continue singing the praises of circular short-term mobilities, particularly regarding development. In general, mobile lifestyles appear "less of a choice" (Büscher 2014: 227) than is often assumed. Instead, many feel the "burden of mobility" (Cass, Shove, and Urry 2005). Labor immobility, on the other hand, is not so much a confined rational or irrational choice. To a large extent, it escapes such a strict economic choice-reasoning (Van Houtum and Van der Velde 2004). A decision to leave a certain job or position, too, is not made frequently; and if someone decides to take up another job (in other words to become occupationally mobile), this does not automatically imply some cross-border spatial mobility.

NOTES

1. Lilischkis (2003) also includes a fifth type, namely "on-site movers," who move back and forth, locally, on a fixed site (e.g., farmers, security agents, and hospital doctors).

2. Historically, a significant portion of European migrants to the United States became known as "birds of passage," describing migrants who crossed the Atlantic more than once. Sometimes this was part of an intentional pattern of circular migration, but in other instances a migrant's level of financial security determined how often he would move. Many of these "birds of passage" dreamed of making their fortunes abroad and then returning to their home villages to purchase land or establish small businesses. As Michael Piore (1979: 3) points out, "Migrants initially see themselves as temporary workers and plan to return home; however, many of them fail to realize their plans and either never return or come back repeatedly ... becoming more or less permanent members of the labor force."

3. Other, related, terms are serial migration, transient migration, pendular migration, return migration, swallow migration, recycling migration, and nomadic work.

4. There are a number of theoretical approaches explaining the global reorganization of late-capitalist accumulation, including dependency theory, world systems theory, and the new international division of labor theory (see Kearney 1986).

5. A career is understood here as an occupation or profession undertaken for a significant period of a person's life, with opportunities for advancement (both in terms of position and salary). Careers connect people with organizations and other social institutions over time. This means that the control over a career is in the hands of multiple stakeholders.

6. This interpretation of the term "expatriate" is relatively new (Green 2009). In general, the meaning of expatriation varies depending on who is initiating the act, and whether it is (perceived as) voluntary or not.

7. Temporary migrants often accept low-status jobs because they do not consider themselves to be part of the social structure of their adopted country; their social identity and status gains are rooted in their place of origin (Piore 1979).

8. In an historical context, highly skilled migration typically involved the forced movement of professionals as a result of political conflicts, followed by the emergence of the "brain drain" in the 1960s (Iredale 2001).

9. Others have termed these different directions of career mobility respectively "career mobility" versus "occupational upgrading" (Masso, Eamets, and Mõtsmees 2013: 10).

10. The term indicates the gender bias in expatriate work, which continues to be male-dominated (this in contrast with lower-skilled jobs).

11. The less resources available, the more the economic motivation becomes dominant. Research on working holidays overseas among New Zealanders, for instance, revealed that people partaking in such practices are mostly motivated by cultural and social incentives (Inkson and Myers 2003). Career development, while apparently substantial, is largely serendipitous.

12. The mantras about migrants as major agents of development are part of this new global labor regime. International financial institutions have made migrant remittances a growing industry just at the moment when people may be less interested in transnational strategies and yet less able to choose to settle permanently in another country (Glick Schiller 2009).

13. The other three are the free movement of goods, the free movement of capital, and the free movement of services. These four freedoms were enshrined by the Treaty of Rome (1957). The free movement of workers was widened in the Maastricht Treaty (1992) to the free movement of people (including limited rights for the "non-economically active"). These four fundamental (economic) principles ensure the functioning of the internal EU market.

14. Europe is taken to be less mobile than the United States: the stereotype of the "old world" of ingrained privilege, tradition, and slow moving social change is often set against the (imagined) "new world" of opportunity, achievement, and flux.

15. "EURES: The European Job Mobility Portal." European Commission website, accessed 28 February 2018, http://ec.europa.eu/eures/public/en/homepage.

16. Different international organizations have adopted positions on the interest in and the benefit of this "permanent" mobility system. In 2005, the Global Commission on International Migration (2005: 33) called on developed countries to promote Circular Migration through mechanisms that would enable the quick and easy movement of workers between countries of origin and destination. The Organization for Economic Cooperation and Development (2007: 108) emphasized that in all probability the circular migration model is, currently, the most recommended way for development in many countries of origin.

17. By recruiting people for a limited period, restricting their labor market and residence rights, and minimizing family reunion, the idea was to provide a "mobile labor potential" (as German employers put it). The approach was known as "rotation": the labor reserves of southern Europe, Turkey, and northern Africa could provide a constant flow of workers, but few would settle permanently, so there would be no significant social or cultural consequences for the receiving country (Castles 2006).

18. The work cycle of an MEP consists of enormous mobility, which is experienced as extremely stressful—always "on the go," always in transition from one meeting to the next, from one country and meeting place to the next, from one kind of audience to the next.

19. "Campaign for a Single Seat for the European Parliament" (online petition), accessed 28 February 2018, http://www.singleseat.eu/; "Let Europe's Heart Beat in Strasbourg: Sign One City!" One City. Strasbourg: One Parliament for Europe (website), 8 October 2008. Accessed 28 February 2018 via Wayback Machine Internet Archive, http://web.archive.org/web/20081008170744/; http://www.one-city.eu:80/en/index.

6

Life's "Pilgrimage"
Travel, Travail, Transformation

Sometimes it's a little better to travel than to arrive.

—Robert M. Pirsig, *Zen and the Art of Motorcycle Maintenance*

After having spent six intense years at various universities and graduating with multiple degrees in the 1990s, I took my first "sabbatical." Despite having some excellent career options, I really felt I needed some time to fully recharge my batteries. I ended up as a volunteer in Taizé, a popular retreat center in Burgundy, France, a place I had gotten to know through its globally circulating contemplative music. Because of my language skills, I was put in charge of the community's welcome infrastructure. I saw thousands of "pilgrims" arriving, most between seventeen and thirty years old. They came from across the world (although the largest numbers obviously were Europeans). After a couple of months, I left with a group of volunteers to Vienna, Austria, to organize Taizé's twentieth "Pilgrimage of Trust on Earth." We had three months to prepare all the logistics of a four-day event that would involve over eighty thousand participants. My involvement in previous editions in Prague, Budapest, Munich, Wroclaw, and Stuttgart was of great help. When I returned to the village of Taizé after this urban "pilgrimage," I became responsible for the "House of Silence," where people came for silent retreats. This seemed to be very popular among high profile professionals from France and beyond. I met many people that I had seen before on television or read about in newspapers or magazines. They all hoped that the quiet days in Taizé would somehow bring some (permanent) "change" to their busy lifestyles.

***

The idea of personal transformation through "travel," broadly interpreted, has always fascinated people (Lean, Staiff, and Waterton 2014; Ricci 2014). In the Mediterranean region, for example, Moses's biblical exodus or Homer's *Odyssey* are two legendary transformative journey narratives.[1] The Mesopotamian *Epic of Gilgamesh* narrates the makeover the king of Uruk undergoes through traveling. The story of Jason and the Argonauts, one of the most popular from Greek mythology, is an epitome of the human "quest"—journeying to reach a destination or a destiny. In the Persian tale of *Shahnameh*, Rostam and his son Sohrab undertake journeys and suffer to win the title of a hero. The Celtic monks in the *immrama*, Old Irish stories concerning voyages to the Otherworld, would travel "without a specific goal, albeit in search of a promised land in the far west; but they followed no set path, travelling where God's will took them" (Barber 1991). The medieval theme of the pilgrim on the road of life appears in the opening verse of Dante Alighieri's *Divina Commedia* (*Divine Comedy*) and is also employed by Geoffrey Chaucer in his *Canterbury Tales*.[2] This topic exists in a broad range of cultural fields: in myths, folklore, and fairy tales, in arts and music, film, poetry, novels, and other literary genres, and in psychological theory and therapy (Birkeland 2005: 6).

The significance of such travel tales for meaning-making across the globe becomes evident when considering the importance of journeying in the lives of religious figures such as Jesus, Buddha, and Mohammed, but also people like Saint Paul (Christianity) or Lao-Tsu (Taoism). The transformation described, particularly when it is consciously sought after, is mostly about "inner" psychological development or growth, a striving toward "a superior existential mode of 'being-in-the-world'" (Morgan 2010: 248). In actual transformative travels, then, "a movement through geographical space is transformed into an analogue for the process of introspection" (Galani-Moutafi 2000: 205). Such journeys are closely linked to the more widespread role of travel (and displacement) in age-old rites of passage and transition in many cultures (see previous chapters).[3] It is no exaggeration to state, in general, that "travel and mobility are central for the development of subjectivity and identity" (Birkeland 2005: 64). In this chapter, then, I focus on the transformative potential that people associate with translocal travel that is not directly associated with (formal) education or work. Starting from pilgrimage, the archetypical form of such journeys, I explore various contemporary ways in which people search for meaning through "travel."

This was the most difficult chapter of this book in terms of methodology. Because of the highly personal nature of the object of study, I decided to include a substantial amount of autoethnographic data (based on personal experiences in the period 1990–2010 in Taizé, Machu Picchu, the road to Santiago de Compostela, and Arusha). This was enriched by secondary data sources and occasional interviews and exchanges with people engaging in the practices under study. Many of the ideas presented here were discussed with the graduate students taking my "Anthropology and Travel" course at the University of Leuven (since 2014). Once again, most examples given are European or related to Europeans (including myself).

Pilgrimage

> And just as the pilgrim who walks along a road on which he has never traveled before believes that every house which he sees from afar is an inn, and finding it not so fixes his expectations on the next one, and so moves from house to house until he comes to the inn, so our soul, as soon as it enters upon this new and never travelled road of life, fixes its eyes on the goal of its supreme good, and therefore believes that everything it sees which seems to possess some good in it is that supreme good.
>
> —Dante, *Il Convivio*

Because I grew up in a Catholic environment, I was sent to a Catholic school. Every year in May, the "month of Mary," the oldest pupils would travel on foot to a nearby sanctuary of Our Lady. I was too young to grasp why we would walk there instead of simply taking the bus. Only years later, when I walked on the Camino de Santiago in Spain, did I come to understand the value of this type of practice. The repetitive walking rhythm really helped me to reflect, and it felt very rewarding to arrive at the destination after such a straining physical exercise. My grandparents also went regularly on pilgrimages. They seemed to be particularly fond of Lourdes in France. However, they traveled always by train or by car. For them, the holy place was far more important than the journey toward it. Their walking pilgrimage was symbolically replaced by perambulating the local "Way of the Cross."

***

Undertaking a journey for spiritual growth, better known as "pilgrimage," is a near universal phenomenon (Coleman and Elsner 1995). It is one of the oldest and most basic forms of human mobility and often of great personal significance. It is estimated that each year more than two hundred million people go on a pilgrimage—for hours, for days, for weeks, and even for months. India is at the top of the list, with various huge pilgrimages, such as the Kumbh Mela, in which millions of Hindus gather to bathe in a sacred river. Every year, around twenty million Catholic pilgrims visit Our

Lady of Guadalupe in Mexico; fourteen million people travel to the Shinto shrine of Ise in Japan; ten million to the Buddhist Nanputuo Temple in China; and an estimated three to five million Muslims make the hajj (the annual Muslim pilgrimage to Mecca, see below).[4]

In current usage, the term "pilgrimage" connotes a (spiritual) journey of a pilgrim. Stemming etymologically from the Latin *peregrinus* (foreigner, traveler), the term allows broader interpretations than a religious traveler to a holy place, including "foreigner, wanderer, exile, and traveler, as well as newcomer and stranger" (V. Smith 1992: 1). In essence, pilgrims are "travelers who leave their native land and are, conversely, strangers in the lands through which they travel" (Frey 1998: 257). In other words, the main connotations of the word pilgrim have to do with traveling. As Peter Jan Margry (2008: 44) points out, "It is possibly due to the focus in English-language pilgrimage studies on travelling and the early medieval *peregrinatio* idea that the wandering, travelling, tourism element has remained so strong in the pilgrimage concept."[5]

Alan Morinis (1992: 4) defines pilgrimage as "a journey undertaken by a person in quest of a place or a state that he or she believes to embody a valued ideal." By characterizing pilgrimage as a human quest, he makes a connection with the idea of the early Christian *peregrination*, a quest and a long-distance journey. While pilgrimages obviously constitute physical movement from one place to another, they entail at the same time—owing to the power of the religious imagination they involve—spiritual or temporal movement. Contemporary European "pilgrims" often do not realize that their venturing out to discover something true about themselves and the world has a long history in Christianity and Western philosophy, centered on the debate over whether the locus of change is to be found in stasis or mobility. Indeed, despite the model of pilgrimage as a physical act, the positive valuation of such a journey is part of a more philosophical debate about whether truth or enlightenment is found in sedentary contemplation or movement (Frey 1998).

It was not until the twelfth century that the imagery of journeying became a popular expression of the spiritual quest. The mediaeval conception of *Homo viator*, a wanderer between two worlds, is fundamental to early Christian thought (Ladner 1967). Dante Alighieri (1990), for instance, describes human life as the journey of a pilgrim who, if he is a good wayfarer (*buono camminatore*) on the straight road (*ottima e diritissima via*), will finally reach his place of rest in city and inn (*posa, albergo, cittade*). The monk as *Homo viator* is represented as a stranger, one who can never settle but must wander from his birthplace, leaving his family and becoming estranged from all worldly ties. In other words, the pilgrim stood for foreigner, and the pilgrimage for a state of alienation. The journey served not merely as a devotional act; it also marked a new spiritual departure, an exodus toward self-transformation. In addition, the homelessness and exile that were part of such *peregrinatio* served as penitential acts. The necessity of arduous travel was thus first linked to a form of (internal) penance before it became connected with more general ideas of self-transformation.

The value of physical movement in relation to personal growth underwent various shifts throughout history. Nancy Frey (1998: 268) superbly summarizes these shifts:

> With the decline of pilgrimage during the Reformation, travel as primarily a holy adventure was transformed into travel as a secular educational adventure. Again, in the late nineteenth century another shift is visible among the romantic writers such as Emerson and Thoreau. Through Thoreau's ascetic Walden experiment he argues that the world and the important mysteries of life are not found through travel to exotic locales or visits to gurus but are present in each moment in each individual. With the contemporary pilgrimage comes the reappearance of the positive valuation and association of mobility with personal discovery and enlightenment, whether it be oriented toward salvation (Middle Ages), education (Renaissance), or personal search (modernity/postmodernity). Through venturing out literally to the thousand regions that lie beyond home, under one's own power, it is currently believed that the physical journey will lead to greater understanding of one's own inner regions.

In anthropology, there has been increasing interest in pilgrimage as a form of "motion." Pioneers Simon Coleman and John Eade (2004) identify four perspectives on pilgrimage-as-movement: (1) movement as performative action, or the sense that movement can effect (not always consciously) certain social and cultural transformations; (2) movement as embodied action, in which corporeal co-presence as well as corporeal testing may sometimes explicitly be valorized; (3) movement as part of a semantic field of local cultural understandings of mobility; and (4) movement as metaphor in discourses that may evoke movement rather than require its physical instantiation.

In some forms of pilgrimage, part of the goal seems to be movement along the journey itself, from the familiar to something extraordinary, until this new "Other" becomes integrated into a new sense of self (Morinis 1992). The movement of pilgrims is recognized as "twofold, exterior and interior, the simultaneous movement of the feet and the soul through time as well as space" (Cousineau 1998: 94). Physical movement is thus an inherent part of pilgrimage. That also explains why undertaking a spiritual journey on foot is preferred over faster means of transport: "Whereas formerly the journey was a necessary evil, nowadays it is seen as 'tradition' or as pilgrimage heritage, and more and more frequently a pilgrimage is only seen as a 'real' pilgrimage if it is completed on foot" (Margry 2008: 26). The walking serves to increase the physical challenge, the degree of embodied engagement with the environment, and to slow the pace down to facilitate contemplation.[6] Our concept of "travel" derives from "travail," hinting at the physical danger and toil that was historically experienced in traveling.

According to Jean Slavin (2003), the journey is no longer an experience to fulfill a physical need but rather a means to incorporate spirituality in the embodied self-seeking enlightenment. Traveling through the unknown, pilgrims step out of their "comfort zone" and can reflect on their identity and their relationship with spirituality or the world. The physical experience of the journey becomes the epitome and the metaphor of the quest for the spiritual and the searching self. The most extreme form is what William Schmidt (2009: 69) calls a "wandering pilgrimage," a type of pilgrimage that is "not guided by a specific destination as such, but by the spiritual impulse arising out of journeying for its own sake." The wandering pilgrim reveals that the objectives are not necessarily tied to time and space but to a seeking of spiritual intensification of some sort, realized through the act of going forth. However, while the journey (more than the sacred goal) can be an end in itself, it is questionable whether "motion can be assumed to be the primary constitutive element of the pilgrimage as a universal phenomenon" (Margry 2008: 27). Sometimes movement has simply become ritualized, such as circumambulation of (sacred) sites.

Transformation

> A pilgrimage is a ritual journey with a hallowed purpose. Every step along the way has meaning. The pilgrim knows that the journey will be difficult and that life-giving challenges will emerge. A pilgrimage is not a vacation: it is a transformational journey during which significant change takes place. New insights are given. Deeper understanding is attained …. On return from the pilgrimage, life is seen with different eyes. Nothing will ever be quite the same again.
>
> —Macrina Wiederkehr, *Behold Your Life: A Pilgrimage through Your Memories*

As historian Eric Leed (1991) documents, physical travel has a long association with personal transformation—meaningful emotional, physical, or psychological progression from one state of being to another. There are many links between concepts for travel, transition, and experience, especially the prevalence of journeying metaphors to describe all manners of change, along with life itself. Garth Lean (2012) develops the notion of "transformative travel" to denote the long-term changes some individuals attribute to their physical travel experiences.[7] Jeffrey Kottler (1997) suggests that many people attempt to facilitate their transformation and spiritual development through travel, while others do so by going on a spiritual pilgrimage. The starting point is an assertion and realization of one's inadequacy, and the journey—within the self or beyond the external world—is one in which the character is further humbled as he or she seeks that which will give life meaning.

In its most general sense, such travels are understood to indicate a significant and signifying movement that transforms people in the process. These are journeys both outward, to new, strange, dangerous places, and inward, to spiritual improvement, whether through increased self-knowledge or through the braving of physical dangers. The physical journey is secondary to the inner one. The transforming encounter between the self (the familiar) and the Other is at the very heart of the pilgrimage experience (Morinis 1992: 26). In other words, pilgrimage entails "the practice of journeying undertaken, in part, as a process of self-transformation, as a labor through which the self is worked on through bodily practices and adopting a particular relation to the self, thus moving the focus from destination to practice" (Dawney 2014: 129). Spirituality is thus both an aspect of the inner self and of the journey, which is neither material nor external. Far from being a triumphant proving of the self, the pilgrimage is an arduous search for understanding, and the outcome is not so much a demonstration of the pilgrim's worth as a reevaluation and transformation of his or her self.

The crossing of boundaries is a central element of pilgrimage. Because it requires going beyond the physical and mental boundaries of ordinary life, pilgrimage is a liminal activity. Victor and Edith Turner (1978: 253–54) use the term "liminoid" to distinguish the pilgrim's journey from the neophyte's liminality experienced during a rite of passage. Edith Turner (in Turner and Turner 1978: xiii) calls pilgrimage "a kinetic ritual." Regardless of the fleeting nature of identity construction, an essential characteristic of pilgrimage that remains a constant is movement—movement across a landscape that seeks to transform both person and place. The theme of movement forms part of Turner and Turner's (1978) arguments about pilgrimage as embodiment of populist, spontaneously articulated "anti-structure." Journeying is said to bring the possibility of creating social and psychological transformation, even if only on a temporary basis (cf. van Gennep [1909] 1960).

It is often through travel to "foreign" lands (which may be within one's own country) that people can be changed irrevocably and permanently because of what they encountered and what they learned. Romantic images of pilgrimage as being strenuous, hazardous, and a constant form of penance have been added to the picture (Swatos and Tomasi 2002). Hardship, challenge, risk, and strain are not accidental to a pilgrimage experience. The ancient Greeks taught that obstacles were the tests of the gods, and the medieval Japanese believed that the sorrows of travel were challenges to overcome and transform into poetry and song. Hardship seems a necessary component of pilgrimage whether one is dealing with physical challenges, emotional challenges, the cognitive adjustment to new awareness, or adaptation to unforeseen and unplanned events. Pilgrims are often pushed beyond their known comforts and familiarities into realms that demand alertness and self-care. But pilgrimage is not a spiritualized form of adventure tourism. The pilgrim's commitment to a journey of hardship and challenge is not to assert one's power in achievement, but to open oneself to a process where one's primal vulnerability can lead to a spiritual encounter.

While some would argue that "all movement transforms: spaces, places, people and environments" (Lean, Staiff, and Waterton 2014: 14), most authors identify transformation as a natural consequence of the pilgrim's journey (Cousineau 1998). Pilgrims return home believing that "the transformation of the world around us will be the result of personal transformation" (Westwood 2003: 222). A journey is often viewed as a metaphor for individuation, personal development, change, and transformation. In general, travel has been characterized as an exemplary case of personal change, a way of becoming whole and the best that one can be (Birkeland 2005: 7). An argument for "measurable" transformation would need to rest on empirical data that demonstrate continued difference well after the journey itself is over. However, similar to the other mobilities described in this book, while actual transformation is certainly sought after by many engaging in these practices, also social recognition for the transformative type of traveling undertaken plays a role, irrespective of the actual outcome.

In sum, transformation through travel is a complex sociocultural phenomenon. As Lean (2012: 169) writes,

> Everyone is transformed by travel to some degree, whether perceived or not, or labelled as "transformation" or by another title—change, shift or personal growth/development. Identities, relationships, realities and performances come to be constructed, maintained and transformed through historical and contemporary travels, not simply as bodily movement but conceptualised as mobility in its totality, facilitated by corporeal, communicative, virtual and imaginative mobilities. It is not physical mobility alone that acts as an agent of transformation.

Transformation through physical travel becomes entwined in a much larger process—the socially mobile de/construction of reality.

Transformative Travels

Traveling is a return to the essential.

—Tibetan proverb

Having sketched the broader conceptual background, we can now have a closer look at some concrete examples of anticipated transformative travel. The idea that certain journeys can initiate deep and enduring changes within a person is not new and has been discussed in contexts as diverse as pilgrimage, backpacking, international sojourn, volunteer tourism, and wellness travel (Kirillova, Lehto, and Cai 2016).

Walking "The Way"

Caminante, son tus huellas el camino, y nada más;
caminante, no hay camino, se hace camino al andar.
Al andar se hace camino, y al volver la vista atrás
se ve la senda que nunca se ha de volver a pisar.

[Wayfarer, your footprints are the road, nothing else;
wayfarer, there is no road, the road is created as you walk.
As you walk, the road is created, and when you look back
you see the path that you will never tread again.]

—Antonio Machado, *Fields of Castile*

Santiago de Compostela in Spain has been associated with pilgrims since the early Middle Ages. The journey to Santiago ranked, together with those to Rome and Jerusalem, among the great pilgrimages of the medieval European church. The birth of Santiago de Compostela is linked to the presumed discovery of the remains of the apostle St. James in the ninth century. Two centuries later, a Romanic cathedral was built, and from then onward, pilgrimages began increasing, turning Santiago de Compostela into one of the most important sacred Christian sites in the world. The *Camino Frances* is the best known and most traveled of the routes (of almost 500 miles / 800 kilometers long).[8] In 1985, the Old Town of Santiago de Compostela was recognized by UNESCO as a cultural World Heritage site.[9] Since then, the numbers of pilgrims, which were in decline, have again increased dramatically: from 3,500 in 1986 to 272,000 in 2010.[10]

The real turnaround came in 1987, when the Council of Europe declared the Camino a symbol of European unity and identity, and the route network was designated as the first "European Cultural Itinerary" (later renamed as "Cultural Route").[11] In that same year, the Brazilian novelist Paulo Coelho published *O Diário de Um Mago* (translated in English as *The Pilgrimage*). Based on recollections of Coelho's own journey along the Camino in 1986, the book explores the need to find one's own path. The book was translated into thirty-seven languages, and together with *O Alquimista* (*The Alchemist*)—Coelho's 1988 narrative of a spiritual quest in which the main character, Santiago, broadens his horizons by travels and experiences in distant countries (a bestseller translated in sixty-seven

Figure 6.1: Pilgrims arriving at their hostel after a long day of walking along the Camino to Santiago de Compostela, Navarra, Spain. (Photographer: Noel B. Salazar)

languages)—had a huge impact on the Camino. In 1993, the Route of Santiago de Compostela was inscribed on UNESCO's World Heritage list.[12]

The *Camino de Santiago* (Way of St James) has been described as a journey not only to a physical destination but to the interior of oneself. The Camino is both the path to Santiago, but also a metaphorical path not bound to space. It is the "between" of "from" and "to." As has been pointed out by other scholars, it is important to acknowledge that "this pilgrimage is not representative of mainstream pilgrimage culture" (Coleman and Eade 2004: 11). For many Camino pilgrims, the movement on foot seems to be more important than reaching the tomb of St. James. The Camino itself, the road to Santiago, rather than the cathedral that hosts the remains of the apostle, can now be distinguished as the major focus of this pilgrimage (see figure 6.1). Most pilgrims do the Camino on foot; many are young people, and only a minority give a religious motivation for undertaking the journey (but motivations become blurred in the process of walking itself). Many of these walkers hope that the physical act of traveling to Santiago will help them achieve a parallel inner journey of self-discovery and self-transformation (Mendel 2015).

Walking the Camino is a nice illustration of how the body serves as a catalyst for enlightenment as the rhythmic movement pulls the body away from material attachments, allowing walkers to produce a profoundly spiritual experience (Slavin 2003). Movement of the body by walking is closely related to movement of the mind (Ingold and Vergunst 2008). The way of walking, body posture, pace, and physical challenges go hand in hand with a mental process of learning and understanding. The physical journey ends in Santiago de Compostela, but the inner journey, the healing process, will continue in daily life as the experiences of the Camino are incorporated and relived. This type of "transit pilgrimage does not really have a beginning or an end, or at any rate they are not relevant. Moving, walking, the accessibility and freedom of the ritual, being in nature, and tranquility are all elements which have contributed to its success" (Margry 2008: 24). The experience of doing the Camino on foot suits contemporary styles of mobility in which images, symbols, feelings, and concerns about nature and culture become central (Herrero 2008).

Pilgrimage of Trust on Earth

Walk forward on your way, because it exists only by your walking.

—Frère Roger de Taizé

Taizé is a small village in Burgundy, France, hosting the Taizé Community, an ecumenical monastic order comprised of more than a hundred Brothers from around the world.[13] Founded in 1940, the community started attracting young people in the 1960s (Escaffit and Rasiwala 2008). In 1966, the first international young adults' meeting was organized, with fourteen hundred participants from thirty countries. In 1974, in response to the second Vatican Council, Taizé organized a "Council of Youth," which gathered over twenty thousand people. At the end of the 1970s, the meetings and surrounding activities began to be referred to as a "Pilgrimage of Trust on Earth."[14] The idea behind this is that the Taizé Community never wanted to start a new global group or movement but instead sends "pilgrims" back from their youth meetings to local churches, parishes, groups, or communities, to continue the pilgrimage back home.

Taizé has become one of the world's most important sites of Christian pilgrimage (and it also receives visitors from other religions, as well as atheists). Over a hundred thousand young people from around the world make pilgrimages to Taizé each year for prayer, Bible study, sharing, and communal work. Contrary to the Camino, physical endurance is not associated with Taizé.[15] Rather, the focus shifts from the body and the individual to communal bonds and conversations taking place among pilgrims. Different from other forms of pilgrimage in which the journey represents an essential element of pilgrims' transformative experience, journeying to the village of Taizé is virtually indistinguishable from traveling for tourism purposes.

However, in addition to welcoming pilgrims in France, small groups of Brothers travel around the globe, sharing and learning with church groups. The Brothers of Taizé have thus become pilgrims themselves, traveling to the cities from which people begin their journeys to Taizé, suggesting a kind of "reciprocity of pilgrimage" (Pritchard 2015: 69). The Pilgrimage of Trust on Earth combines the ongoing meetings in Taizé with meetings in cities throughout the world, organized in collaboration with local churches. In 1978, a first European meeting was held in Paris, France. Since then, similar annual meetings have been organized across Europe. Particularly significant were the first meetings after 1989, when young people from Eastern and Western Europe could finally meet and welcome one another (see figure 6.2). Because of this, the European meetings in the 1990s easily attracted around a hundred thousand participants (whereas the current numbers are more around thirty thousand).

As Elizabeth Pritchard (2015: 69) argues, "Taizé is not a single destination, then, but entails multiple flows of persons in varying directions." This is what William Swatos (2006: x) calls a "movement pilgrimage," not constituted by site but space. Thus, although the Taizé Community may

Figure 6.2: Thousands of young people gathering during the 1991 Pilgrimage of Trust on Earth, organized by the Community of Taizé in Budapest, Hungary. (Photographer: Noel B. Salazar)

be physically located in a village in France, it cannot be confined to this location. In his *Unfinished Letter*, published after his death, Taizé founder Brother Roger proposed to "widen" the Pilgrimage of Trust on Earth.[16] Consequently, intercontinental young adult meetings have begun to take place, beginning in Kolkata, India, in 2006. So far, these meetings have covered all continents, except for Oceania. In sum, Taizé is an interesting example of how boundary-crossing mobility and (spiritual) transformation are combined in innovative ways.

Elsewhere too ...

As you start to walk on the way, the way appears.

—Rumi

In Islam, many *hadiths* describe the benefits of travel in relation to the rewards that travelers receive (Eickelman and Piscatori 1990).[17] The most known form is the hajj, the pilgrimage to the holy city of Mecca (and one of the five pillars of the Islamic faith).[18] During the six days of hajj, the pilgrims must go through several stages, including walking from Mina to the plain of Arafat and circumambulating the holy Ka'aba shrine in Mecca. As a major factor of individual mobility in premodern society, the pilgrimage was a complex phenomenon. Through literature, we learn about the networked nature of Muslim mobility that stresses the hajj but also extends beyond it to privilege travel of all kinds to many places (Euben 2006). Although with the speed of contemporary travel technologies the journey to Mecca and back can be completed in a week or two, rather than the many months that used to be involved, the emphasis of the hajj is still on the need for proper spiritual preparation for the journey. Today, people often lament that air travel and packaged tours remove too much travail (toil) from the hajj, turning it into just another shopping spree.[19]

An analysis of who participates in the hajj pilgrimage is important for understanding it as an agent of personal social mobility and change. Internal expectations of change appear to be associated with social mobility, cultural and political identity, prestige, and a sense of belonging (Eickelman and Piscatori 1990). The pilgrimage is costly, time-consuming, and physically demanding. Most Muslims will never be able to afford it. Islamic scholars are nearly unanimous that no one should make the hajj if it will cause hardship for oneself or one's family. In practice and in principle, the hajj is not an absolute obligation—only a highly desirable duty for those financially and physically capable of making the journey in reasonable safety and comfort.

Movement has also been a constant feature among Hindus and Buddhists, for whom travel is an essential part of their self-identity. The elevated number of Hindu pilgrims participating in pilgrimages across India confirms this (see above). While for many the journey aspect is perhaps less important, the traveling *sadhus* (holy people) prove quite the contrary (Hausner 2007).[20] For close to three thousand years, these religious ascetics have wandered the Indian subcontinent. For many Buddhists, too, the act of travel may be regarded as an external indication of the inner spiritual journey. That the journey reflects an application of positive human values such as compassion, caring, and sharing as part of the improvement of self in this life in preparation for the next is as important as an avowed desire to follow in the path of the Buddha; in fact, the two are inseparable. From a Buddhist perspective, therefore, "how a person travels in relation to others is more important than the act of traveling itself" (Hall 2005: 180).

The transformative aspects of pilgrimage can resonate through the rest of a person's life. Iain Reader's (2005) research on the Shikoku pilgrimage for Buddhists in Japan illustrates how pilgrimages, rather than being marginal and transient, can be central organizing themes in the lives of participants. The Shikoku pilgrimage is an 870-mile / 1,400-kilometer pilgrimage route that circles the island of Shikoku and involves the pilgrims visiting eighty-eight Buddhist temples on the way. As with the Camino in Spain, the number of pilgrims has increased, and more people choose again to walk (instead of traveling in organized groups by bus). Reader (2005) notes how some participants are confronted with the addictive nature of the pilgrimage. Many maintain a continuing association with the pilgrimage afterward, and some become "recurrent" (Reader 2005: 255) or even "permanent pilgrims" (250). This is facilitated by the circular nature of the pilgrimage, with no fixed or defined finishing point.[21] It offers people a means of continually improving themselves spiritually, linked to Buddhist notions of "repeating practices over and again as a means of spiritual advancement" (Reader 2005: 262). Repeated pilgrimage activity provides participants with a sense of status and empowerment.

What about Tourism?

When a friend of mine who was working for a development NGO told me at the beginning of the new millennium that they were setting up tourism trips to their projects in developing countries, I knew I had immediately found a topic for my master's thesis in anthropology. It turned out to be hard to combine the relaxed atmosphere of a holiday with the manifold challenges raised by development projects. A couple of years later (in 2007), while I was in Tanzania conducting doctoral fieldwork, I was confronted again with the theme. I soon discovered that the guesthouse at which I was staying was also the preferred accommodation for "voluntourists." Especially during the summer months, the place was packed with Westerners who participated in one of the many programs offered by volunteer organizations. Many were undergraduate students who had paid outrageous amounts of money to teach Tanzanian farmers about sustainable agriculture or to take care of (supposed) HIV/AIDS orphans. During their first week, these voluntourists would learn some words of Swahili and receive some general information. After that, they were sent off to "the field" to start their volunteering experience. Most would end their stay with either a safari or an attempt to climb nearby Mt. Kilimanjaro. The voluntourists had good intentions and usually did not think of the potential negative impacts of their actions. They certainly judged what they did as beneficial to their own development (and career building).

***

Whereas pilgrimage is almost automatically linked to transformation and the quest for self-realization, tourism is more often seen as an activity that confirms people's identity and worldview rather than transforming them. The ethnographic work of Edward Bruner (1991: 238), for instance, shows that, although "tourist discourse promises the tourist a total transformation of self," often the very opposite occurs, namely that the tourist self is changed very little by tourism. Indeed, for most tourists, tourism involves more hedonism and conspicuous consumption than learning or understanding. However, Dean MacCannell (1976) has suggested that tourism is a form of (secular) pilgrimage where people seek to escape the shallowness and alienation of modern life and discover the "authentic." Erik Cohen (1979) points out that it is inaccurate to assume that all tourists are either dopes or secular pilgrims. According to him, most are simply out to have a good time—"travelling for pleasure." Only a few of the non-institutionalized variety (also known as "independent travelers") look for meaning in their lives by touring the world inhabited by the "Other."

Many scholars have characterized tourism metaphorically as "pilgrimages" (something experts of religion have repeatedly criticized). Some seem to suggest that tourism evolved out of pilgrimage. While tourist, as a concept, only appeared at the beginning of the nineteenth century in English and French, one can identify what we would call "tourists," as well as the practices in which they engage, long before that. The term itself, derived from the Greek *tornos* (a carpenter's tool for drawing a circle), refers to an individual who makes a circuitous journey (usually for pleasure) and returns to the starting point (Salazar 2014b). Valene Smith (1992: 2) argues that "tourist encounters can be just as compelling [as pilgrimage] and almost spiritual in personal meaning." She sees social approval (received "back home") as the most important factor differentiating tourists from pilgrims. The fact that many contemporary pilgrims are after social recognition as well shows the increasing blurring between these different types of travel categories.

Tommi Mendel's documentary, *Common Roads* (2013), shows this nicely. Whereas the label of pilgrim is still mostly associated with devout persons leaving home for purely religious motives, young people taking to the road as backpackers are perceived as pleasure seeking adventurous globetrotters. Questioning these stereotypes, Mendel (2015) followed one young woman along the Camino through Spain and another one along backpacking routes through Thailand, Cambodia, and Laos. Documenting their ideas and hopes, experiences, and encounters over a period of three years, his ethnographic film reveals intriguing parallels on various levels between what appear as two different ways of traveling, at the same time providing a mirror image of today's society.

Another blurring occurs with new ways of touring old sites. The Camino is the best documented example, but there are others too. In Peru, for instance, alternative ways of experiencing the archaeological complex of Machu Picchu are reconfiguring its meaning toward the "sacred" (Arellano 2007). The recent wave of spiritual travelers is expanding, as several pilgrimages to the lost city invite a mystic tourism clientele to recover lost wisdom and transform spiritually. One such traveler, with intentions to merge realities on his hike on the Inca Trail to the archeological ruins of Machu Picchu in Peru, shared his intentions, saying, "I want to enter the city [Machu Picchu] as the original inhabitants did. It was more important to me that my steps echoed the Incas" (Ross 2010).

Over the last decade, the Inca trail has become a tourism rite of passage that aims for the "real Inca experience":

> A "healthy" tourist who does not enter Machu Picchu by trekking the Inca trail has not "experienced" or felt what it was like to live in the Inca era. The 4-day trek is essential to reaching this sensuous "state," as the long-distance walk and camping among nature, beauty and ancient civilization allows the achievement of a reflexive awareness of the body and senses and, therefore, a fully corporeal experiencing of the sacred site. (Arellano 2007: 94)

The trail, sometimes dubbed "the Inca trial" (Arellano 2007: 94), is a challenging rite of passage and a unique experience that requires physical and mental conditioning. Alexandra Arellano (2007: 89) calls it a "transformational pilgrimage."

Already in the 1980s, Nelson Graburn (1983: 13) juxtaposed travel as rite of passage with other rites of passage in stating that "the touristic forms [of rites of passage] are usually self-imposed (and thereby more exceptional and personally meaningful) as one might expect in complex society." Backpackers can be conceived of as rite-of-passage tourists, because they are usually young adults and they favor lengthy trips that are often mentally and physically challenging. Their trips are a type of "self-testing wherein the individuals prove to *themselves* that they can make life long changes" (Graburn 1983: 13).

In "voluntourism" (travel-related volunteering), the hoped for altruistic transformation of the self is coupled with a transformation of the (impoverished) "Other," promised by the providers (Mostafanezhad 2014). For some participants, being a volunteer tourist provides an opportunity to undergo a rite of passage and display independence while seeking new experiences possibly unavailable to them at home (Lyons and Wearing 2008). The supposed transformative effects of this special interest type of tourism or pro bono volunteering in either tourists or "hosts" has long been questioned (Salazar 2004). For some, voluntourism, as an activity thought to be of higher (moral) value, is one of the ways in which they try to distinguish themselves from regular "tourists" (cf. Munt 1994).

Even if no transformation is achieved, the participation in voluntourism can still be rewarded by endowing the participating tourists with symbolic capital (particularly of the social and cultural type). This is unrelated to whether there is a genuine interest to help or not. Providers do sell voluntourism as "career development." As pointed out earlier (see Introduction), this type of tourism is a typical activity appearing at moments when there is a transition in the cycle of people's lives (Amit 2007: 6). While voluntourism is found in all age ranges, the more long-term engagements are particularly popular among young adults and also (nearly) retired people.[22] In the latter case, people often want to use (administrative, engineering, IT, medical, or technical) skills they have accumulated in their professional life, a phenomenon that has been termed "skilled volunteering" (Garlinghouse and Dorsey 2015).[23]

Do All Roads Lead to Rome?

> We travel, initially, to lose ourselves, and we travel, next, to find ourselves.
>
> —Pico Iyer, *Why We Travel*

People build their worlds (and identities) in the movement between "home" and "(far) away." The promise of travel for fulfillment and/or enlightenment is the possibility of personal transformation or, as Victor Turner puts it in regards to liminality, the potential for "what may be" (in Turner and Turner 1978: 3). Therefore, the journey is oriented toward the unknown future as it may become (see figure 6.3). It is the movement toward the (imagined) unknown and uncertain, through geographical and symbolic separation, that is believed to be a core component for the self to develop and progress. "Immersion without drowning, then, seems to be the balancing act of most significant journeys" (Beckstead 2010: 387). Thus it becomes important "more to travel than to arrive anywhere" (Pirsig 1974: 5).

Pilgrimages are the archetypical journeys of becoming, voyages toward new identities, new selves, and a more fulfilling way of being-in-the-world. Pilgrimage can involve a metaphorical journey that brings deeper meaning to an experience of change in a person's life. Those who suffer travail undergo a transformation and metamorphosis during their journeys, and gain new insights and reach self-understanding. Their worldview, identity, and horizon of understanding can be transformed in the course of travel (Islam 1996).

For it to be a positive experience, mobility is required to refresh one's connection with places and peoples in order to transform selfhood. It is important to remain an "outsider" through the practice of (temporary) relocation to embark on new routes. Returns represent new mobilities, or new trajectories within place and self (Frey 2004; and see chapter 1 of this volume). Some people become "serial pilgrims," constantly planning the next journey, never settling long enough to live any other way, and using that as a badge of authenticity. Such trajectories demonstrate a commitment to fluidity and identity creation rather than "finding oneself" or one place to belong. Others return home and start support groups with other pilgrimage veterans, gathering to share stories and raise funds for support of the pilgrimage.

As Tim Ingold (2011: 148) argues, "Lives are led not inside places but through, around, to and from them, from and to places elsewhere." He uses the term "wayfaring" to describe "the embodied experience of this perambulatory movement." Importantly, "the wayfarer has no final destination, for wherever he is, and so long as life goes on, there is somewhere further he can go" (Ingold 2011: 150). In Ingold's (2011: 12) words, "To be ... is not to be *in* place but to be *along* paths. The path, and not the place, is the primary condition of being, or rather of becoming." This idea of wayfaring is very well evoked in pilgrimage, which can be transformed

Figure 6.3: Different people find different ways in search of "balance" in their lives, Brussels, Belgium. (Photographer: Noel B. Salazar)

into a lifestyle, a life-long inner journey. The physical goal is an integral part of the pilgrimage, but the real purpose is to find a new inner goal in life or a better lifestyle (Davidsson Bremborg 2013). Going on a wayfaring journey has long been used as a metaphor for understanding our lives in general. To link pilgrimage with a continuous way of life is, however, not necessary, as most pilgrims view pilgrimage more as a temporary break from ordinary life, to which they will eventually return. In other words, the pilgrimage functions more as a recovery, rather than a radical "life switch" or lifestyle.

Journeys that follow prescribed itineraries or scripts are unlikely to produce transformative consequences (which is the criticism that most types of tourism receive). They might prompt transformation, but only if one stumbles across something unexpected during a carefully planned trip. In an interconnected world, it becomes increasingly difficult for individuals to distance themselves from their "world" (the one they left behind). They may be physically removed from "home" but still very much connected through their laptops, tablets, and smart phones. The increasing inability to "disconnect" is a challenge for contemporary pilgrims or "serious" tourists, as well as for anthropologists conducting fieldwork. Paradoxically, the connectedness is precisely what is needed to receive more instantaneous social rewards for the transformative travel one is trying to experience.

NOTES

1. The word "odyssey" itself has come to indicate a difficult and transformative journey.
2. Metaphorically, many cultural views of the afterlife have been rooted in travel to an "otherworld."
3. One could also think here of the tales of shamanic transformation journeys to the edge, where trials are undergone and power is confronted, then won.
4. Except for the hajj, most of these pilgrimages can be classified as "domestic."
5. In the Middle Ages, *peregrinatio* referred to a self-imposed exile and wandering for the love of God. This type of "true" travel (*peregrinari*) was contrasted with aimless and useless rambling or purposeless vagrancy (*vagary*), thereby revealing a deeply embedded concern over the morality of voyaging (Stagl 1995: 71).
6. There are also links here with the idea of "slow travel" (Dickinson and Lumsdon 2010). Slow travel undoes the pejorative overtones commonly associated with slowness (Parkins and Craig 2006). It parallels the various other slow movements (Honoré 2004) and related ideas linked to de-growth, de-development, downshifting, and simple living.
7. Transformative Travel website, accessed 22 February 2018, http://www.transformativetravel.org/.

8. Saint James Way website, Council of Europe, accessed 22 February 2018, http://www.saintjamesway.eu/en/.

9. Santiago de Compostela (Old Town) World Heritage inscription website, UNESCO, accessed 22 February 2018, http://whc.unesco.org/en/list/347.

10. Estadísticas, Oficina de Acogida al Peregrino, accessed 22 February 2018, http://oficinadelperegrino.com/estadisticas/.

11. Santiago de Compostela Pilgrim Routes website, Council of Europe, accessed 22 February 2018, http://www.coe.int/en/web/cultural-routes/the-santiago-de-compostela-pilgrim-routes.

12. Routes of Santiago de Compostela World Heritage inscription website, UNESCO, accessed 22 February 2018, http://whc.unesco.org/en/list/669.

13. Taizé Community website, accessed 22 February 2018, http://taize.fr/en.

14. "A pilgrimage of trust on earth," Taizé Community, 31 January 2012. Accessed 22 February 2018, http://www.taize.fr/en_article58.html and "Taizé - European Meetings," Vimeo, accessed 22 February 2018, http://vimeo.com/11838114.

15. If a pilgrim decides to spend the afternoon walking around St. Stephen's Source, a network of paths in a wooded area of the community, or in the hilly neighborhood surrounding the village, he or she is free to do so.

16. "Brother Roger's unfinished letter," Taizé Community, 12 December 2005. Accessed 22 February 2018, http://www.taize.fr/en_article2964.html.

17. A *hadith* is one of various accounts describing the words, actions, or habits of the Islamic prophet Muhammad.

18. Another telling example is that of Tablighi Jama'at, a global movement that encourages its members to do at least one three-day trip a month, one forty-day trip a year, and one four-month trip in a lifetime (Masud 2000). The amount of time spent in (missionary) travel is thus quite significant; a committed Tablighi spends at least one-fifth of his lifetime journeying.

19. The enormous death tolls during recent pilgrimages show that hajjis still face many of the old dangers, as well as new ones. Most of the truly life-threatening situations now appear in Mecca itself rather than on the way. Sunstroke and dehydration are as pernicious as ever, and even more lives are lost to stampeding crowds and exploding stoves.

20. Hausner (2007), however, explains that also lay Hindu pilgrims travel in the spirit of asceticism.

21. While this would be impossible on the Camino, some pilgrims there do not stop in Santiago either, but continue until the "edge of the world" at Cape Finisterre (55 miles / 90 kilometers from Santiago) (Herrero 2008). Some people decide to return home walking backwards on the Camino while others become "serial pilgrims" (Frey 1998).

22. Over 50 and Overseas website, accessed 22 February 2018, http://www.over-50andoverseas.com/.

23. Career Volunteer website, accessed 22 February 2018, http://www.careervolunteer.co.uk/.

Mobile Futures

We construct borders, literally and figuratively, to fortify our sense of who we are; and we cross them in search of who we might become.

—Frances Stonor Saunders, "Where on Earth are You?"

The findings presented in this book illustrate how meaning-making through momentous mobilities is the product of a wide variety of boundary-crossing as well as boundary-creating processes. Indeed, new boundaries are constructed even as borders are crossed, and such boundaries are multiple and multifaceted. Therefore, it is necessary to question mobility ideologies that associate certain forms of movement (or the lack thereof) with specific meanings and causalities. Through culturally inflected notions of mobility, social class distinctions are made, which ultimately feed back into the production of the social (R. Thomson and Taylor 2005). An important aspect of the momentous mobilities described here is the degree to which they become embedded as regularized and prescribed parts of the lives of individuals, families, and organizations (Frändberg 2006).

(Im)Mobility

Motion can be imagined as creating a global regime, whether of freedom or governmentality, only to the extent that motion is imagined as loosening the grip of local practice. Yet the closer we examine social and geographical mobility, the less useful it seems to think in terms of overcoming such friction. This is where movement as mobility and mobilization can be of use. Movement helps us visualize forms of mobility with cultural and political definition—not just transcendent freedom. The specificity of the trajectory of movement is important for what results. Furthermore, there must be mobilization—the movement of the heart—for travel to remake the world. Mobilization refigures identities even as it draws from foreign connections and comparisons.

—Anna L. Tsing, *Friction: An Ethnography of Global Connection*

Mobility, particularly of the transnational type, remains formidably difficult for many; sometimes more so than before. There are myriad contradictory rules, regulations, and regimes to face. The currently dominant mobility discourse affirms the structural inequalities between those who are voluntarily mobile and those who cannot or are forced to move. To understand mobility, we thus need to pay attention to immobility, to the structures (which, once again, are changing too) that facilitate certain movements while impeding others (Khan 2016). Each kind of mobility is constrained by different sets of restrictions, which differ not only in degree, but also in quality. Categories of movement, including the momentous mobilities described in this work, are always formed relationally, vis-à-vis other groups. Normative ideologies operate in shaping mobility as well as spatial relations, with people who are on the move as well as with those who remain put. Mobility transforms the experience of life, no matter one's own movements or the lack thereof: "The paradigmatic experience of global modernity for most people ... is that of staying in one place but experiencing the 'dis-placement' that global modernity *brings to them*" (Tomlinson 1999: 9). As political scientist Roxanne Euben (2006: 29) notes,

> The association of travel, imagination, curiosity, knowledge and reflexive self-understanding simultaneously produces an image of the people who do not or cannot travel, whether they are those "left behind" or those "exotics" at the end of the journey. If immobility is implicitly linked to stasis, inertia, narrowness and complacency, those who do not travel come to be characterized by an absence of curiosity, lack of philosophical reflectiveness, or both.

Despite the normalization of mobility in many societies and cultures, mobile practices are still too often regarded as phenomena that are to be examined under specific headings such as migration studies or tourism studies. It is useful, at least analytically, to expand and redefine these separate thematic lines as a subset of mobility studies. The examples discussed in this book, in various sociocultural contexts, and domains as varied as education, work, or "lifestyle," illustrate the widespread importance of mobility in people's lives. If we seek a more in-depth understanding of momentous human movements, then drawing on multiple theories, perspectives, and methods will add profoundly to the more formal economic, demographic, and sociological models upon which many previous studies have been built.

Instead of closing the discussion on momentous mobilities, the research presented in this monograph adds new questions to it, issues that can only be addressed properly by future collaborative and interdisciplinary work on this complex topic.

Michael Hardt and Antonio Negri (2000) rightly point out that circulation, mobility, and flexibility are not, in themselves, "liberatory." There is an inherent paradox in the contemporary idealization of the freedom of movement: "'Freedom' entails developing the infrastructure to defend the free movement and operation of some, and to strictly curtail the freedom of others" (James 2005: 27). After all, not all movements are valued equally positively, and the processes that produce global movements also result in immobility and exclusion (Cunningham and Heyman 2004; Salazar and Smart 2011). Restrictions on mobility also limit people's freedom to circulate (Abram et al. 2017). Paradoxically, as the Indonesian case in chapter 2 illustrated, this situation often leads to a higher rate of permanent migration and to discouraging people from returning, temporarily or not, to their point of departure, particularly in the context of work (cf. Holmes 2013).

Anthropology of Mobility

> Can the tree, symbol of rootedness and stability, be reconciled with the canoe, symbol of journeying and unrestricted wandering?
>
> —Joël Bonnemaison, *The Tree and the Canoe*

An anthropology of mobility and its associated imaginaries, as developed in this book, directs new questions toward traditional social science topics. Mobility is all-pervading as a metaphor for the contemporary world, both in its physical forms and its imaginative implications. Mobility may well have become the key difference- and otherness-producing machine of our age, involving significant inequalities of speed, risk, rights, and status (Heyman and Campbell 2009), with both "movers" and "stayers" being engaged in the construction of complex politics of fixity and movement (Salazar and Smart 2011). Mobility gains meaning and becomes momentous through its embeddedness within societies, culture, politics, and histories (which are themselves, to a certain extent, mobile). It does not mark the obsolescence of the social, but brings about new configurations of it, not as a territorially bounded entity, but shaped through dynamics and processes that can take variable forms. The question is not so much about the overall rise or decline of mobility, but how various mobilities are formed, regulated, and distributed, and how the formation, regulation, and distribution of these mobilities are shaped and patterned by existing social, political, and economic structures.

The sociocultural assumptions, meanings, and values attached to (im)mobility need to be empirically problematized rather than assumed (Jónsson 2011; Salazar 2010b). The meaningful and ideological coding of mobility reflects contextual societal attitudes and cultural practices. The various case studied presented in this book show that the ideological associations of mobility with liberty, freedom, and universalism contain serious shortcomings and neglect the social costs. For one, "freedom as mobility" is composed both of opportunities to travel (when and where one pleases) and of the feasibility of "voluntary immobility," the choice not to move at all (Bergmann and Sager 2008; B. Turner 2007).

This book reaffirms that sociocultural anthropologists are well equipped to challenge the (Western) assumptions embedded within much current mobility theory. Founding fathers such as Franz Boas and Bronislaw Malinowski, while missing the extent to which their epistemological project was predicated on their own mobility or how anthropological knowledge derives from movement, showed how the liminal positioning of anthropologists among the humanities and social sciences, with constant methodological and theoretical boundary crossings, offers promise for a fruitful and grounded analysis (Salazar 2013a). Anthropology—with its methodical skepticism and interest in holism—holds the potential to act as a catalyst, bringing different fields together in mobility studies, and this in novel and fruitful ways.

Anthropology can contribute to the current debate in the social sciences by detailing how human mobility is a contested construct involving much more than mere physical movement. It can assess, for instance, how imaginary activities and social relations concerning mobility are variously materialized, enacted, and inculcated across the globe. As hinted at in this book, the distinct contribution of anthropology to debates on mobility lies in its capacity to show the actual limits of the fantasies that imaginaries of mobility produce. An in-depth empirical focus enables anthropologists to document the many ways in which mobility, in association with processes of globalization, transforms (everyday) life, both for those on the move and for those who stay behind. The findings of my own research, for example, show in which ways widespread imaginaries and personal aspirations about boundary-crossing human mobilities are interconnected but also contradicting each other (Salazar 2014a). Such insights invite us to critically question what it means to be (im)mobile, mobility rich, or mobility poor. In sum, an anthropology of mobility imaginaries reveals how local lifeworlds in global contexts are always negotiated, contested, and constantly under transformation.

Belonging and Becoming

> Circulez, mais ne vous éloignez pas trop!
> [Circulate, but do not stray too far.]
>
> —Franck Michel, *Routes: Éloge de l'Autonomadie*

> Home is the journey we make.
>
> —Ronald Talney, "Writing Portlandia"

> We leave to come back. The final point of each journey is, again, home, if not in the direct physical sense, then at least in the mental or symbolic sense …. Way back home is the last stage of a journey. Departure and arrival happen in the same place. Journey to the home is a circle.
>
> —Kaia Lehari, "The Road that Takes and Points"

The opening quote of this book referred to the fact that humans have always been mobile (Goytisolo 2004: 1). At the same time, people are and will remain social animals. The momentous, boundary-crossing mobilities I have discussed in the context of education, work, or "lifestyle" nicely illustrate how the act of returning is always implied (at least initially) in the act of leaving. People feel the need to belong to a social group. The appeal of the idea of return is nurtured in contemporary societies by a strong feeling that human beings have "roots" and that these conflate with culture and territory (Malkki 1995). However, as noted in chapter 1, the process of return is more complex than the simple act of going back. As Alfred Schutz (1945) pointed out a long time ago, to the homecomer, "home" shows an unaccustomed face, at least in the beginning. This is often accompanied by feelings of nostalgia for a (past) home/world that has been lost. Moreover, the homecomer witnesses an unexpected sense of isolation when he or she finds that those at home have only stereotyped views of the experience abroad. Home itself, then, is no longer "home" but has become uncharted territory (Blunt and Dowling 2006).

Spending time away "elsewhere" can provide people with an opportunity to see "home" from multiple angles. This can result in a changed meaning of home (see figure 7.1). The concept develops and extends. Contrary to what many think, belonging "almost always involve(s) diverse forms of mobility," so that people dwell "in and through being at home and away, through the dialectic of roots and routes" (Urry 2000: 132–33). Translocal mobility itself can be conceived as a form of return (Sinatti 2011). Therefore, we need to "develop a new conceptual understanding of the interplay between mobility and belonging" (Papastergiadis 2010: 354). For one, research on human mobility shows how people can make, imagine, or remember their "home" in this world in one place, in multiple places, or while being on the move. Home, then, does not contradict mobility, for it refers to people's ability to make themselves feel "at home" in different places, with different people (Rapport and Dawson 1998).

Another phenomenon that blurs commonly used categories is that of "lifestyle travelers" who are seeking regular relocation to new places to promote some kind of identity transformation (S. Cohen 2011). Multiple selves can be explored and tested, and multiple "homes" established along the way (S. Cohen, Duncan, and Thulemark 2013). Amy Goldmacher (2008) draws on and expands on the concept of "located mobility," capturing the meaning of obligation and belonging to more than one place at the same time, attempting to demonstrate presence in both. This fluid form of agency and social belonging has reignited social and political

Figure 7.1: Feeling at "home" while on the move. A man carrying a home for pigeons, somewhere on the road around Blantyre, Malawi. (Photographer: Noel B. Salazar)

debates on "cosmopolitanism," the idea of belonging to a global community (Acharya 2016; Salazar 2015).

The mobility experience many people aim for is less about regularly moving back and forth between "home" and "elsewhere," but encompasses a broader understanding of movement, which includes a variety of locations that emerge and/or are abandoned organically in an individual's trajectory (Baas 2010). Therefore, a semiotic analysis of mobility seems in place, a nonbinary inquiry into the meanings of home, of being away, and the consequences certain articulations of home, mobility, and the wider world might have for the constructions of self and place (Teampău and Van Assche 2009). Or, in the words of Tim Ingold (2011: 12), "We need a different understanding of movement: … not the *trans-port* (carrying across) of completed being, but the *pro-duction* (bringing forth) of perpetual becoming."

The Road Less Traveled

The journey, not the arrival, matters; the voyage, not the landing.

—Paul Theroux, *The Old Patagonian Express*

A more general understanding of mobility is not only missing in public debates, but has been a lacuna in the social sciences. What is mobility—a state, a force, a set of shifting co-ordinates? How does the definition of mobility shape social attitudes and personal experiences?

—Nikos Papastergiadis, "Wars of Mobility"

People are on the move in multiple directions. There is no single model or grand theory that can explain the complexity of human mobility, certainly not on a global scale. In this book, I have focused particularly on people who journey "elsewhere" (usually abroad) in the hope of attaining something—call it a contemporary way of "questing." As Mark Neumann (1992: 178) points out, this type of travel is often related to a search for (cultural) identity:

As people assign meaning and significance to their travel experiences, they reveal how culture and identity become incorporated through travel, the kinds of selves people find and lose when away from home, how identities are made as people confront others, and the peculiar and paradoxical ways that everyday life reappears as people seek to escape in their journeys.

Somehow, this all goes back to the widely shared idea that by undertaking a journey that involves a profound engagement with unfamiliar places and peoples, a person may experience a degree of disruption to their subjective orientation to the world (worldview or inner consciousness), sufficient to engender "transformative learning" (Morgan 2010). This explains the widespread role of travel (and displacement) in age-old rites of passage and transition in many cultures. The assumed association between travel and transformation, apart from being a metaphorical one with spatial or geographical metaphors, is embedded in the etymology of the word "travel" (from "travail," see chapter 6).[1] Those who suffer travail are believed to undergo a transformation and metamorphosis during their journeys, gaining new insights and reaching self-understanding. However, the examples discussed in this book also show that, in many cases, the social recognition or cultural capital accumulated through momentous mobilities can be of greater importance than the promise (whether realized of unfulfilled) to return personally enriched or transformed.

As a "cultural practice," translocal mobilities are an act of exploration, research, escape, transformation, and encountering the Other, through which a person hopes to reach a cultural perception and self-recognition. In other words, the types of mobility described in this book are strongly believed to be central to the development of subjectivity and identity, be it in the context of education, work, or lifestyle. As such, they remain promoted socially as possible agents of change (although, as we have seen, not universally). Not surprisingly, some have started confusing mobility itself as a goal to be achieved instead of a means to obtain some economic, social, or cultural "gain" (e.g., symbolic capital). Future research should determine to which extent the patterns and practices described here are found in other places and contexts.

Another issue that requires our future attention and research is the environmental impact of human mobility. This impact is becoming continuously greater because of the number and frequency of human movements across the planet and because of the (polluting) means of transport used. An important part of the sustainability debate has been rooted in the assumption that environmental problems cannot be solved by relying only on technology but must imply changes in present-day lifestyle, including "slowing down." The idea of "slow travel," then, is about finding the right speed with which to move, in a way that values quality over quantity, long-term benefits over short-term gains, and wellbeing of the many over the few. However, this is a mere luxury approach limited to those with the requisite time and resources. In general, the whole (environmental) sustainability argument seems to have very limited impact on how most people imagine, experience, and value translocal mobilities. The fact that the theme of sustainability hardly came up in the many talks I had for this book confirms this. This is a huge challenge, one that will only grow in the near future.

Related to sustainability and the means of travel used is the distinction between people who are "moving" (self-powered motion) or "being moved" (e.g., by an engine-driven transportation system). Very few scholars in mobility studies have paid attention to the sensuous body-in-motion and to what mobility (and everything associated with it) does to the human body. This is another topic that warrants more future research. Some of the issues discussed in chapter 6 already hint at the importance of this. Moving, and thinking with and through movement, is foundational to being a body that is alive—that is, a dynamically embodied person. Anthropology has largely succeeded in decentering the normative subject from theoretical assumptions, but we still have much work to do to capture the intersubjective experiences and modes of mobile embodiment that remain.

In sum, *Momentous Mobilities* constitutes just one small step on a long road toward disentangling how people imagine, experience, and value travels to an "elsewhere." In many cultures and societies, these travels form an essential part of the ongoing quest of becoming fully human. Therefore, we need to study them, anthropologically and otherwise.

NOTE

1. The term "motion" is etymologically linked with "emotion." Movement expresses emotion, and during spatial mobility people are in the presence of an emotion linked to the fact of moving in space. People are *moved* by movement: emotional processes shape mobilities, and vice versa (Svasek 2012). At the same time, the importance of the physical motion involved in the mobilities discussed in this book (except for the examples discussed in chapter 6) often remain at the metaphorical level.

References

Abelmann, Nancy, Nicole Newendorp, and Sangsook Lee-Chung. 2014. "East Asia's Astronaut and Geese Families: Hong Kong and South Korean Cosmopolitanisms." *Critical Asian Studies* 46(2): 259–86.

Abram, Simone, Bela Feldman-Bianco, Shahram Khosravi, Noel Salazar, and Nicholas de Genova. 2017. "The Free Movement of People around the World Would Be Utopian." *Identities: Global Studies in Culture and Power* 24(2): 123–55.

Acharya, Malasree Neepa. 2016. "Cosmopolitanism." In *Keywords of Mobility: Critical Engagements*, ed. Noel B. Salazar and Kiran Jayaram, 33–54. Oxford: Berghahn.

Ackers, Louise. 2008. "Internationalisation, Mobility and Metrics: A New Form of Indirect Discrimination?" *Minerva* 46: 411–35.

Adey, Peter. 2010. *Mobility*. London: Routledge.

Adey, Peter, David Bissell, Kevin Hannam, Peter Merriman, and Mimi Sheller, eds. 2013. *The Routledge Handbook of Mobilities*. London: Routledge.

Adler, Judith. 1985. "Youth on the Road: Reflections on the History of Tramping." *Annals of Tourism Research* 12(3): 335–54.

Aínsa, Fernando. 1986. "From the Golden Age to El Dorado: Metamorphosis of a Myth." *Diogenes* 34(133): 20–46.

Ali, Mariam M. 1996. "Ethnic Hinterland: Contested Spaces between Nations and Ethnicities in the Lives of Baweanese Labor Migrants." Ph.D. Dissertation. Cambridge, MA: Harvard University.

Allende, Isabel. 2003. *My Invented Country: A Nostalgic Journey through Chile*, trans. Margaret S. Peden. New York: HarperCollins.

Amit, Vered, ed. 2007. *Going First Class? New Approaches to Privileged Travel and Movement*. Oxford: Berghahn.

Andersson, Ruben. 2014. *Illegality, Inc.: Clandestine Migration and the Business of Bordering Europe*. Oakland, CA: University of California Press.

Andresen, Maike, Akram Al Ariss, and Matthias Walther, eds. 2013. *Self-Initiated Expatriation: Individual, Organizational, and National Perspectives*. New York: Routledge.

Appadurai, Arjun. 1996. *Modernity at Large: Cultural Dimensions of Globalization*. Minneapolis, MN: University of Minnesota Press.

Arellano, Alexandra. 2007. "Religion, Pilgrimage, Mobility and Immobility." In *Religious Tourism and Pilgrimage Festivals Management: An International Perspective*, ed. Razaq Raj and Nigel D. Morpeth, 89–97. Wallingford: CABI.

Århem, Kaj. 1985. *Pastoral Man in the Garden of Eden: The Maasai of the Ngorongoro Conservation Area, Tanzania*. Uppsala: University of Uppsala.

Arthur, Michael B., and Denise M. Rousseau, eds. 1996. *The Boundaryless Career: A New Employment Principle for a New Organizational Era.* New York: Oxford University Press.

Augé, Marc. 1995. *Non-Places: Introduction to an Anthropology of Supermodernity*, trans. John Howe. London: Verso.

Baas, Michiel. 2010. *Imagined Mobility: Migration and Transnationalism among Indian Students in Australia.* New York: Anthem Press.

Baeza, Cecilia. 2010. "Des Exilés aux Globe-Trotters: La Redéfinition du Statut de L'expatrié dans la Transition Démocratique Chilienne (1990-2006)." In *Loin Des Yeux, PrèS Du Coeur: Les ÉTats Et Leurs ExpatriéS*, ed. Stéphane Dufoix, Carine Guerassimoff, and Anne de Tinguy, 285–304. Paris: Presses de la Fondation Nationale des Sciences Politiques.

Baeza, Manuel Antonio. 2008. *Mundo Real, Mundo Imaginario Social: Teoría Y Práctica De Sociología Profunda.* Santiago: RIL Editores.

Bagnoli, Anna. 2009. "On 'an Introspective Journey': Identities and Travel in Young People's Lives." *European Societies* 11(3): 325–45.

Baker, Beth. 2016. "Regime." In *Keywords of Mobility: Critical Engagements*, ed. Noel B. Salazar and Kiran Jayaram, 152–70. Oxford: Berghahn.

Banai, Moshe, and Wes Harry. 2004. "Boundaryless Global Careers: The International Itinerants." *International Studies of Management & Organization* 34(3): 96–120.

Barber, Richard W. 1991. *Pilgrimages.* Woodbridge: Boydell Press.

Barendregt, Bart. 2002. "The Sound of 'Longing for Home': Redefining a Sense of Community through Minang Popular Music." *Bijdragen tot de Taal- Land- en Volkenkunde* 158(3): 411–50.

———. 2008. "Sex, Cannibals, and the Language of Cool: Indonesian Tales of the Phone and Modernity." *Information Society* 24(3): 160–70.

Barfield, Thomas J. 1993. *The Nomadic Alternative.* Englewood Cliffs, NJ: Prentice Hall.

Barker, Joshua, and Johan Lindquist. 2009. "Figures of Indonesian Modernity." *Indonesia* 87: 35–72.

Barth, Fredrik. 1969. *Ethnic Groups and Boundaries: The Social Organization of Culture Difference.* Boston, MA: Little Brown.

Bauman, Zygmunt. 1998. *Globalization: The Human Consequences.* New York: Columbia University Press.

———. 2000. *Liquid Modernity.* Cambridge: Polity Press.

———. 2007. *Liquid Times: Living in an Age of Uncertainty.* Cambridge: Polity Press.

Beaverstock, Jonathan V. 2005. "Transnational Elites in the City: British Highly-Skilled Inter-Company Transferees in New York City's Financial District." *Journal of Ethnic and Migration Studies* 31(2): 245–68.

Beck, Ulrich. 2000. *What Is Globalization?* Cambridge: Polity Press.

Beckstead, Zachary. 2010. "Liminality in Acculturation and Pilgrimage: When Movement Becomes Meaningful." *Culture & Psychology* 16(3): 383–93.

Bedford, Richard. 1973. *New Hebridean Mobility: A Study of Circular Migration.* Canberra: Australian National University.

Bell, Martin, and Gary Ward. 2000. "Comparing Temporary Mobility with Permanent Migration." *Tourism Geographies* 2(1): 87–107.

Benhabib, Seyla, and Judith Resnik, eds. 2009. *Migrations and Mobilities: Citizenship, Borders, and Gender.* New York: New York University Press.

Benjamin, Walter. 1999. *The Arcades Project.* Cambridge, MA: Belknap Press.

Benson, Michaela, and Karen O'Reilly, eds. 2009. *Lifestyle Migration: Expectations, Aspirations and Experiences.* Farnham: Ashgate.

Bergmann, Sigurd, and Tore Sager, eds. 2008. *The Ethics of Mobilities: Rethinking Place, Exclusion, Freedom and Environment.* Aldershot: Ashgate.

Bernard, H. Russell. 2006. *Research Methods in Anthropology: Qualitative and Quantitative Approaches.* 4th ed. Lanham, MD: AltaMira.

Birkeland, Inger J. 2005. *Making Place, Making Self: Travel, Subjectivity, and Sexual Difference.* Aldershot: Ashgate.

Blunt, Alison, and Robyn M. Dowling. 2006. *Home.* New York: Routledge.

Bogue, Ronald. 2004. "Apology for Nomadology." *Interventions: International Journal of Postcolonial Studies* 6(2): 169–79.

Bonnemaison, Joël. 1984. "The Tree and the Canoe: Roots and Mobility in Vanuatu Societies." *Pacific Viewpoint* 25(2): 117–51.

Böröcz, József. 1992. "Travel-Capitalism: The Structure of Europe and the Advent of the Tourist." *Comparative Studies in Society and History* 34(4): 708–41.

Bourdieu, Pierre. 1984. *Distinction: A Social Critique of the Judgement of Taste*, trans. Richard Nice. Cambridge, MA: Harvard University Press.

———. 1986. "The Forms of Capital." In *Handbook of Theory and Research for the Sociology of Education*, ed. John G. Richardson, 241–58. Westport, CT: Greenwood Press.

———. 1988. *Homo Academicus.* Cambridge: Polity Press.

Braidotti, Rosi. 1994. *Nomadic Subjects: Embodiment and Sexual Difference in Contemporary Feminist Theory.* New York: Columbia University Press.

Briggs, Charles L. 2013. "Contested Mobilities: On the Politics and Ethnopoetics of Circulation." *Journal of Folklore Research* 50(1–3): 285–99.

Brodersen, Meike. 2014. "Mobility: Ideological Discourse and Individual Narratives." In *Globalisierung, Bildung und Grenzüberschreitende Mobilität*, ed. Jürgen Gerhards, Silke Hans, and Sören Carlson, 93–108. Wiesbaden: Springer.

Brubaker, Rogers. 2010. "Migration, Membership, and the Modern Nation-State: Internal and External Dimensions of the Politics of Belonging." *Journal of Interdisciplinary History* 41(1): 61–78.

Bruner, Edward M. 1991. "Transformation of Self in Tourism." *Annals of Tourism Research* 18(2): 238–50.

———. 2002. "The Representation of African Pastoralists: A Commentary." *Visual Anthropology* 15(3): 387–92.

Bude, Heinz, and Jörg Dürrschmidt. 2010. "What's Wrong with Globalization? Contra 'Flow Speak'—Towards an Existential Turn in the Theory of Globalization." *European Journal of Social Theory* 13(4): 481–500.

Burawoy, Michael, ed. 2000. *Global Ethnography: Forces, Connections, and Imaginations in a Postmodern World.* Berkeley, CA: University of California Press.

Büscher, Monika. 2014. "Nomadic Work: Romance and Reality." *Computer Supported Cooperative Work* 24(2): 223–38.

Büscher, Monika, John Urry, and Katian Witchger, eds. 2011. *Mobile Methods*. London: Routledge.

Canihuante, Gabriel. 2006. *Turismo En Chile: Paisajes Y Culturas Del Pasado, Presente Y Futuro*. La Serena: Fondo Editorial.

Cano, Verónica, and Magdalena Soffia. 2009. "Los Estudios sobre Migración Internacional en Chile: Apuntes y Comentarios para Una Agenda de Investigación Actualizada." *Papeles de Población* 15(61): 129–67.

Canzler, Weert, Vincent Kaufmann, and Sven Kesselring, eds. 2008. *Tracing Mobilities: Towards a Cosmopolitan Perspective*. Aldershot: Ashgate.

Cartus. 2012. *Global Mobility Policy & Practices Survey: 2012 Trends in Global Relocation*. Danbury, CT: Cartus.

Casimir, Michael J., and Aparna Rao, eds. 1992. *Mobility and Territoriality: Social and Spatial Boundaries among Foragers, Fishers, Pastoralists, and Peripatetics*. New York: Berg.

Cass, Noel, Elizaebeth Shove, and John Urry. 2005. "Social Exclusion, Mobility and Access." *Sociological Review* 53(3): 539–55.

Castells, Manuel. 2000. *The Rise of the Network Society*. 2nd ed. Oxford: Blackwell.

———. 2004. *The Power of Identity*. 2nd ed. Malden, MA: Blackwell.

Castillo Sandoval, Roberto. 2005. "Nostalgia de la Buena (Nostalgia de Futuro)," Noticias Secretas blog, 8 November 2005. Accessed 28 February 2018, http://noticiassecretas.blogspot.be/2005/11/nostalgia-de-la-buena-nostalgia-de.html.

———. 2008. "El 'Negrito de Harvard'," Noticias Secretas blog, 4 June 2008. Accessed 28 February 2018, http://noticiassecretas.blogspot.be/2008/06/el-negri-to-de-harvard.html.

Castles, Stephen. 2006. "Back to the Future? Can Europe Meet Its Labour Needs through Temporary Migration?" IMI Working Paper. Oxford: International Migration Institute.

Castoriadis, Cornelius. 1987. *The Imaginary Institution of Society*, trans. Kathleen Blamey. Cambridge, MA: MIT Press.

Céline, Louis-Ferdinand. 1934. *Journey to the End of the Night*, trans. John H.P. Marks. Boston, MA: Little, Brown.

Cerdin, Jean-Luc, and Jan Selmer. 2014. "Who Is a Self-Initiated Expatriate? Towards Conceptual Clarity of a Common Notion." *International Journal of Human Resource Management* 25(9): 1281–301.

Chapman, Murray, and R. Mansell Prothero, eds. 1985. *Circulation in Population Movement: Substance and Concepts from the Melanesian Case*. London: Routledge.

Chou, Cynthia. 2003. *Indonesian Sea Nomads: Money, Magic, and Fear of the Orang Suku Laut*. London: RoutledgeCurzon.

Chu, Julie Y. 2010. *Cosmologies of Credit: Transnational Mobility and the Politics of Destination in China*. Durham, NC: Duke University Press.

Clifford, James. 1997. *Routes: Travel and Translation in the Late Twentieth Century*. Cambridge, MA: Harvard University Press.

Coast, Ernestina. 2000. "Maasai Demography." Ph.D. dissertation. London: University College London.

_____. 2002. "Maasai Socioeconomic Conditions: A Cross-Border Comparison." *Human Ecology* 30(1): 79–105.

Cohen, Erik. 1977. "Expatriate Communities." *Current Sociology* 24(3): 5–90.

_____. 1979. "A Phenomenology of Tourist Experiences." *Sociology* 13(2): 179–201.

Cohen, Jeffrey H. 2004. *The Culture of Migration in Southern Mexico.* Austin, TX: University of Texas Press.

Cohen, Scott A. 2011. "Lifestyle Travellers: Backpacking as a Way of Life." *Annals of Tourism Research* 38(4): 1535–55.

Cohen, Scott A., Tara Duncan, and Maria Thulemark. 2013. "Lifestyle Mobilities: The Crossroads of Travel, Leisure and Migration." *Mobilities* 10(1): 155–72.

Cohen, Scott A., and Stefan Gössling. 2015. "A Darker Side of Hypermobility." *Environment and Planning A* 47(8): 1661–79.

Coleman, Simon, and John Eade, eds. 2004. *Reframing Pilgrimage: Cultures in Motion.* London: Routledge.

Coleman, Simon, and John Elsner. 1995. *Pilgrimage: Past and Present in the World Religions.* Cambridge, MA: Harvard University Press.

Coles, Tim Edward, and Dallen J. Timothy, eds. 2004. *Tourism, Diasporas, and Space.* London: Routledge.

Colic-Peisker, Val. 2010. "Free Floating in the Cosmopolis? Exploring the Identity-Belonging of Transnational Knowledge Workers." *Global Networks* 10(4): 467–88.

Collier, Simon, and William F. Sater. 2004. *A History of Chile, 1808–2002.* 2nd ed. Cambridge: Cambridge University Press.

Connell, John. 2008. "Niue: Embracing a Culture of Migration." *Journal of Ethnic and Migration Studies* 34(6): 1021–40.

Contardo, Óscar. 2008. *Siútico: Arribismo, Abajismo Y Vida Social En Chile.* Santiago: Vergara.

Corbett, Michael. 2004. "'It Was Fine, If You Wanted to Leave': Educational Ambivalence in a Nova Scotian Coastal Community 1963–1998." *Anthropology and Education Quarterly* 35(4): 451–71.

Council of the European Union. 2009. *Council Conclusions of 12 May 2009 on a Strategic Framework for European Cooperation in Education and Training ('Et 2020') [2009/C 119/02].* Brussels: Council of the European Union.

Cousineau, Phil. 1998. *The Art of Pilgrimage: The Seeker's Guide to Making Travel Sacred.* Berkeley, CA: Conari Press.

Cresswell, Tim. 1997. "Imagining the Nomad: Mobility and the Postmodern Primitive." In *Space and Social Theory: Interpreting Modernity and Postmodernity*, ed. Georges Benko and Ulf Strohmayer, 360–79. Oxford: Blackwell.

_____. 2006. *On the Move: Mobility in the Modern Western World.* London: Routledge.

Csedő, Krisztina, 2008. "Negotiating Skills in the Global City: Hungarian and Romanian Professionals and Graduates in London." *Journal of Ethnic and Migration Studies* 34(5): 803–23.

Cunningham, Hilary, and Josiah Heyman. 2004. "Introduction: Mobilities and Enclosures at Borders." *Identities: Global Studies in Culture and Power* 11(3): 289–302.

D'Andrea, Anthony. 2007. *Global Nomads: Techno and New Age as Transnational Countercultures in Ibiza and Goa*. London: Routledge.

Dante, Alighieri. 1990. *Il Convivio (The Banquet)*, trans. Richard H. Lansing. New York: Garland.

Dauvergne, Catherine, and Sarah Marsden. 2014. "The Ideology of Temporary Labour Migration in the Post-Global Era." *Citizenship Studies* 18(2): 224–42.

Davidsson Bremborg, Anna. 2013. "Creating Sacred Space by Walking in Silence: Pilgrimage in a Late Modern Lutheran Context." *Social Compass* 60(4): 544–60.

Dawney, Leila. 2014. "Temporality, Technologies and Techniques of the Self: Long-Distance Walking as Secular Pilgrimage." In *Travel and Transformation*, ed. Garth Lean, Russell Staiff, and Emma Waterton, 125–37. Farnham: Ashgate.

Dayton-Johnson, Jeff, et al. 2007. *Gaining from Migration: Towards a New Mobility System*. Paris: OECD Development Centre.

de Bruijn, Mirjam, Rijk van Dijk, and Dick Foeken, eds. 2001. *Mobile Africa: Changing Patterns of Movement in Africa and Beyond*. Leiden: Brill.

De Moor, Bart, and Piet Henderikx. 2013. "International Curricula and Student Mobility." LERU Advice Paper No. 12. Leuven: League of European Research Universities.

de Ridder-Symoens, Hilde. 1992. "Mobility." In *A History of the University in Europe: Universities in the Middle Ages*, Hilde de Ridder-Symoens, 280–304. Cambridge: Cambridge University Press.

_____. 1996. "Mobility." In *A History of the University in Europe: Universities in Early Modern Europe (1500–1800)*, ed. Hilde de Ridder-Symoens, 416–8l. Cambridge: Cambridge University Press.

Dean, Bartholomew. 2016. "Freedom." In *Keywords of Mobility: Critical Engagements*, ed. Noel B. Salazar and Kiran Jayaram, 55–72. Oxford: Berghahn.

del Pozo Artigas, José, ed. 2006. *Exiliados, Emigrados, Retornados: Chilenos En América Y Europa, 1973–2004*. Santiago: RIL Editores.

Deleuze, Gilles, and Félix Guattari. 1986. *Nomadology: The War Machine*, trans. Brian Massumi. New York: Semiotext(e).

Dickinson, Janet, and Les Lumsdon. 2010. *Slow Travel and Tourism*. London: Earthscan.

DICOEX. 2005. *Chilenos En El Exterior: Donde Viven, Cuántos Son Y Qué Hacen Los Chilenos En El Exterior*. Santiago: Ministerio de Relaciones Exteriores, Dirección para la Comunidad de Chilenos en el Exterior.

Doherty, Noeleen, and Michael Dickmann. 2009. "Exposing the Symbolic Capital of International Assignments." *International Journal of Human Resource Management* 20(2): 301–20.

Donaghey, Jimmy, and Paul Teague. 2006. "The Free Movement of Workers and Social Europe: Maintaining the European Ideal." *Industrial Relations Journal* 37(6): 652–66.

Dorfman, Ariel. 1999. *The Nanny and the Iceberg*. New York: Farrar, Straus, Giroux.

_____. 2011. *Feeding on Dreams: Confessions of an Unrepentant Exile*. Boston: Houghton Mifflin Harcourt.

Duany, Jorge. 2002. "Mobile Livelihoods: The Sociocultural Practices of Circular Migrants between Puerto Rico and the United States." *International Migration Review* 36(2): 355–88.

Dubow, Jessica. 2004. "The Mobility of Thought: Reflections on Blanchot and Benjamin." *Interventions: International Journal of Postcolonial Studies* 6(2): 216–28.

Easthope, Hazel. 2009. "Fixed Identities in a Mobile World? The Relationship between Mobility, Place, and Identity." *Identities: Global Studies in Culture and Power* 16(1): 61–82.

EC. 2001. *New European Labour Markets, Open to All, with Access for All*. Brussels: European Commission.

———. 2006. *Europeans on the Move: Portraits of 31 Mobile Workers*. Luxembourg: Office for Official Publications of the European Communities.

Eickelman, Dale F., and James P. Piscatori, eds. 1990. *Muslim Travellers: Pilgrimage, Migration, and the Religious Imagination*. Berkeley, CA: University of California Press.

Elliot, Alice. 2016. "Gender." In *Keywords of Mobility: Critical Engagements*, ed. Noel B. Salazar and Kiran Jayaram, 73–92. Oxford: Berghahn.

Elliot, Alice, Roger Norum, and Noel B. Salazar, eds. 2017. *Methodologies of Mobility: Ethnography and Experiment*. Oxford: Berghahn.

Elliott, Anthony, and John Urry. 2010. *Mobile Lives*. London: Routledge.

Elmhirst, Rebecca. 2007. "Tigers and Gangsters: Masculinities and Feminised Migration in Indonesia." *Population, Space and Place* 13(3): 225–38.

Engebrigtsen, Ada Ingrid. 2017. "Key Figure of Mobility: The Nomad." *Social Anthropology* 25(1): 42–54.

Escaffit, Jean-Claude, and Moïz Rasiwala. 2008. *Histoire De Taizé*. Paris: Éditions du Seuil.

Euben, Roxanne Leslie. 2006. *Journeys to the Other Shore: Muslim and Western Travelers in Search of Knowledge*. Princeton, NJ: Princeton University Press.

Eurobarometer. 2011. *Flash Eurobarometer 319b: Youth on the Move*. Budapest: The Gallup Organization.

European Commission. 2014. *The Erasmus Impact Study: Effects of Mobility on the Skills and Employability of Students and the Internationalisation of Higher Education Institutions*. Luxembourg: Publications Office of the European Union.

European Migration Network. 2011. *Temporary and Circular Migration: Empirical Evidence, Current Policy Practice and Future Options in Eu Member States*. Luxembourg: Publications Office of the European Union.

———. 2012. *Asylum and Migration Glossary 2.0*. Luxembourg: Publications Office of the European Union.

European Parliament. 2010. *Improving the Participation in the Erasmus Programme*. Brussels: European Parliament.

Eurostat. 2013. *Key Figures on Europe: 2013*. Luxembourg: Eurostat.

Evans, Gareth. 2009. *Merantau*. Jakarta: Pt. Merantau Films.

Ezra, Elizabeth, and Antonio Sánchez. 2005. "L'auberge Espagnole (2002): Transnational Departure or Domestic Crash Landing?" *Studies in European Cinema* 2(2): 137–48.

Faist, Thomas. 2013. "The Mobility Turn: A New Paradigm for the Social Sciences?" *Ethnic and Racial Studies* 36(11): 1637–46.

_____. 2014. "On the Transnational Social Question: How Social Inequalities Are Reproduced in Europe." *Journal of European Social Policy* 24(3): 207–22.

Favell, Adrian. 2008. *Eurostars and Eurocities: Free Movement and Mobility in an Integrating Europe.* Malden, MA: Blackwell.

_____. 2009. "Immigration, Migration and Free Movement in the Making of Europe." In *European Identity*, ed. Jeffrey C. Checkel and Peter J. Katzenstein, 167–89. Cambridge: Cambridge University Press.

Favell, Adrian, Miriam Feldblum, and Michael P. Smith. 2007. "The Human Face of Global Mobility: A Research Agenda." *Social Science and Modern Society* 44(2): 15-25.

Favell, Adrian, and Ettore Recchi. 2011. "Social Mobility and Spatial Mobility." In *Sociology of the European Union*, ed. Adrian Favell and Virginie Guiraudon, 50–75. Basingstoke: Palgrave Macmillan.

Fechter, Anne-Meike, and Katie Walsh. 2010. "Examining 'Expatriate' Continuities: Postcolonial Approaches to Mobile Professionals." *Journal of Ethnic and Migration Studies* 36(8): 1197–210.

Feldman, Gregory. 2012. *The Migration Apparatus: Security, Labor, and Policymaking in the European Union.* Stanford, CA: Stanford University Press.

Fernandez-Gimenez, Maria E., and Sonya Le Febre. 2006. "Mobility in Pastoral Systems: Dynamic Flux or Downward Trend?" *International Journal of Sustainable Development & World Ecology* 13(5): 341–62.

Fernández Herrero, Beatriz. 1994. "América, La Utopía Europea Del Renacimiento." *Cuadernos Hispanoamericanos* 529/530: 103–14.

Findlay, Alan M. 1988. "From Settlers to Skilled Transients: The Changing Structure of British International Migration." *Geoforum* 19(4): 401–10.

Ford, Michele, and Lenore Lyons. 2006. "The Borders Within: Mobility and Enclosure in the Riau Islands." *Asia Pacific Viewpoint* 47(2): 257–71.

Forshee, Jill. 2000. *Between the Folds: Stories of Cloth, Lives, and Travels from Sumba.* Honolulu, HI: University of Hawaii Press.

_____. 2006. *Culture and Customs of Indonesia.* Westport, CT: Greenwood Press.

Frändberg, Lotta. 2006. "International Mobility Biographies: A Means to Capture the Institutionalisation of Long-Distance Travel?" *Current Issues in Tourism* 9(4–5): 320–34.

Franz, Carlos. 2000. "Ainogatap, La Anti-Utopía, O El Fin Del Mundo Al Revés." *Quehacer* 124(May–June): 52–58.

Frello, Birgitta. 2008. "Towards a Discursive Analytics of Movement: On the Making and Unmaking of Movement as an Object of Knowledge." *Mobilities* 3(1): 25–50.

Frey, Nancy L. 1998. *Pilgrim Stories: On and Off the Road to Santiago.* Berkeley, CA: University of California Press.

_____. 2004. "Stories of the Return: Pilgrimage and Its Aftermaths." In *Intersecting Journeys: The Anthropology of Pilgrimage and Tourism*, ed. Ellen Badone and Sharon R. Roseman, 89–109. Urbana, IL: University of Illinois Press.

Friedman, Jonathan. 2002. "From Roots to Routes: Tropes for Trippers." *Anthropological Theory* 2(1): 21–36.

Fumerton, Patricia. 2006. *Unsettled: The Culture of Mobility and the Working Poor in Early Modern England*. Chicago, IL: University of Chicago Press.

Galani-Moutafi, Vasiliki. 2000. "The Self and the Other: Traveler, Ethnographer, Tourist." *Annals of Tourism Research* 27(1): 203–24.

Galaty, John G. 2002. "How Visual Figures Speak: Narrative Inventions of "the Pastoralist" in East Africa." *Visual Anthropology* 15(3–4): 347–67.

Gallez, Caroline, and Vincent Kaufmann. 2015. "Aux Racines de la Mobilité en Sciences Sociales." In *De L'histoire Des Transports À L'histoire De La Mobilité*, ed. Mathieu Flonneau and Vincent Guigueno, 51–55. Rennes: Presses Universitaires de Rennes.

García-Huidobro Mac Auliffe, Cecilia. 2008. *Tics De Los Chilenos: Vicios Y Virtudes Nacionales Según Nuestros Grandes Cronistas*. Santiago: Catalonia.

Garlinghouse, Meg, and Alison Dorsey. 2015. "The Power and Unrealized Promise of Skilled Volunteering." In *Volunteer Engagement 2.0: Ideas and Insights Changing the World*, ed. Robert J. Rosenthal, 197–209. Hoboken, NJ: Wiley.

GCIM. 2005. *Migration in an Interconnected World: New Directions for Action* Geneva: Global Commission on International Migration.

General Assembly. 2006. *International Migration and Development: Report of the Secretary General*. New York: UN General Assembly.

Germond-Duret, Celine. 2016. "Tradition and Modernity: An Obsolete Dichotomy? Binary Thinking, Indigenous Peoples and Normalisation." *Third World Quarterly* 37(9): 1537–58.

Geschiere, Peter. 2009. *The Perils of Belonging: Autochthony, Citizenship, and Exclusion in Africa and Europe*. Chicago, IL: University of Chicago Press.

Gherardi, Laura. 2011. "Human Costs of Mobility: On Management in Multinational Companies." In *The Politics of Proximity: Mobility and Immobility in Practice*, ed. Giuseppina Pellegrino, 105–19. Farnham: Ashgate.

Gill, Lesley. 2004. *The School of the Americas: Military Training and Political Violence in the Americas*. Durham, NC: Duke University Press.

Gingrich, Andre, and Richard G. Fox, eds. 2002. *Anthropology, by Comparison*. London: Routledge.

Glick Schiller, Nina. 2009. "A Global Perspective on Migration and Development." *Social Analysis* 53(3): 14–37.

Glick Schiller, Nina, and Noel B. Salazar. 2013a. "Regimes of Mobility across the Globe." *Journal of Ethnic and Migration Studies* 39(2): 183–200.

_____. eds. 2013b. *Regimes of Mobility: Imaginaries and Relationalities of Power*. Theme issue, *Journal of Ethnic and Migration Studies* 39(2).

Gluesing, Julia C., Tracy L. Meerwarth, and Brigitte Jordan. 2008. "Conclusion: Patterns of Mobile Work and Life." *NAPA Bulletin* 30: 148–55.

Goldmacher, Amy. 2008. "Located Mobility: Living and Working in Multiple Places." *NAPA Bulletin* 30: 118–27.

Goss, Jon, and Bruce Lindquist. 2000. "Placing Movers: An Overview of the Asian-Pacific Migration System." *The Contemporary Pacific* 12(2): 385–414.

Goytisolo, Juan. 2004. *Metafores de la Migracio/Metaphors of Migration*. Barcelona: Generalitat Catalunya.

Green, Nancy L. 2009. "Expatriation, Expatriates, and Expats: The American Transformation of a Concept." *American Historical Review* 114(2): 307–28.

Greenblatt, Stephen, ed. 2009. *Cultural Mobility: A Manifesto*. Cambridge: Cambridge University Press.

Hahn, Hans Peter, and Georg Klute, eds. 2007. *Cultures of Migration: African Perspectives*. Berlin: Lit.

Haines, David. 2012. "'More Aware of Everything': Exploring the Returnee Experience in American Higher Education." *Journal of Studies in International Education* 17(1): 19–38.

Hall, C. Michael. 2005. "Buddhism, Tourism and the Middle Way." In *Tourism, Religion, and Spiritual Journeys*, ed. Dallen J. Timothy and Daniel H. Olsen, 172–85. New York: Routledge.

Hall, C. Michael, and Allan M. Williams, eds. 2002. *Tourism and Migration: New Relationships between Production and Consumption*. Boston, MA: Kluwer.

Hamilton, Gary G. 1985. "Temporary Migration and the Institutionalization of Strategy." *International Journal of Intercultural Relations* 9(4): 405–25.

Hannam, Kevin, Mimi Sheller, and John Urry. 2006. "Editorial: Mobilities, Immobilities and Moorings." *Mobilities* 1(1): 1–22.

Hannerz, Ulf. 2002. "Where We Are and Who We Want to Be." In *The Postnational Self: Belonging and Identity*, ed. Ulf Hedetoft and Mette Hjort, 217–32. Minneapolis, MN: University of Minnesota Press.

Hardt, Michael, and Antonio Negri. 2000. *Empire*. Cambridge, MA: Harvard University Press.

Hartung, Paul J., and Linda Mezydlo Subich, eds. 2011. *Developing Self in Work and Career: Concepts, Cases, and Contexts*. Washington, DC: American Psychological Association.

Hau'ofa, Epeli. 2008. *We Are the Ocean. Selected Works*. Honolulu, HI: University of Hawaii Press.

Hausner, Sondra L. 2007. *Wandering with Sadhus: Ascetics in the Hindu Himalayas*. Bloomington, IN: Indiana University Press.

Herrero, Nieves. 2008. "Reaching Land's End: New Social Practices in the Pilgrimage to Santiago De Compostela." *International Journal of Iberian Studies* 21(2): 131–49.

Hew, Cheng Sim. 2003. *Women Workers, Migration and Family in Sarawak*. London: Routledge.

Heyman, Josiah McC., and Howard Campbell. 2009. "The Anthropology of Global Flows: A Critical Reading of Appadurai's 'Disjuncture and Difference in the Global Cultural Economy.'" *Anthropological Theory* 9(2): 131–48.

Hibbert, Christopher. 1969. *The Grand Tour*. New York: Putnam.

Hinde, Sidney L., and Hildegarde B. Hinde. 1901. *The Last of the Masai*. London: W. Heinemann.

Hodgson, Dorothy L. 2000. "Taking Stock: State Control, Ethnic Identity and Pastoralist Development in Tanganyika, 1948-1958." *Journal of African History* 41(1): 55-78.

_____. 2001. *Once Intrepid Warriors: Gender, Ethnicity, and the Cultural Politics of Maasai Development*. Bloomington, IN: Indiana University Press.

_____. 2011. *Being Maasai, Becoming Indigenous: Postcolonial Politics in a Neoliberal World*. Bloomington, IN: Indiana University Press.

Hoey, Brian A. 2003. "Nationalism in Indonesia: Building Imagined and Intentional Communities through Transmigration." *Ethnology* 42(2): 109-26.

Holdsworth, Clare. 2009. "'Going Away to Uni': Mobility, Modernity, and Independence of English Higher Education Students." *Environment and Planning A* 41(8): 1849-64.

Holmes, Seth M. 2013. *Fresh Fruit, Broken Bodies: Migrant Farmworkers in the United States*. Berkeley, CA: University of California Press.

Honoré, Carl. 2004. *In Praise of Slowness: How a Worldwide Movement Is Challenging the Cult of Speed*. San Francisco, CA: Harper.

Hughes, Lotte. 2006a. "'Beautiful Beasts' and Brave Warriors: The Longevity of a Maasai Stereotype." In *Ethnic Identity: Problems and Prospects for the Twenty-First Century*, ed. Lola Romanucci-Ross, George A. de Vos, and Takeyuki Tsuda, 246-94. Lanham, MD: Altamira.

_____. 2006b. *Moving the Maasai: A Colonial Misadventure*. Basingstoke: Palgrave Macmillan.

Hugo, Graeme J. 1982. "Circular Migration in Indonesia." *Population and Development Review* 8(1): 59-83.

_____. 2005. "The New International Migration in Asia: Challenges for Population Research." *Asian Population Studies* 1(1): 93-120.

Hui, Allison. 2016. "The Boundaries of Interdisciplinary Fields: Temporalities Shaping the Past and Future of Dialogue between Migration and Mobilities Research." *Mobilities* 11(1): 66-82.

Ibn Khaldūn. 1967. *The Muqaddimah: An Introduction to History*. 2nd ed., trans. Franz Rosenthal. Princeton, NJ: Princeton University Press.

Ingold, Tim. 2011. *Being Alive: Essays on Movement, Knowledge and Description*. London: Routledge.

Ingold, Tim, and Jo Lee Vergunst, eds. 2008. *Ways of Walking: Ethnography and Practice on Foot*. Aldershot: Ashgate.

Inkson, Kerr, Hugh Gunz, Shiv Ganesh, and Juliet Roper. 2012. "Boundaryless Careers: Bringing Back Boundaries." *Organization Studies* 33(3): 323-40.

Inkson, Kerr, and Barbara A. Myers. 2003. "'The Big Oe': Self-Directed Travel and Career Development." *Career Development International* 8(4): 170-81.

IOM. 2009. *Temporary and Circular Labour Migration: Experiences, Challenges and Opportunities*. Colombia: International Organization for Migration.

Iredale, Robyn. 2001. "The Migration of Professionals: Theories and Typologies." *International Migration* 39(5): 7-24.

Islam, Syed Manzurul. 1996. *The Ethics of Travel: From Marco Polo to Kafka*. Manchester: Manchester University Press.

Iyer, Pico. 2000. "Why We Travel," *Salon*, 18 March 2000. Accessed 28 February 2018, http://www.salon.com/2000/03/18/why/.

Jackson, Michael. 2008. "The Shock of the New: On Migrant Imaginaries and Critical Transitions." *Ethnos* 73(1): 57–72.

Jacobs, Alan H. 1965. "African Pastoralists: Some General Remarks." *Anthropological Quarterly* 38(3): 144–54.

James, Paul. 2005. "Global Enchantment: A Matrix of Ideologies." In *Global Matrix: Nationalism, Globalism and State-Terrorism*, ed. Tom Nairn and Paul James, 19–29. London: Pluto Press.

Jayaram, Kiran. 2016. "Capital." In *Keywords of Mobility: Critical Engagements*, ed. Noel B. Salazar and Kiran Jayaram, 13–32. Oxford: Berghahn.

Jedlicki, Fanny. 2001. "Les Exilés Chiliens Et L'affaire Pinochet: Retour Et Transmission De La Mémoire." *Cahiers de l'Urmis* 7(June): 33–51.

_____. 2007. "De L'exilé Héroïque À L'illégitimité Du Retornado: Les Retours Des Familles De Réfugiés Chiliens En France." *Anuario de Estudios Americanos* 64(1): 87–110.

Jones, Gill. 1999. "'The Same People in the Same Places'? Socio-Spatial Identities and Migration in Youth." *Sociology* 33(1): 1–22.

Jónsson, Gunvor. 2011. "Non-Migrant, Sedentary, Immobile, or 'Left Behind'? Reflections on the Absence of Migration." IMI Working Paper. Oxford: International Migration Institute.

Kabachnik, Peter. 2010. "England or Uruguay? The Persistence of Place and the Myth of the Placeless Gypsy." *Area* 42(2): 198–207.

_____. 2012. "Nomads and Mobile Places: Disentangling Place, Space and Mobility." *Identities: Global Studies in Culture and Power* 19(2): 210–28.

Kaplan, Caren. 1996. *Questions of Travel: Postmodern Discourses of Displacement*. Durham, NC: Duke University Press.

Kato, Tsuyoshi. 1982. *Matriliny and Migration: Evolving Minangkabau Traditions in Indonesia*. Ithaca, NY: Cornell University Press.

Kaufmann, Vincent. 2002. *Re-Thinking Mobility: Contemporary Sociology*. Aldershot: Ashgate.

Kaufmann, Vincent, Manfred M. Bergman, and Dominique Joye. 2004. "Motility: Mobility as Capital." *International Journal of Urban and Regional Research* 28(4): 745–56.

Kearney, Michael. 1986. "From the Invisible Hand to Visible Feet: Anthropological Studies of Migration and Development." *Annual Review of Anthropology* 15: 331–61.

Kedit, Peter M. 1993. *Iban Bejalai*. Kuala Lumpur: Ampang Press.

Kennedy, Paul. 2010. "Mobility, Flexible Lifestyles and Cosmopolitanism: EU Postgraduates in Manchester." *Journal of Ethnic and Migration Studies* 36(3): 465–82.

Khan, Nichola. 2016. "Immobility." In *Keywords of Mobility: Critical Engagements*, ed. Noel B. Salazar and Kiran Jayaram, 93–112. Oxford: Berghahn.

Khazanov, Anatoly M. 1994. *Nomads and the Outside World*. 2nd ed., trans. Julia Crookenden. Madison, WI: University of Wisconsin Press.

Khosravi, Shahram. 2010. *"Illegal" Traveller: An Auto-Ethnography of Borders*. Basingstoke: Palgrave Macmillan.

Killias, Olivia. 2010. "'Illegal' Migration as Resistance: Legality, Morality and Coercion in Indonesian Domestic Worker Migration to Malaysia." *Asian Journal of Social Science* 38(6): 897–914.

Kim, Terri. 2009. "Transnational Academic Mobility, Internationalization and Interculturality in Higher Education." *Intercultural Education* 20(5): 395–405.

King, Russell, and John Connell, eds. 1999. *Small Worlds, Global Lives: Islands and Migration*. London: Pinter.

Kirillova, Ksenia, Xinran Lehto, and Liping Cai. 2016. "Tourism and Existential Transformation: An Empirical Investigation." *Journal of Travel Research* 56(5): 638–50.

Kloppenburg, Sanneke, and Peter Peters. 2012. "Confined Mobilities: Following Indonesian Migrant Workers on Their Way Home." *Tijdschrift voor Economische en Sociale Geografie* 103(5): 530–41.

Knowles, Joan. 1993. "Power, Influence and the Political Process among Iloitai Maasai." Ph.D. dissertation. Durham, NC: Durham University.

Kottler, Jeffrey A. 1997. *Travel That Can Change Your Life: How to Create a Transformative Experience*. San Francisco, CA: Jossey-Bass.

Kuznetsov, Yevgeny, ed. 2006. *Diaspora Networks and the International Migration of Skills: How Countries Can Draw on Their Talent Abroad*. Washington, DC: World Bank.

LaBianca, Øystein S., and Sandra A. Scham, eds. 2004. *Connectivity in Antiquity: Globalization as a Long-Term Historical Process*. London: Equinox.

Ladner, Gerhart B. 1967. "Homo Viator: Mediaeval Ideas on Alienation and Order." *Speculum* 42(2): 233–59.

Larsen, Jonas, John Urry, and Kay Axhausen. 2006. *Mobilities, Networks, Geographies*. Aldershot: Ashgate.

Latour, Bruno. 2005. *Reassembling the Social: An Introduction to Actor-Network Theory*. Oxford: Oxford University Press.

Lean, Garth L. 2012. "Transformative Travel: A Mobilities Perspective." *Tourist Studies* 12(2): 151-72.

Lean, Garth, Russell Staiff, and Emma Waterton, eds. 2014. *Travel and Transformation*. Farnham: Ashgate.

Leed, Eric J. 1991. *The Mind of the Traveler: From Gilgamesh to Global Tourism*. New York: Basic Books.

Lehari, Kaia. 2000. "The Road That Takes and Points." In *Place and Location*, ed. Kaia Lehari and Virve Sarapik, 53–62. Tallinn: Estonian Academy of Arts.

Leinonen, Johanna. 2012. "'Money Is Not Everything and That's the Bottom Line': Family Ties in Transatlantic Elite Migrations." *Social Science History* 36(2): 243–68.

Leivestad, Hege Høyer. 2016. "Motility." In *Keywords of Mobility: Critical Engagements*, ed. Noel B. Salazar and Kiran Jayaram, 133–51. Oxford: Berghahn.

Lien, Marianne E., and Marit Melhuus, eds. 2007. *Holding Worlds Together: Ethnographies of Knowing and Belonging.* Oxford: Berghahn.

Lilischkis, Stefan. 2003. "More Yo-Yos, Pendulums and Nomads: Trends of Mobile and Multi-Location Work in the Information Society." STAR (Socio-economic Trends Assessment for the digital Revolution) Report No. 36. Databank, Milano.

Lindquist, Johan A. 2009. *The Anxieties of Mobility: Migration and Tourism in the Indonesian Borderlands.* Honolulu, HI: University of Hawaii Press.

Lindquist, Johan, Xiang Biao, and Brenda S. A. Yeoh. 2012. "Opening the Black Box of Migration: Brokers, the Organization of Transnational Mobility and the Changing Political Economy in Asia." *Pacific Affairs* 85(1): 7–19.

Lineton, Jacqueline. 1975. "Pasompe' Ugi': Bugis Migrants and Wanderers." *Archipel* 10(1): 173–201.

Liu-Farrer, Gracia. 2009. "Educationally Channeled International Labor Mobility: Contemporary Student Migration from China to Japan." *International Migration Review* 43(1): 178–204.

Liu, Xin. 1997. "Space, Mobility, and Flexibility: Chinese Villagers and Scholars Negotiate Power at Home and Abroad." In *Ungrounded Empires: The Cultural Politics of Modern Chinese Transnationalism*, ed. Aihwa Ong and Donald M. Nonini, 91–114. New York: Routledge.

Lowe, Celia. 2003. "The Magic of Place: Sama at Sea and on Land in Sulawesi, Indonesia." *Bijdragen tot de Taal- Land- en Volkenkunde* 159(1): 109–33.

Lyons, Kevin D., and Stephen Wearing, eds. 2008. *Journeys of Discovery in Volunteer Tourism: International Case Study Perspectives.* Wallingford: CABI.

MacCannell, Dean. 1976. *The Tourist: A New Theory of the Leisure Class.* New York: Schocken Books.

⸻. 1999. *The Tourist: A New Theory of the Leisure Class.* Revised ed. Berkeley, CA: University of California Press.

Machado, Antonio. 2007. *Fields of Castile/Campos De Castilla: A Dual-Language Book*, trans. Stanley Appelbaum. Mineola, NY: Dover Publications.

Madison, Greg. 2010. *Existential Migration: Voluntary Migrants' Experiences of Not Being-at-Home in the World.* Chisinau: Lambert Academic Publishing.

Main, Izabella. 2014. "High Mobility of Polish Women: The Ethnographic Inquiry of Barcelona." *International Migration* 52(1): 130–45.

Malkki, Liisa H. 1995. *Purity and Exile: Violence, Memory, and National Cosmology among Hutu Refugees in Tanzania.* Chicago, IL: University of Chicago Press.

Mantra, Ida Bagus. 1980. "Circular Mobility and Regional Development: A Case Study of Two Dukuh in Yogyakarta Special Region." *Indonesian Journal of Geography* 10(40): 43–54.

Marcus, George E. 1998. *Ethnography through Thick and Thin.* Princeton, NJ: Princeton University Press.

Margry, Peter Jan. 2008. "Secular Pilgrimage: A Contradiction in Terms?" In *Shrines and Pilgrimage in the Modern World: New Itineraries into the Sacred*, ed. Peter Jan Margry, 13–46. Amsterdam: Amsterdam University Press.

Martínez Pizarro, Jorge. 2003. *El Encanto De Los Datos: Sociodemografía De La Inmigración En Chile Según El Censo De 2002*. Santiago: Naciones Unidas.

Maryanski, Alexandra, and Jonathan H. Turner. 1992. *The Social Cage: Human Nature and the Evolution of Society*. Stanford, CA: Stanford University Press.

Marzloff, Bruno. 2005. *Mobilités, Trajectoires Fluides*. La Tour d'Aigues: Editions de l'Aube.

Massey, Doreen B. 1993. "Power Geometry and a Progressive Sense of Place." In *Mapping the Futures: Local Cultures, Global Change*, ed. Jon Bird, 59–69. London: Routledge.

Masso, Jaan, Raul Eamets, and Pille Mõtsmees. 2013. "The Effect of Temporary Migration Experience on Occupational Mobility in Estonia." CESifo Working Paper. Munich: Ludwig Maximilian University.

Masud, Muhammad Khalid, ed. 2000. *Travellers in Faith: Studies of the Tabli Ghi Jama at as a Transnational Islamic Movement for Faith Renewal*. Boston, MA: Brill.

May, Ann. 2003. "Maasai Migrations: Implications for HIV/AIDS and Social Change in Tanzania." Population Aging Center Working Paper. Boulder, CO: University of Colorado, Institute of Behavioral Science.

May, Ann, and Francis N. Ole Ikayo. 2007. "Wearing *Illkarash*: Narratives of Image, Identity and Change among Maasai Labour Migrants in Tanzania." *Development and Change* 38(2): 275–98.

Mayerhofer, Helene, Linley C. Hartmann, Gabriela Michelitsch-Riedl, and Iris Kollinger. 2004. "Flexpatriate Assignments: A Neglected Issue in Global Staffing." *International Journal of Human Resource Management* 15(8): 1371–89.

McCabe, J. Terrence. 2003. "Sustainability and Livelihood Diversification among the Maasai of Northern Tanzania." *Human Organization* 62(2): 100–11.

McKenna, Steve, and Julia Richardson. 2007. "The Increasing Complexity of the Internationally Mobile Professional: Issues for Research and Practice." *Cross Cultural Management* 14(4): 307–20.

Meerwarth, Tracy L. 2008. "Disentangling Patterns of a Nomadic Life." *NAPA Bulletin* 30: 102–17.

Meir, Avinoam. 1997. *As Nomadism Ends: The Israeli Bedouin of the Negev*. Boulder, CO: Westview Press.

Mendel, Tommi. 2015. *Common Roads: Pilgern und Backpacking im 21. Jahrhundert*. Bielefeld: Transcript.

Michel, Franck. 2009. *Routes: Éloge de l'Autonomadie*. Quebec: Les Presses de l'Université Laval.

Mitchell, Katharyne. 2006. "Neoliberal Governmentality in the European Union: Education, Training, and Technologies of Citizenship." *Environment and Planning D: Society and Space* 24(3): 389–407.

Morgan, Alun D. 2010. "Journeys into Transformation: Travel to an 'Other' Place as a Vehicle for Transformative Learning." *Journal of Transformative Education* 8(4): 246–68.

Morinis, E. Alan, ed. 1992. *Sacred Journeys: The Anthropology of Pilgrimage*. Westport, CT: Greenwood Press.

Mostafanezhad, Mary. 2014. *Volunteer Tourism: Popular Humanitarianism in Neoliberal Times*. Farnham: Ashgate.

Mrázek, Rudolf. 1994. *Sjahrir: Politics and Exile in Indonesia*. Ithaca, NY: Southeast Asia Program Publications.

Munt, Ian. 1994. "Eco-Tourism or Ego-Tourism?" *Race and Class* 36(1): 49–59.

Naficy, Hamid. 2001. *An Accented Cinema: Exilic and Diasporic Filmmaking*. Princeton, NJ: Princeton University Press.

Naim, Mokhtar. 1974. "Merantau: Minangkabau Voluntary Migration." Ph.D. Dissertation. Singapore: National University of Singapore.

_____. 1976. "Voluntary Migration in Indonesia." In *Internal Migration: The New World and the Third World*, ed. Daniel Kubát and Anthony H. Richmond, 148–83. Beverly Hills, CA: Sage.

Nakayama, Shigeru. 1984. *Academic and Scientific Traditions in China, Japan, and the West*, trans. Jerry Dusenbury. Tokyo: University of Tokyo Press.

Neumann, Mark. 1992. "The Trail through Experience: Finding Self in the Recollection of Travel." In *Investigating Subjectivity: Research on Lived Experience*, ed. Carolyn Ellis and Michael G. Flaherty, 176–200. Newbury Park, CA: Sage Publications.

Neumann, Roderick P. 1998. *Imposing Wilderness: Struggles over Livelihood and Nature Preservation in Africa*. Berkeley, CA: University of California Press.

Nilsson, Jessika. 2016. "'What Is New about What Has Always Been': Communication Technologies and the Meaning-Making of Maasai Mobilities in Ngorongoro." Ph.D. dissertation. Leuven: University of Leuven.

Nilsson, Jessika, and Noel B. Salazar. 2017. "Embedded and Re-Purposed Technologies: Human Mobility Practices in Maasailand." *Mobilities* 12(3): 445–61.

Nowicka, Magdalena, and Maria Rovisco, eds. 2009. *Cosmopolitanism in Practice*. Farnham: Ashgate.

Noyes, John K. 2000. "Nomadic Fantasies: Producing Landscapes of Mobility in German South-West Africa." *Ecumene* 7(1): 47–66.

_____. 2004. "Nomadism, Nomadology, Postcolonialism: By Way of Introduction." *Interventions: International Journal of Postcolonial Studies* 6(2): 159–68.

Núñez, Javier. 2004. *Ni González Ni Tapia: Clasismo V/S Meritocracia en Chile*. Santiago: Departamento de Economía, Universidad de Chile.

Núñez, Javier, and Cristina Risco. 2004. *Movilidad Intergeneracional Del Ingreso en un País en Desarrollo: El Caso de Chile*. Santiago: Departamento de Economía, Universidad de Chile.

Nyíri, Pál. 2010. *Mobility and Cultural Authority in Contemporary China*. Seattle, WA: University of Washington Press.

OECD. 2007. *Policy Coherence for Development: Migration and Developing Countries*. Paris: Organisation for Economic Co-operation and Development.

_____. 2012. *Education at a Glance 2012: OECD Indicators*. Paris: Organisation for Economic Co-operation and Development.

Ohnmacht, Timo, Hanja Maksim, and Manfred M. Bergman, eds. 2009. *Mobilities and Inequality*. Farnham: Ashgate.

Olsson, Erik. 2010. "Living Next to an Airport: Narratives on the Return to Chile." CEIFO Working Paper 3. Stockholm: Stockholm University.

Olwig, Karen F. 2003. "'Transnational' Socio-Cultural Systems and Ethnographic Research: Views from an Extended Field Site." *International Migration Review* 37(3): 787–811.

Ong, Aihwa. 1999. *Flexible Citizenship: The Cultural Logics of Transnationality*. Durham, NC: Duke University Press.

Ossman, Susan. 2004. "Studies in Serial Migration." *International Migration* 42(4): 111–21.

Oyarzún, Luis. 1967. *Temas de la Cultura Chilena*. Santiago: Editorial Universitaria.

Pajo, Erind. 2007. *International Migration, Social Demotion, and Imagined Advancement: An Ethnography of Socioglobal Mobility*. New York: Springer.

Papadopoulos, Dimitris, Niamh Stephenson, and Vassilis Tsianos. 2008. *Escape Routes: Control and Subversion in the Twenty-First Century*. London: Pluto Press.

Papastergiadis, Nikos. 2000. *The Turbulence of Migration: Globalization, Deterritorialization, and Hybridity*. Cambridge: Polity Press.

_____. 2010. "Wars of Mobility." *European Journal of Social Theory* 13(3): 343–61.

Parkes, Roderick. 2009. "EU Mobility Partnerships a Model of Policy Coordination." *European Journal of Migration and Law* 11: 327–45.

Parkins, Wendy, and Geoffrey Craig. 2006. *Slow Living*. Oxford: Berg.

Peters, John D. 2006. "Exile, Nomadism and Diaspora: The Stakes of Mobility in the Western Canon." In *Visual Culture: Spaces of Visual Culture*, ed. Joanne Morra and Marquard Smith, 17–41. London: Taylor & Francis.

Peters, Richard Stanley. 1973. *The Philosophy of Education*. Oxford: Oxford University Press.

Piore, Michael J. 1979. *Birds of Passage: Migrant Labor and Industrial Societies*. Cambridge: Cambridge University Press.

Pirsig, Robert M. 1974. *Zen and the Art of Motorcycle Maintenance: An Inquiry into Values*. New York: Morrow.

Pizarro, Ana. 2003. "Mitos y Construcción del Imaginario Nacional Cotidiano." *Atenea* (Concepción) 487: 103–11.

PNUD. 2003. *Transformaciones Culturales E Identidad Juvenil En Chile*. Santiago: Programa de las Naciones Unidas para el Desarrollo.

PPMI. 2010. *Mobility of Young Volunteers across Europe*. Vilnius: Public Policy and Management Institute.

Pratchett, Terry. 2004. *A Hat Full of Sky*. New York: HarperCollins.

Pritchard, Elizabeth. 2015. "Pilgrimages and Publics: The Case of Taizé." *Anthropological Theory* 15(1): 68–91.

Prothero, R. Mansell, and Murray Chapman, eds. 1985. *Circulation in Third World Countries*. London: Routledge.

Rapport, Nigel, and Andrew Dawson, eds. 1998. *Migrants of Identity: Perceptions of Home in a World of Movement*. Oxford: Berg.

Reader, Ian. 2005. *Making Pilgrimages: Meaning and Practice in Shikoku*. Honolulu, HI: University of Hawaii Press.

Rebolledo, Loreto, and María Elena Acuña. 2001. "Narrativas del Exilio Chileno." *Anales Nueva Época* 3-4(15): 223-41.

Recchi, Ettore. 2008. "Cross-State Mobility in the EU: Trends, Puzzles and Consequences." *European Societies* 10(2): 197-224.

Recchi, Ettore, and Adrian Favell, eds. 2009. *Pioneers of European Integration: Citizenship and Mobility in the EU.* Cheltenham: Edward Elgar.

Reed-Danahay, Deborah, ed. 1997. *Auto/Ethnography: Rewriting the Self and the Social.* Oxford: Berg.

Reed-Danahay, Deborah, and Caroline Brettell. 2008. *Citizenship, Political Engagement, and Belonging: Immigrants in Europe and the United States.* New Brunswick: Rutgers University Press.

Ricci, Gabriel R., ed. 2014. *Travel, Discovery, Transformation.* New Brunswick: Transaction Publishers.

Robertson, Susan L. 2006. "Brain Drain, Brain Gain and Brain Circulation." *Globalisation, Societies and Education* 4(1): 1-5.

_____. 2010. "Critical Response to Special Section: International Academic Mobility." *Discourse: Studies in the Cultural Politics of Education* 31(5): 641-47.

Rodgers, Susan, ed. 1995. *Telling Lives, Telling History: Autobiography and Historical Imagination in Modern Indonesia.* Berkeley, CA: University of California Press.

Rojek, Chris, and John Urry, eds. 1997. *Touring Cultures: Transformations of Travel and Theory.* London: Routledge.

Römhild, Regina. 2003. "Practised Imagination: Tracing Transnational Networks in Crete and Beyond." Working Paper. Frankfurt: Research Group Transnationalism.

Ross, Susan L. 2010. "Transformative Travel: An Enjoyable Way to Foster Radical Change." *ReVision* 32(1): 45-61.

Rudnyckyj, Daromir. 2004. "Technologies of Servitude: Governmentality and Indonesia Transnational Labor Migration." *Anthropological Quarterly* 77(3): 407-34.

Rutten, Marcel, and Moses Mwangi. 2012. "Mobile Cash for Nomadic Livestock Keepers: The Impact of the Mobile Phone Money Innovation (M-Pesa) on Maasai Pastoralists in Kenya." In *Transforming Innovations in Africa: Explorative Studies on Appropriation in African Societies,* ed. Jan-Bart Gewald, André Leliveld, and Iva Pesa, 79-101. Leiden: Brill.

Sager, Tore. 2006. "Freedom as Mobility: Implications of the Distinction between Actual and Potential Travelling." *Mobilities* 1(3): 465-88.

Said, Edward W. 1994. *Orientalism.* Revised ed. New York: Vintage Books.

Salazar, Noel B. 2004. "Developmental Tourists vs. Development Tourism: A Case Study." In *Tourist Behaviour: A Psychological Perspective,* ed. Aparna Raj, 85-107. New Delhi: Kanishka Publishers.

_____. 2006. "Touristifying Tanzania: Global Discourse, Local Guides." *Annals of Tourism Research* 33(3): 833-52.

_____. 2009. "Imaged or Imagined? Cultural Representations and the 'Tourismification' of Peoples and Places." *Cahiers d'Études Africaines* 49(193-194): 49-71.

_____. 2010a. *Envisioning Eden: Mobilizing Imaginaries in Tourism and Beyond.* Oxford: Berghahn.

_____. 2010b. "Towards an Anthropology of Cultural Mobilities." *Crossings: Journal of Migration and Culture* 1(1): 53–68.

_____. 2011a. "The Power of Imagination in Transnational Mobilities." *Identities: Global Studies in Culture and Power* 18(6): 576–98.

_____. 2011b. "Tanzanian Migration Imaginaries." In *Migration and Culture*, ed. Robin Cohen and Gunvor Jónsson, 673–87. Cheltenham: Edward Elgar.

_____. 2012. "Tourism Imaginaries: A Conceptual Approach." *Annals of Tourism Research* 39(2): 863–82.

_____. 2013a. "Anthropology." In *The Routledge Handbook of Mobilities*, ed. Peter Adey, David Bissell, Kevin Hannam, Peter Merriman, and Mimi Sheller, 55–63. London: Routledge.

_____. 2013b. "Imagining Mobility at the 'End of the World.'" *History and Anthropology* 24(2): 233–52.

_____. 2014a. "Migrating Imaginaries of a Better Life … until Paradise Finds You." In *Understanding Lifestyle Migration: Theoretical Approaches to Migration and the Quest for a Better Way of Life*, ed. Michaela Benson and Nicholas Osbaldiston, 119–38. Basingstoke: Palgrave.

_____. 2014b. "To Be or Not to Be a Tourist: The Role of Concept-Metaphors in Tourism Studies." *Tourism Recreation Research* 39(2): 259–65.

_____. 2015. "Becoming Cosmopolitan through Traveling? Some Anthropological Reflections." *Journal of English Language & Literature* 61(1): 51–67.

Salazar, Noel B., and Jamie Coates, eds. 2017. *Key Figures of Mobility*. Theme issue, *Social Anthropology* 25(1).

Salazar, Noel B., and Nina Glick Schiller, eds. 2014. *Regimes of Mobility: Imaginaries and Relationalities of Power*. London: Routledge.

Salazar, Noel B., and Kiran Jayaram, eds. 2016. *Keywords of Mobility: Critical Engagements*. Oxford: Berghahn.

Salazar, Noel B., and Isabelle Rivoal, eds. 2013. *Contemporary Ethnographic Practice and the Value of Serendipity*. Theme issue, *Social Anthropology* 21(2).

Salazar, Noel B., and Alan Smart, eds. 2011. *Anthropological Takes on (Im)Mobility*. Theme issue, *Identities: Global Studies in Culture and Power* 18(6).

Saunders, Frances Stonor. 2016. "Where on Earth Are You?" *London Review of Books* 38(5): 7–12.

Schapendonk, Joris. 2011. "Turbulent Trajectories: Sub-Saharan African Migrants Heading North." Ph.D. dissertation. Nijmegen: Radboud Universiteit Nijmegen.

Schiermeier, Quirin. 2011. "Career Choices: The Mobility Imperative." *Nature* 470: 563–64.

Schmidt, William S. 2009. "Transformative Pilgrimage." *Journal of Spirituality In Mental Health* 11(1–2): 66–77.

Schneider, Leander. 2006. "The Maasai's New Clothes: A Developmentalist Modernity and Its Exclusions." *Africa Today* 53(1): 101–31.

Scholz, Fred, and Günther Schlee. 2015. "Nomads and Nomadism in History." In *International Encyclopedia of the Social and Behavioral Sciences*, ed. James D. Wright, 838–43. Amsterdam: Elsevier.

Schrooten, Mieke, Noel B. Salazar, and Gustavo Dias. 2016. "Living in Mobility: Trajectories of Brazilians in Belgium and the UK." *Journal of Ethnic and Migration Studies* 42(7): 1199–215.

Schuster, Liza. 2005. "The Continuing Mobility of Migrants in Italy: Shifting between Places and Statuses." *Journal of Ethnic and Migration Studies* 31(4): 757–74.

Schütz, Alfred. 1945. "The Homecomer." *American Journal of Sociology* 50(5): 369–76.

Scott, Heidi V. 2010. "Paradise in the New World: An Iberian Vision of Tropicality." *Cultural Geographies* 17(1): 77–101.

Scott, James C. 1998. "Compulsory Villagization in Tanzania: Aesthetics and Miniaturization." In *Seeing Like a State: How Certain Schemes to Improve the Human Condition Have Failed*, ed. James C. Scott, 223–61. New Haven, CT: Yale University Press.

Sennett, Richard. 1998. *The Corrosion of Character: The Personal Consequences of Work in the New Capitalism*. New York: Norton.

Shore, Cris. 2000. *Building Europe: The Cultural Politics of European Integration*. London: Routledge.

Siegel, James T. 2000. *The Rope of God*. Ann Arbor, MI: University of Michigan Press.

Sigalas, Emmanuel. 2010. "Cross-Border Mobility and European Identity: The Effectiveness of Intergroup Contact during the Erasmus Year Abroad." *European Union Politics* 11(2): 241–65.

Silvey, Rachel M. 2000a. "Diasporic Subjects: Gender and Mobility in South Sulawesi." *Women's Studies International Forum* 23(4): 501–15.

————. 2000b. "Stigmatized Spaces: Gender and Mobility under Crisis in South Sulawesi, Indonesia." *Gender, Place & Culture* 7(2): 143–61.

————. 2006. "Consuming the Transnational Family: Indonesian Migrant Domestic Workers to Saudi Arabia." *Global Networks* 6(1): 23–40.

Sinatti, Giulia. 2011. "'Mobile Transmigrants' or 'Unsettled Returnees'? Myth of Return and Permanent Resettlement among Senegalese Migrants." *Population, Space and Place* 17(2): 153–66.

Siu, Paul C. 1952. "The Sojourner." *American Journal of Sociology* 58(1): 34–44.

Slavin, Jean. 2003. "Walking as Spiritual Practice: The Pilgrimage to Santiago de Compostela." *Body & Society* 9(3): 1–18.

Smith, Andrew. 2006. "'If I Have No Money for Travel, I Have No Need': Migration and Imagination." *European Journal of Cultural Studies* 9(1): 47–62.

Smith, Michael P., and Adrian Favell. 2006. *The Human Face of Global Mobility: International Highly Skilled Migration in Europe, North America and the Asia-Pacific*. New Brunswick: Transaction Publishers.

Smith, Valene L. 1992. "Introduction: The Quest in Guest." *Annals of Tourism Research* 19(1): 1–17.

Snee, Helene. 2014. *A Cosmopolitan Journey? Difference, Distinction and Identity Work in Gap Year Travel*. Farnham: Ashgate.

Sobania, Neal. 2002. "But Where Are the Cattle? Popular Images of Maasai and Zulu across the Twentieth Century." *Visual Anthropology* 15(3): 313–46.

Söderström, Ola, Didier Ruedin, Shalini Randeria, Gianni D'Amato, and Francesco Panese, eds. 2013. *Critical Mobilities*. London: Routledge.

Sopher, David E. 1977. *The Sea Nomads: A Study of the Maritime Boat People of Southeast Asia*. Singapore: National Museum.

Spaan, Ernst. 1994. "Taikongs and Calos: The Role of Middlemen and Brokers in Javanese International Migration." *International Migration Review* 28(1): 93–113.

Spear, Thomas T., and Richard Waller, eds. 1993. *Being Maasai: Ethnicity and Identity in East Africa*. London: James Currey.

Stagl, Justin. 1995. *A History of Curiosity: The Theory of Travel, 1550–1800*. Australia: Harwood Academic Publishers.

Stepputat, Finn. 2004. *Dynamics of Return and Sustainable Reintegration in a 'Mobile Livelihoods' Perspective*. Copenhagen: Danish Institute for International Studies.

Strauss, Claudia. 2006. "The Imaginary." *Anthropological Theory* 6(3): 322–44.

Stuven, Ana María. 2007. *Chile Disperso: El País En Fragmentos*. Santiago: Editorial Cuarto Propio.

Subercaseaux, Benjamín. 1973. *Chile o una Loca Geografía*. Santiago: Editorial Universitaria.

Svasek, Maruska, ed. 2012. *Emotions and Human Mobility: Ethnographies of Movement*. London: Routledge.

Swatos, William H., ed. 2006. *On the Road to Being There: Studies in Pilgrimage and Tourism in Late Modernity*. Boston, MA: Brill.

Swatos, William H., and Luigi Tomasi, eds. 2002. *From Medieval Pilgrimage to Religious Tourism: The Social and Cultural Economics of Piety*. Westport, CT: Praeger.

Syed, Ali. 2007. "'Go West Young Man': The Culture of Migration among Muslims in Hyderabad, India." *Journal of Ethnic and Migration Studies* 33(1): 37–58.

Tagliacozzo, Eric. 2009. "Navigating Communities: Race, Place, and Travel in the History of Maritime Southeast Asia." *Asian Ethnicity* 10(2): 97–120.

Talney, Ronald. 2010. "Writing Portlandia." *Oregon State Bar Bulletin* 38: 38.

Tarrius, Alain. 2000. *Les Nouveaux Cosmopolitismes: Mobilités, Identités, Territoires*. Paris: Editions de l'Aube.

Taylor, Charles. 2004. *Modern Social Imaginaries*. Durham, NC: Duke University Press.

Teampău, Petruța, and Kristof Van Assche. 2009. "Migratory Marginalities: Making Sense of Home, Self and Mobility." *Ethnologia Balkanica* 13: 147–62.

Teichler, Ulrich. 2012. "International Student Mobility in Europe in the Context of the Bologna Process." *Journal of International Education and Leadership* 2(1): 1–13.

Teichler, Ulrich, Irina Ferencz, and Bernd Wächter. 2011. *Mapping Mobility in European Higher Education*. Brussels: Directorate General for Education and Culture, European Commission.

Theroux, Paul. 1979. *The Old Patagonian Express: By Train through the Americas*. Boston, MA: Houghton Mifflin.

Thomson, Joseph. 1885. *Through Masailand*. London: Sampson Low, Marston, Searle and Rivington.

Thomson, Rachel, and Rebecca Taylor. 2005. "Between Cosmopolitanism and the Locals: Mobility as a Resource in the Transition to Adulthood." *Young* 13(4): 327–42.

Thorn, Kaye. 2009. "The Relative Importance of Motives for International Self-Initiated Mobility." *Career Development International* 14(5): 441–64.

Thurlow, Crispin, and Adam Jaworski. 2006. "The Alchemy of the Upwardly Mobile: Symbolic Capital and the Stylization of Elites in Frequent-Flyer Programmes." *Discourse and Society* 17: 99–135.

Tirtosudarmo, Riwanto. 2009. "Mobility and Human Development in Indonesia." Human Development Reports Research Paper. New York: United Nations Development Programme.

Tomlinson, John. 1999. *Globalization and Culture*. Chicago: University of Chicago Press.

Torche, Florencia. 2005. "Unequal but Fluid: Social Mobility in Chile in Comparative Perspective." *American Sociological Review* 70(3): 422–50.

Torre, Carlos Antonio, Hugo Rodríguez Vecchini, and William Burgos, eds. 1994. *The Commuter Nation: Perspectives on Puerto Rican Migration*. Río Piedras: Editorial de la Universidad de Puerto Rico.

Tremblay, Karine. 2005. "Academic Mobility and Immigration." *Journal of Studies in International Education* 9(3): 196–228.

Triandafyllidou, Anna, ed. 2013. *Circular Migration between Europe and Its Neighbourhood: Choice or Necessity?* Oxford: Oxford University Press.

Tsing, Anna L. 1993. *In the Realm of the Diamond Queen: Marginality in an Out-of-the-Way Place*. Princeton, NJ: Princeton University Press.

———. 2000. "The Global Situation." *Cultural Anthropology* 15(3): 327–60.

———. 2005. *Friction: An Ethnography of Global Connection*. Princeton, NJ: Princeton University Press.

Tsong, Yuying, and Yuli Liu. 2009. "Parachute Kids and Astronaut Families." In *Asian American Psychology: Current Perspectives*, ed. Nita Tewari and Alvin N. Alvarez, 365–79. New York: Psychology Press.

Turner, Bryan S. 2007. "The Enclave Society: Towards a Sociology of Immobility." *European Journal of Social Theory* 10(2): 287–303.

Turner, Victor W., and Edith L. B. Turner 1978. *Image and Pilgrimage in Christian Culture: Anthropological Perspectives*. New York: Columbia University Press.

UNDP. 2009. *Human Development Report 2009. Overcoming Barriers: Human Mobility and Development*. New York: United Nations Development Program.

UNESCO. 2012. *Global Education Digest 2012: Opportunities Lost*. Montreal: UNESCO Institute for Statistics.

United Nations. 2013. *Trends in International Migrant Stock: The 2013 Revision*. New York: United Nations.

Universidad Católica. 2008. *Encuesta Nacional Bicentenario UC Adimark*. Santiago: Pontificia Universidad Católica de Chile.

Ure, John. 2003. *In Search of Nomads: An Anglo-American Obsession from Hester Stanhope to Bruce Chatwin*. London: Constable.

Uriely, Natan. 1994. "Rhetorical Ethnicity of Permanent Sojourners: The Case of Israeli Immigrants in the Chicago Area." *International Sociology* 9(4): 431–45.

Urry, John. 2000. *Sociology Beyond Societies: Mobilities for the Twenty-First Century*. London: Routledge.

——. 2007. *Mobilities*. Cambridge: Polity Press.

Uteng, Tanu Priya, and Tim Cresswell, eds. 2008. *Gendered Mobilities*. Aldershot: Ashgate.

Valdés, Juan Gabriel. 1995. *Pinochet's Economists: The Chicago School in Chile*. Cambridge: Cambridge University Press.

van Gennep, Arnold. (1909) 1960. *The Rites of Passage*, trans. Monika B. Vizedom and Gabrielle L. Caffee. Chicago, IL: University of Chicago Press.

Van Houtum, Henk, and Martin Van der Velde. 2004. "The Power of Cross-Border Labour Market Immobility." *Tijdschrift voor Economische en Sociale Geografie* 95(1): 100–7.

Vannini, Phillip. 2011. "Constellations of Ferry (Im)Mobility: Islandness as the Performance and Politics of Insulation and Isolation." *Cultural Geographies* 18(2): 249–71.

Verstraete, Ginette. 2010. *Tracking Europe: Mobility, Diaspora, and the Politics of Location*. Durham, NC: Duke University Press.

Vertovec, Steven. 2007. "Circular Migration: The Way Forward in Global Policy?" IMI Working Paper. Oxford: International Migration Institute.

Vertovec, Steven, and Robin Cohen, eds. 1999. *Migration, Diasporas, and Transnationalism*. Cheltenham: Edward Elgar.

Vickers, Adrian. 2004. "The Country and the Cities." *Journal of Contemporary Asia* 34(3): 304–17.

——. 2009. "Southeast Asian Studies after Said." *Arts: The Journal of the Sydney University Arts Association* 31: 58–72.

Villegas, Fernando. 2008. *Ruego a Ud. Tenga la Bondad de Irse a la Cresta*. Santiago: Editorial Sudamericana.

Vredenbregt, Jacob. 1964. "Bawean Migrations." *Bijdragen tot de Taal-, Land- en Volkenkunde* 120(1): 109–39.

Wächter, Bernd. 2003. "An Introduction: Internationalisation at Home in Context." *Journal of Studies in International Education* 7(1): 5–11.

Waters, Johanna L. 2015. "Dysfunctional Mobilities: International Education and the Chaos of Movement." In *Handbook of Children and Youth Studies*, ed. Johanna Wyn and Helen Cahill, 679–88. New York: Springer.

Welch, Anthony R. 2005. "From Peregrinatio Academica to Global Academic: The Internationalisation of the Profession." In *The Professoriate: Profile of a Profession*, ed. Anthony R. Welch, 71–96. Dordrecht: Springer.

——. 2008. "Myths and Modes of Mobility: The Changing Face of Academic Mobility in the Global Era." In *Students, Staff and Academic Mobility in Higher Education*, ed. Mike Byram and Fred Dervin, 292–311. Newcastle: Cambridge Scholars Publishing.

West, Anne, and Eleanor Barham. 2009. "Student Mobility, Qualifications and Academic Recognition in the EU." *Assessment in Education: Principles, Policy & Practice* 16(1): 25–37.

Westwood, Jennifer. 2003. *On Pilgrimage: Sacred Journeys around the World*. Mahwah: HiddenSpring/Paulist Press.

Wickramasekara, Piyasiri. 2011. *Circular Migration: A Triple Win or a Dead End*. Geneva: International Labour Organization.

Wiederkehr, Macrina. 2000. *Behold Your Life: A Pilgrimage through Your Memories*. Notre Dame, IN: Ave Maria Press.

Williams, Allan M. 2009. "Employability and International Migration: Theoretical Perspectives." In *Refugees, Recent Migrants and Employment: Challenging Barriers and Exploring Pathways*, ed. Sonia McKay, 23–34. New York: Routledge.

Williams, Catharina P. 2007. *Maiden Voyages: Eastern Indonesian Women on the Move*. Singapore: Institute of Southeast Asian Studies.

Wilson, Iain. 2011. "What Should We Expect of 'Erasmus Generations'?" *Journal of Common Market Studies* 49(5): 1113–40.

Wilson, Thomas M., and Hastings Donnan, eds. 2012. *A Companion to Border Studies*. Hoboken, NJ: Wiley Blackwell.

Wokler, Robert. 2007. "Rites of Passage and the Grand Tour: Discovering, Imagining and Inventing European Civilization in the Age of Enlightenment." In *Finding Europe: Discourses on Margins, Communities, Images*, ed. Anthony Molho and Diogo Ramada Curto, 205–22. Oxford: Berghahn Books.

Wright, Thomas C., and Rody Oñate Zúñiga. 1998. *Flight from Chile: Voices of Exile*. Albuquerque, NM: University of New Mexico Press.

———. 2007. "Chilean Political Exile." *Latin American Perspectives* 34(4): 31–49.

Xiang, Biao, Brenda S. A. Yeoh, and Mika Toyota, eds. 2013. *Return: Nationalizing Transnational Mobility in Asia*. Durham, NC: Duke University Press.

Yépez del Castillo, Isabel, and Gioconda Herrera, eds. 2007. *Nuevas Migraciones Latinoamericanas a Europa: Balances y Desafíos*. Quito: Facultad Latinoamericana de Ciencias Sociales.

Index

www.ingramcontent.com/pod-product-compliance
Lightning Source LLC
Chambersburg PA
CBHW070928030426
42336CB00014BA/2578